How to Prepare a Dissertation Proposal

How to Prepare a Dissertation Proposal

Suggestions for Students in Education and the Social and Behavioral Sciences

David R. Krathwohl
Nick L. Smith

Distributed by Syracuse University Press

ISBN 0-8156-8141-0

Produced and distributed by Syracuse University Press,
Syracuse, New York 13244-5160

The author suggests cataloguing as follows: LB2369.K73 2005.

Manufactured in the United States of America

Contents

Illustrations

WORKSHEETS

Preface

CHAPTER CONTENTS

HOW SHOULD YOU READ THIS BOOK?

This book will guide you through the steps of drafting a dissertation proposal. It is an assembly manual that will (1) identify and explain the components of a dissertation proposal, (2) assist you in constructing the needed elements, and (3) guide you in combining the pieces to produce a complete and convincing proposal. There are several ways you can use this book.

> "I learn best when you tell me what to do, give me some examples to study, and then show me how to practice it."

> "I like to figure out how to do things for myself from some examples and then check my process against the instructions to be sure I didn't miss anything."

> "An example and a checklist are worth a thousand words of instruction!"

Would you just as soon be given instructions and then see some illustrations of their use? Or are you one of those people who learns best from examples? Or does your preference depend on the material you are mastering? Depending on how you prefer to learn, you may want to read this book's chapters in an atypical order. Let us explain why this is so.

This book is organized into six parts. Part 1 deals with the definition of a proposal, its different functions, and the basic logic that underlies many studies. Everyone should start with it.

Part 2 presents the core elements of any proposal, the problem statement and the method statement, while part 3 shows how those elements are modified to convey the strengths of particular kinds of studies, such as qualitative investigations, experimental tests, demonstrations, etc.

Part 4 both explains the additional material needed to complete a full proposal and discusses the process of getting your proposal reviewed and approved.

Part 5 reproduces three actual student proposals of different types (chapters: 11, Warters; 12, Beissner; and 13, Phelan) with interspersed annotations that refer back to the advice given in parts 2, 3, and 4.

Part 6 discusses getting the proposal funded.

Most of us expect to have a procedure explained and then be shown examples of its application. Those of you who prefer this will want to proceed by reading parts 1, 2, 3, and 4 in order, looking ahead to see how those ideas are implemented in the annotated student proposals of part 5. We have provided worksheets at the end of each chapter in parts 1, 2, 3, and 4 to help you make practical use of the material you have just read.

If you empathized with the quotes above about starting with examples, however, after reading part 1, you may want to proceed to part 5, first working through the examples and then reading parts 2, 3, and 4 to see in more detail the rationale for the annotations. If you learn best by working on specific tasks related to a problem, then you may want to pay particular attention to the worksheets at the end of each chapter. They will help you work through each step in the process and give you a checklist for reviewing your progress.

Maybe you'll want to work back and forth between the parts as you proceed. Since parts 2 and 3 frequently cite examples in the annotated proposals of part 5 to show what is meant by their advice, and since part 5 indicates where in parts 2 and 3 the topic of the annotation is covered, it is easy to move back and forth between them. So you may choose this alternative. See what works best for you.

Remember that this is a "how-to-do-it" instruction manual. You don't read an instruction manual just once, but alternately refer to different sections as you encounter various parts of the assembly process. For example, if you are designing a quantitative experimental study as part of your dissertation, you will probably need to refer repeatedly to part 3, chapter 8, on experiments and to the corresponding sample proposal in part 5, chapter 12. Read through the book once, then use it selectively to assemble your own proposal.

If you are reading the book selectively, concentrating on those parts that seem most relevant to your situation, you may miss two discussions of importance. One concerns the problem of "how much is enough for a dissertation." While this is discussed in the context of philosophical and historical studies, it can be a problem in almost any type of study, so include pp. 139–41 in your reading. Include as well pp. 115–16 that refer to the problem of doing the proposal after the dissertation is started, which you may consider doing. Also don't forget to consult part 6 if you anticipate needing additional resources to support your work.

AN ASSEMBLY MANUAL WITH A DIFFERENCE

We have referred to this book as an assembly manual. But where our usual conception of a manual is something that guides you mechanically through a series of steps, this manual is much more than that. We want you to understand the "why" of what is called for, how your proposal can advance your relations with your faculty mentors, how each part of the proposal fits into and contributes to a larger whole, and the logic that constitutes the larger whole that will be represented in your proposal. If you understand the "whys" and bear in mind the logic of the larger picture, then as you formulate the steps in your proposal you will be able to creatively translate what is suggested here into what you propose to do. So, yes, this is an assembly manual, but one with a difference.

WHAT DO WE ASSUME YOU BRING TO READING THE BOOK?

An assembly manual, whether for assembling a child's swing set, a new computer system, or a dissertation proposal, must assume that the user has all the needed materials, tools, and skills at hand to do the work. In writing this book, we too have had to make certain assumptions about what background you bring to it. Specifically, we assume:

1. You already have a dissertation topic or know enough about a possible topic that you can sort among the various dissertation proposal formats to find the one or those few that are relevant to your study. In order to develop an effective proposal, you must tailor it to the specific details of a particular problem.

2. You have had enough research background and are willing to look up the appropriate references when you come across a research aspect you don't understand, so that we don't have to make this both a research text as well as a "how-to" manual.

We make the first assumption because we start the book at that point in the dissertation process where you either are close to having a topic or already have one. For this reason, we did not include a chapter on finding a dissertation topic. If you are still looking for one, reading chapter 5, "Finding a Problem," in Krathwohl (1998/2004) or a similar chapter in a research methods book may help you.

Why the second assumption? Because in order to include all the background provided in a research methods text would have produced a book requiring you to reinforce your bookshelf. When providing advice regarding a part of the proposal, we try to supply enough detail for you to know what to write about and how to describe it without going into the detail you would expect to find in a research text.

A good example of the boundaries of this book's coverage is the matter of ruling out alternative explanations. If you are explaining a phenomenon, you don't want your explanation to be rivaled by a plausible alternative. We have supplied one or two examples so that you are clear about what we mean by alternative explanations. But there are many, many others we don't mention. If you don't know the ones to protect against in your study, you need to find out about them by reviewing a research methods text, studying prior research, or consulting a fellow researcher.

Another boundary example: As a proposal assembly manual, this book will demonstrate how the results of your literature review should be used in the proposal to strengthen your research argument, but it will not provide instruction on how to conduct literature searches. Further, the book emphasizes the importance of clear, direct, well-written English in producing a convincing proposal, but does not offer instruction in how to write well. The goal of this book, therefore, is to help you with the specific task of assembling an effective dissertation proposal, and so it assumes you either have certain required related knowledge and skills or will seek out and acquire them.

WHAT IS DISTINCTIVE ABOUT THIS BOOK?

Here are some of the distinctive aspects of this book:

1. *The definition of a proposal and the variety of its functions.* We all have some idea of what a proposal is, but chapters 1 and 2 challenge you to consider it more broadly. The definition presented in chapter 1 is curious and thought provoking, deals with both attitude and content, and has implications for how the proposal is written. The different functions a proposal can serve described in chapter 2 also affect how it is written, as well as how it is judged by various audiences.

2. *How the chain of reasoning organizes and integrates the proposal.* One of the most important functions of the proposal is to present a rationale for the study. Chapter 3 shows how the presentation of that rationale (as well as how you later present the findings of your study) is analogous to a particular pattern of metal chain, its properties and characteristics. Keeping the chain analogy in mind helps you develop a strong and integrated proposal.

3. *How to write the various parts of the proposal is described in detail.* Chapters 4 and 5 describe in considerable detail what is to be included in the core sections of the proposal. Chapter 4 describes how you present what you hope to study and shows how it builds on past research. Chapter 5 indicates how you describe what you will operationally do in pursuing the problem. Chapter 6 provides the various assurances that your chair, committee, and institution need in

order to feel confident that you have appropriate background knowledge, adequate understanding of your procedure, every intent to observe ethical cautions, and adequate time and fiscal resources. Chapter 10 gives tips and invites consideration of other aspects of the process not covered elsewhere.

4. *How to adapt the typical proposal format to a wide variety of types of studies.* Chapters 7 through 9 discuss how the proposal differs depending on the types of studies that can be pursued for the doctorate. Chapter 7 does this for qualitative studies such as case studies, philosophical and conceptual studies, and historical investigations. Chapter 8 does the same for quantitative investigations such as experimental, causal modeling, and meta-analysis studies. Chapter 9 likewise covers studies that combine both qualitative and quantitative approaches such as sample survey studies, evaluation studies, development projects, and demonstration and action projects.

5. *The inclusion of annotated sample proposals.* Because so much can be learned from examples, this book includes not just one, but three annotated proposals, each different with respect to method and topic.

6. *Worksheets for working through the proposal development process.* The worksheets provided with each chapter help you put the material just presented into actual practice. Collectively, they guide you through the development process and provide you with criteria for checking your progress.

In this book, we have provided a variety of paths and tools to help you in putting together a convincing and effective dissertation proposal. Become familiar with the entire volume, so you can refer to the separate chapters as needed in assembling your proposal.

Remember that complicated products often require refitting and reassembly until the parts fit just as you want them. Developing a dissertation proposal is a complicated and difficult task, but with persistence, you can produce a proposal to be proud of. Good luck!

PART ONE

Concepts Fundamental to Proposal Writing

Before preparing your proposal, you should become familiar with the information in this part; it provides concepts fundamental to all proposals. It may also broaden your conception of what proposals are and the variety of problems they encompass. This part consists of three chapters:

Chapter 1 defines a dissertation proposal in terms you may not have considered.

Chapter 2 describes the functions that are served by proposals and how these functions may vary depending on the kind of problem posed. A fundamental function served by all proposals is the presentation of an argument to justify conducting the study.

Chapter 3 describes how presenting that argument is like a chain of reasoning and explores some of the consequences of that analogy for writing the proposal.

CHAPTER 1

What Is a Proposal?

CHAPTER CONTENTS

DEFINITION OF A PROPOSAL

What is a proposal? "That's obvious," you say, "let's get on with it!" We would agree with you, except that it always pays to have a precise idea of where one is going; it makes it so much easier to get there! So here are some things to consider:

- What you will be proposing as your dissertation research has never been done exactly as you propose to do it. So you, your doctoral chairperson, and your committee[1] are sharing some risk if it is approved. Shared decision making is a much more appropriate frame of mind when professional reputations, energy, time, and resources are ventured by both sides.
- Sharing the decision making takes maximum advantage of your chairperson's and committee's ability to test the worth of the ideas you pro-

1. Institutions vary; some require a committee that works with a chairperson to guide the student's work, some require only a chairperson, or advisor, and use readers to review the final product. All, however, require someone who serves as a mentor. Throughout this book we will refer to the mentor as chairperson, and those who work with her as the committee. Note also that because of the lack of a neutral pronoun, masculine and feminine forms will be used randomly throughout the book to avoid the awkward "he/she" and "his/her" forms of expression.

pose. Students who approach the presentation of their ideas more as a hurdle requiring a strong sales pitch than as a chance to try them out lose this advantage.

- A sales job may not stand up on sober reflection, but a carefully formulated problem is more likely to. Indeed, if you later need to make substantial changes or get help or additional resources, a solidly based document is more likely to result in the chairperson's and committee's serious commitment to the project—a stance conducive to getting the help you need. Further, proposal development is part of the process of building your relationship with your chairperson in particular and your committee in general. You want those relations to be solid!

- If, even though you have presented your ideas adequately, your chairperson (and/or your committee) turns the proposal down for substantive reasons, she may have done you a favor (although it may take a bit of time to realize it). You may have been saved from venturing a substantial amount of your time and energy in a useless quest. Shared decision making may save you a misstep.

As noted below, you will have chosen your dissertation chairperson and committee members for their experience and special qualifications for making the judgments needed to guide and improve the quality of your work. Since they also function as gatekeepers to the profession, some students may view them with apprehension. In reality, faculty want good ideas to succeed. Indeed, having accepted membership on your committee, they want you to succeed. In addition to their interest in you as a person, your success reflects favorably on them! Keeping their concern for you in mind results in a more positive attitude; let that attitude show through in your writing!

All of the above assumes that in the proposal you presented your case in such a way that the chairperson and committee could fully encounter it and could make what you consider a fair judgment based on their perceptions of the ideas and actions that you intend. Someone once said, "Books exist in the minds of readers. It really doesn't matter what the author intended at all." Of course it matters! It matters a great deal to you. You want what "exists in the minds of readers" to be what you meant. It is because the reviewer's image of both the proposal and the proposer is so often not what was intended—the case for the study was not made as well as it could have been—that books like this have value. Adequate and appropriate presentation of an idea is a skill that can be learned. This book's intent is to help you learn it.

So we have begun defining a proposal by explaining some considerations underlying it. To help you with the material that follows, however, we need a more explicit definition, one that is compatible with the considerations with which we began yet amplifies and specifies what is to be done. So, what is a proposal?

Basically, a dissertation proposal describes a plan of work to learn something of real or potential significance about an area of interest. It is a logical presentation. Its opening problem statement draws the reader into the plan: showing its significance, describing how it builds upon previous work (both substantively and methodologically), and outlining the investigation. The overall plan of action flows from the problem statement: specific steps are described in the methods section, their sequence is illuminated graphically in the work plan (and, if one is included, by the time schedule), and their feasibility is shown by the availability of resources. The enthusiasm of the proposal carries the reader along; the reader is impressed with the proposal's perspective on the problem, is reassured by the technical and scholarly competence shown, and is provided with a model of the clarity of thought and writing that can be expected in the final write-up. The reader comes away feeling that the opportunity to support this research should not be missed.

Perhaps you are thinking, "That is a great definition, but hardly compatible with all the talk about not being a sales pitch!" Not true. First, it simply recognizes that if you are not enthusiastic about your ideas, you cannot expect others to be. Material can be written interestingly and still presented with integrity. Your writing doesn't have to be boring to be good.

Second, the definition points out that the proposal is an integrated chain of reasoning that makes strong logical connections between your problem statement and the coherent plan of action you are proposing to undertake. This point is discussed further in chapter 3.

Third, as this modified definition makes clear, it is not only your idea and action plan that are subject to consideration, but also your capability to successfully carry them through.

Alright now, let's pull it together and add a few realities. Once more, "What is a proposal?"

Your dissertation proposal is an opportunity for you to present your idea and proposed actions for consideration in a shared decision-making situation. You, with all the integrity at your command, are helping your chairperson and/or doctoral committee to see how you view the situation, how the work you propose fills a need, how it builds on what has been done before, how it will proceed, how pitfalls will be avoided, why pitfalls not avoided are not a serious threat, what the consequences of your efforts are likely to be, and what significance they are likely to have. It is a carefully prepared, enthusiastic, interestingly written, skillful presentation. Your presentation displays your ability to assemble the foregoing materials into an internally consistent chain of reasoning.

Is that what you thought a proposal was? Well, whether it was or not, now you know where we want to go. And that makes it easier to get there. Helping you get there is what this book is about.

TYPICAL DISSERTATION PROPOSAL SECTIONS

The content and format of dissertation proposals vary across institutions, departments, and committees. Some have strict requirements or formal guidelines, while others allow the student considerable latitude. Although we present a range of alternatives, to learn what is expected of you, you should search out your school's officially stated requirements, review prior proposals accepted in your department, and discuss expectations with your chairperson.

A conventional format of a completed dissertation consists of five chapters:

Chapter 1: Problem Statement
Chapter 2: Literature Review
Chapter 3: Method Statement
Chapter 4: Study Results
Chapter 5: Interpretation and Conclusions

Some departments therefore expect the dissertation proposal to consist of the first three chapters of the final dissertation, either in annotated outline form, substantially developed, or possibly even in full draft form. (The reasons for some of these requirements are discussed further in the next chapter.) Students are often allowed, or even encouraged, to develop a *prospectus* prior to the development of the full proposal. The prospectus provides an overview of the same topics as the Problem Statement, Literature Review, and Method Statement, but in a much abbreviated two—to ten-page presentation. A prospectus is especially useful for initiating discussions about possible dissertation studies, recruiting dissertation committee members, and soliciting potential study participants.

OVERVIEW OF THE DISSERTATION PROPOSAL PROCESS

Producing a dissertation proposal involves not only preparing the proposal document, but also preparing yourself to do the dissertation research.

Preparing Yourself

Before even considering a dissertation proposal, of course, you have spent several years of graduate education preparing to do a dissertation study. You will continue to improve your knowledge and skills throughout the proposal development process, the actual dissertation study, and the rest of your professional career. At this point, the key question is, "How prepared are you to begin the proposal development process?" To what extent have you already:

Developed a research interest? Completing a dissertation requires a major time, resource, and ego investment; do you have a dissertation topic of sufficiently strong personal interest? If not, how close are you to finding one?

Accumulated required knowledge? Do you have or do you still need to attain adequate knowledge about the phenomena and problem of interest? About how others have studied this problem? About your own motivation, inquiry skills, work style and preferences?

Acquired Necessary Skills? Considering your possible research, do you have, or will you need to develop, sufficient skills to conduct literature searches, design studies, develop instrumentation, create interventions and treatments, collect and analyze data, communicate orally and in technical writing, use computers and technology, and manage resources and time?

Garnered Adequate Resources? Do you have, or can you obtain, the resources needed to develop the proposal, including technical assistance (including a chairperson), study resources, and sufficient time, financial, and personal support to develop the proposal?

How well prepared should you be *before* starting to develop the proposal, as opposed to developing the needed knowledge and skills as you work on the proposal? The answer varies, and this is a good question to discuss with your chairperson, researchers working in your area of interest, and fellow students already past the proposal development stage.

Part of what makes doing dissertations interesting is the occurrence of the unexpected. So you can't prepare for every eventuality, but adequate preparation makes the process easier. Therefore, we have provided Worksheet 1.1: Self-Assessment and Worksheet 1.2: Environmental Assessment to help you review your readiness to begin drafting the dissertation proposal. Think of them as assembly-manual lists that ensure you will have the necessary parts when you begin the assembly process.

There are a variety of ways of gaining this assurance. Additional course work is often the fastest and most efficient way to make major improvements in knowledge or skills, but also consider independent study, tutoring, workshops and short-term training sessions, and consultant help. If, more than further instruction, you need increased experience with your topic of interest and how to research it, then consider apprenticeships, volunteer positions, on-the-job training, and, of course, pilot testing some of your preliminary ideas. Nothing improves a proposal like drawing on your own personal experiences of what does and does not work.

Preparing the Proposal

So you are ready to start on the proposal; how do you proceed? It is true that your proposal will typically follow a logical chain of reasoning from problem to literature review to method, etc. But, depending on circumstances, the process of its preparation may start in any number of places such as reviewing the literature, investigating research methods, or working to understand the problem better through observation or pilot studies.

The central task of the proposal preparation process is to transform a personal interest into a researchable problem: dissertation studies are typically constructed, not discovered. They develop through a process of reading, writing, review and discussion, rewriting, further discussion, additional reading, redrafting, and so on. The work of this process is *thinking*; the proposal document records the results of that thinking.

- Reading is important; read selectively and critically to gain understanding and insight.
- Writing is important; use it as a means of clarifying and making explicit your own ideas so you can communicate them to others.
- Reviews and discussions are important; use them to capture the strengths and repair the weaknesses of your and others' thinking.

You redraft and rethink, move from problem analysis to method considerations and back again, until an acceptable balance of study importance, technical quality, and practical feasibility is reached.

Although this describes the internal process of proposal development, there are also common external milestones of progress. While this process varies, the following describes typical events in developing a dissertation proposal.

1. After relevant course work, extensive reading, and informal conversations, the student either verbally tries out or drafts an initial "think piece" about a possible dissertation topic.
2. The student works with the chairperson through successive drafts to develop a short but adequate prospectus.
3. The prospectus is used to feel out potential committee members regarding their interest, the student's likely compatibility with them, and their suggestions for further revisions.
4. The student works with the chairperson and committee to further develop the problem and method statements.
5. The chairperson and committee give the student provisional approval for initial field and development work.
6. The student works to develop the full proposal, possibly including development of instrumentation, interventions, or treatments; initial qualitative fieldwork; development and submission of Institutional Review Board clearances; and the design and conduct of pilot tests.
7. The student increasingly interacts with professional colleagues: peers for personal support, other researchers for procedural advice, and methodologists for assistance with instrument development, data collection, analysis plans, etc.

8. With the chairperson's prior approval, the student presents and defends the full dissertation proposal, either at a meeting of just the committee or possibly at a public oral defense.
9. After making requested revisions, obtaining all required permissions and approvals, and possibly submitting the proposal for external funding, the student proceeds to implement the proposal and conduct the dissertation research.

There are also subtle aspects of this process not made explicit in the above steps that require an understanding of the variety of functions the proposal serves in addition to providing one a "green light" on the road to a degree—a topic we take up in the next chapter.

Self-Assessment

Am I Ready to Begin the Dissertation Proposal?

For each item in the table, rate your level of preparation, and note how you could become better prepared to begin working on the dissertation proposal.

How Well Prepared Am I?	Strong– Ready to Go	Adequate– Good Enough To Start	Weak–I Need To Work on This	To Strengthen This Area, I Should:	Already Past This Point or Don't Plan or Need to Do
Do I Have Sufficient Knowledge To . . . ?					
Identify a short list of important, feasible, and personally interesting dissertation topics?					
Specify in some detail the nature and importance of each topic?					
Briefly summarize enough of the relevant empirical research, theoretical positions, and practical knowledge to help choose among these topics?					
Discuss general research approaches possibly relevant to studying these topics?					
Discuss my personal interest in these subjects as dissertation topics?					
Discuss how my current motivation, circumstances, and work style may both help and hinder me in completing the proposal?					

(Continued on next page)

How Well Prepared Am I?	Strong–Ready to Go	Adequate–Good Enough To Start	Weak–I Need To Work on This	To Strengthen This Area, I Should:	Already Past This Point or Don't Plan or Need to Do
Do I Have Sufficient Skills To...?					
Conduct a paper-based literature search?					
Conduct a computer-based literature search using electronic databases and the Internet?					
Use software to assist in analyzing the relevant literature?					
Conduct a meta-analysis of empirical research?					
Critique alternative inquiry approaches possibly appropriate to my topics?					
Discuss the purposes, strengths, weaknesses, and necessary conditions of alternative study designs appropriate to my topics?					
Select, develop, and implement data collection procedures needed for my study?					
Select or develop any instrumentation needed for my study?					
Analyze and interpret the different kinds of data I may collect in my study?					

(Continued on next page)

11

How Well Prepared Am I?	Strong– Ready to Go	Adequate– Good Enough To Start	Weak–I Need To Work on This	To Strengthen This Area, I Should:	Already Past This Point or Don't Plan or Need to Do
Use appropriate equipment, including computers, needed in my study?					
Communicate effectively, orally and in writing, with my chairperson, committee members, colleagues, and study participants?					
Write effectively in professional technical English (i.e. the language of the written dissertation)?					
Manage my proposal and study time and resources in light of competing professional, occupational, familial, social, religious, and personal demands?					

Environmental Assessment

What Resources Are Available?

For each item in the table, rate how sufficient the resource is, and note what steps you can take to increase needed resources before starting on the proposal.

What Resources Are Available?	Plenty– Ready to Go	Adequate– Enough to Get Started	Weak–More Help Is Needed Here	To Strengthen This Resource I Should:
Do I Have Sufficient Resources To . . . ?				
Devote significant time each week working on the proposal and dissertation study?				
Devote significant time over several months or years working on the proposal and dissertation study?				
Financially support myself and family while working on the proposal and dissertation study?				
Maintain the needed emotional and personal support required to complete the proposal and dissertation study?				
Are There Sufficient Resources Available to Me in Terms of . . . ?				
Relevant instructional courses?				
Qualified, interested, and available faculty mentors, chairperson, and committee members?				
Technical assistance with computers, research methods, and writing skills?				

(Continued on next page)

What Resources Are Available?	Plenty–Ready to Go	Adequate–Enough to Get Started	Weak–More Help Is Needed Here	To Strengthen This Resource I Should:
Work setting?				
Computer facilities?				
Laboratory facilities?				
Library resources?				
Field settings and study participants?				

CHAPTER 2

The Functions of a Dissertation Proposal

CHAPTER CONTENTS

In this chapter, we review the various functions a proposal can serve in the dissertation process, and how those functions may differ depending on the type of inquiry being proposed. Student examples illustrate some of these differences.

THE FUNCTIONS OF THE PROPOSAL IN THE DISSERTATION PROCESS

Anna[1] was proud of her new dissertation proposal. It had been completed just two weeks after she had started her doctoral program; in fact, approval by a faculty committee was required before she could officially begin her doctoral studies. Having learned about the kind of research her mentors conducted, she had indicated her desire to do similar research, and, after discussing possible projects, had agreed to the work described in her new dissertation proposal. The eight-page statement, which had been

---

1. Because the student examples provided throughout the book are based on actual cases, names and personal details have been changed to preserve confidentiality.

drafted by two faculty members who were to serve as her mentors and supervisors, included a description of the background of the problem, research questions, and a general scope of proposed work. Anna's name did not appear in the document because it would be submitted for funding by her mentors. On receiving the grant, they would employ her for the next four years to study, design, implement, evaluate, and produce research related to alternative coaching procedures for teacher professional development in four international settings.

In contrast, after more than two years of doctoral courses, Laura was still uncertain about her dissertation topic. Her interests were varied, and she had approached several faculty members about the possibility of their working with her. Because she was an outstanding student, most faculty members expressed interest and support, but asked for greater clarity about the nature of her possible research. After choosing an advisor who had agreed to help her through the proposal development process, she decided to conduct extensive field interviews and collect other data in order to find a focus within her general concern, the professional development of medical personnel. As she learned more, however, her shifting interests were reflected in multiple proposal revisions and a changing cast of possible faculty mentors. Finally, after months of difficult fieldwork, Laura produced an extensive dissertation proposal that reflected considerable sophistication about the topic of her research and enabled her to gain the agreement of several faculty members to assist her.

Anna's story reflects an instance in which a dissertation proposal is simply a statement of planned work out of which the student's deeper understanding is to emerge as the problem is engaged (indeed, it is quite possible that the plan of work will change as the work unfolds). This pattern, where the faculty set the problem, is more common in the natural and physical sciences. Laura's story reflects significant understanding of her research problem. This pattern, where the student sets the problem, is common in the social sciences and humanities and is the pattern to which the bulk of this book is addressed. In both cases, however, the proposal provides a set of boundaries for actually doing the dissertation work.

Clearly, *boundary setting* is one role of the proposal, and that enters into some of the other multiple purposes the proposal may play in the dissertation process. This chapter identifies seven possible functions:

- Justification for the dissertation study
- Work plan
- Evidence of ability
- Request for commitment
- Contract
- Evaluative criterion
- Partial dissertation draft

The Proposal as Justification for the Study

A sound argument, a well-grounded or firmly-backed claim, is one which will stand up to criticism . . . [and] deserve[s] a favourable verdict. (Toulmin, 1958, p. 8)

Researchers employ theory, method, evidence, and reasoning to produce findings they claim are important and relevant to the questions of interest. The reasoning producing the findings and relating them to the problem constitutes an argument that is the heart of the dissertation proposal. This argument justifies conducting the study and supports the meaning and utility of the results found. The primary function of the dissertation proposal, then, is to provide this justification for the inquiry.

Therefore, in doing the study, the student develops the following points into a reasoned argument:

1. Why it is worth studying what will be studied.
2. What is already known, how that relates to the proposed study, and how it coalesces into an argument for:
   a. an extrapolation of past knowledge to predict the outcome of the study,
   b. or, if not a prediction, some anticipation of possible outcomes,
   c. or knowledge of where to look for results,
   d. or knowledge of what area to study in order to likely attain payoff. (If much is known about what is to be researched, a, above, is possible. With less prior knowledge, one falls back to b, with still less to c, and finally to d.)
3. How the study will proceed: what method will be used; data gathered; and situations, circumstances, and persons involved.
4. How those data represent future situations, circumstances, and/or persons in such a way as to relate usefully and meaningfully to the problem, question, or area of investigation proposed.

As might be expected, these points relate to the proposal as well as to the dissertation study itself. The first three points are covered in the proposal, the fourth in the dissertation report. As discussed in the next chapter, designing the proposal as a chain of reasoning is an effective way of providing a strong justification for the dissertation study.

The Proposal as Work Plan

This is the most common function a proposal serves. It sets forth what work will be done, why, and with what anticipated result. Most proposals include a scope of work, a list of activities, and possibly a time line and budget. These indicate how the student plans to proceed. The work plan allows faculty to judge the investigation's importance, feasibility, efficiency, and likely success. The material in the following sections of this book will assist you in developing a strong work plan.

The Proposal as Evidence of Ability

A dissertation proposal may also serve as evidence of ability—the student's knowledge of the topic, understanding of the relevant literature, grasp of appropriate inquiry procedures and methods, analytic and design skills, and, certainly, organizational and writing skills are all reflected in the proposal. A student who produces a strong proposal in these respects can have greater confidence that she is indeed prepared to undertake the proposed inquiry. And the faculty, by assessing the proposal's clarity, organization, attention to detail, originality, and level of sophistication, can judge the student's current state of readiness and her need for additional preparation, support, or supervision.

Both Anna's and Laura's dissertation proposals served as work plans, but only Laura's was used as a means of providing evidence of her ability to carry out the planned research. Her proposal helped to certify to the faculty that, after months of extensive investigation and fieldwork, she was prepared to proceed with the full study. In Anna's doctoral program, students were expected to develop all needed abilities as the dissertation proceeded. When she started her dissertation, Anna did not yet have the abilities needed to write "her" proposal.

The Proposal as Request for Commitment

As mentioned earlier, a draft prospectus may be used to identify persons who might serve as collaborators, consultants, or participants in the inquiry. A more complete version may be used to solicit faculty participation on the dissertation committee. Either of these versions may be useful in gaining the approval of gatekeepers of sites from which one hopes to collect data. Often they like to see it in less than final form so they may suggest changes. This both makes the project more acceptable to them and gives them a sense of partial ownership of it. The latter is equally true of faculty being sought as dissertation committee members. As noted below, it also commits the faculty to helping the student meet the challenges the project will present. A full draft of the proposal may be used to seek financial or institutional support.

The Proposal as Contract

A proposal may come to serve as a contract as it changes from a request for commitment to an accepted agreement of work to be done. Approval of the proposal may entail faculty and institutional obligation to provide support, resources, and ultimately a doctoral degree if the work is completed as proposed.[2] Because approval by the dissertation committee may constitute an institutional contract to accept the basic elements of the proposal, a dissertation committee may be particularly careful to ensure that the proposed study is well designed, complies with institutional guidelines and local norms, and is feasible.

> Both Anna's and Laura's proposals served as requests for commitment and subsequently as contracts, but in different ways. In accepting their proposals, the students were expected to conduct the work as outlined in their respective documents. Anna's proposal contained less detail, providing her greater room for subsequent change, but less direction on how to proceed, making her more dependent on her mentors. Laura's proposal was very procedurally specific and detailed, reflecting a direction she had chosen and was now committed to seeing through.

> In both cases, the faculty made commitments to work with the student, but Anna's mentors were agreeing to provide intensive training, consultation, and supervision in her conduct of a study related to their own research. Laura had used early versions of her proposal to identify and solicit faculty to work with her. Her committee was serving more at her invitation to assist in a dissertation that was to be primarily under her direction and initiative. Anna's proposal included guaranteed financial support; Laura was promised only the resources of faculty time and expertise.

The Proposal as Evaluative Criterion

Once accepted, a dissertation proposal can become an evaluative criterion used to judge the direction and quality of the ensuing work. The more specific and detailed the proposal is, the more likely it will be used to monitor the progress of the inquiry. The student may be expected to implement the study as planned, inform the faculty of further details as she works them out, and provide justification when seeking approval for any major changes to the study as proposed. The proposal may also serve as an evaluative criterion in judging the quality of the final dissertation report. Consider Laura's and Anna's situations:

> Because of the detail contained in Laura's proposal, it was used as an evaluative criterion to monitor the progress and direction of her work. As her proposal continued to evolve, periodic restatements of the proposal were produced to ensure that she and her committee all shared the same understanding of the direction of her work. Although she was not forced to comply with the formally accepted proposal, she was required to document and justify any subsequent changes. Further, her proposal did include substantial sections of what were expected to be the first three chapters of her final report.

2. In some institutions, once the student's dissertation committee has formally accepted the proposal, all subsequent reviewers, even at the final dissertation hearing, must accept the basic design decisions contained in the accepted proposal.

Anna's proposal contained only an outline of work to be conducted over a four-year period, and so was not a strong criterion for judging either the progress or the final report of her dissertation. Because she had not written the proposal, it also provided no prior information on the nature or quality of her final report.

Other examples:

Jerry's dissertation committee criticized his final report as not living up to the high quality of work that he had shown in his proposal. They felt he had not taken his study seriously enough and that, in an attempt to finish quickly, he had not done his best work. (Note: Dissertation standards *may* be adjusted to what can be expected of each individual.)

Reviewers at her final dissertation defense criticized Lilly for implementing a study design with serious flaws. Since she had identified many of these flaws herself when she reviewed prior research in her proposal, it was charged that she had already given evidence that she knew better.

Franklin, an international student, had returned home to collect data after his proposal had been approved. He made several major changes to his study design without prior faculty approval. He provided a strong, convincing argument at his defense, however, that the approved proposal design had turned out to be infeasible in his home setting. His study changes gave evidence of his mastery of inquiry design principles and were applauded by his dissertation committee.

A committee member, anticipating using the proposal to monitor and evaluate the implementation of the dissertation study, may request greater procedural detail. A similarly concerned committee member may suggest that the student write the proposal to show sensitivity to possible changing conditions, flexibility to meet them, and, perhaps, how likely deviations from plans will be handled. A student, knowing how others may use the proposal as a criterion to judge her work, uses the opportunity to suggest the basis on which she wants to be judged and to describe the amount of flexibility from plans she anticipates needing.

The Proposal as Partial Dissertation Draft

Each student must adjust the final dissertation format to fit his study. As outlined in chapter 1, however, the conventional pattern employs five chapters:

- The first chapter covers what will be studied and why it is worth studying. It may also foreshadow what is to come in the remainder of the document.
- The second chapter reviews how far previous researchers have taken the

area and how the study relates to and builds on what they have done, both substantively and methodologically.
- The third chapter describes the study method and design.
- The fourth chapter describes what was found and presents the data processed so their meaning can be assessed.
- The fifth chapter interprets what was found in terms of the original study aims.

In some cases, dissertation advisors ask for a proposal that amounts to a partial dissertation draft—the first three chapters: statement of problem, review of the literature, and description of method.[3] Presumably, if there are subsequently no significant changes in the study's process or design, these three early chapter drafts can be used in the final dissertation report with only minor modifications.

For the faculty, a full three-chapter proposal provides the strongest basis for several of the functions of a proposal discussed above (for example, evidence of ability, contractual obligation, and subsequent evaluative criterion). For the student, substantial initial work is required without formal assurance that the study being planned will be acceptable, but once such a proposal is approved, the student is well on his way to completing the entire study.

More often, however, proposals provide a sketchier coverage of the study than the development of chapters implies. This better fits the level of knowledge of the student at the time the proposal is written, as well as allowing for the almost inevitable adjustments required later to fit newly revealed realities. This is less true, however, if the preparation of the proposal is preceded by a pilot study. For empirical studies, a pilot test enables the researcher to cycle through the entire study on a small scale so that an improved argument, inquiry process, and set of questions can be developed for the dissertation proposal. Let's look at Dana's pilot test study as an example of this sequence.

In simplified terms, Dana suspected that undergraduates would do better in philosophy classes if they produced study outlines of the various philosophers' positions they were studying. She developed an argument based on research and theory in cognitive processing, instructional design, and the structural nature of philosophy, which supported her claim that having the student construct outlines would improve both understanding and recall of philosophical positions.

She then designed a study to test her claims. She had an instructor teach students in a philosophy course how to construct study outlines, and, in a comparable course, the

3. Some advisors prefer a four-chapter dissertation format in which the problem statement and literature review are combined in the first chapter. In such cases, the proposal covers only the first two dissertation chapters, thus covering the same items.

same instructor had the students study as they usually did. Dana then ran a pilot test of her study and compared results from the students' course examinations in the two classes. She found no difference between the two groups.

At this point, Dana reexamined why she may have obtained the results she did. Was her argument flawed? (Perhaps outlining really didn't improve performance.) Was the study process she had used a poor way to test her claims? (Perhaps students in both groups already used outlining, or perhaps the course examinations were not a good measure of the kind of increased understanding that outlining provides.) Did the instructor attend more carefully to the class taught outlining?

Dana then went back to the research and theory on the topic, and clarified and strengthened her argument about what outlining should do and why. She developed more careful procedures to rule out the alternative explanations she was encountering (such as more clearly defining the difference in treatments) and developed better measures of the impact of outlining. Because of her pilot test experience, Dana's subsequent data collection and defense of her claims were based on a much more sophisticated argument and collection of evidence.

When Harry was asked at his final dissertation defense what was the one most important thing he had learned from his work, he responded in jest, "How to do this study right!" Seriously, however, that is probably one of the most important lessons you will learn from your dissertation study; pilot testing can help you learn it sooner and can dramatically increase the quality of your proposal and final study.

Summary

A dissertation proposal may serve several functions, then: as justification for the study, as work plan, as evidence of ability to conduct inquiry, as a request for commitment, as the basis for contractual agreements, as an evaluative criterion for judging the progress and final product, and even as a report of the portion of the dissertation work already completed. Anna's and Laura's proposals illustrate two different ways in which a proposal may serve some of these functions; there are, of course, countless other variations. All proposals share in common the first of these functions—they provide an argument that the proposed inquiry addresses a problem worth investigating, in a feasible way, and it is likely to produce meaningful and useful information. Proposals provide a justification for pursuing the proposed inquiry.

HOW FUNCTIONS DIFFER WITH DIFFERENT KINDS OF INQUIRY

An ever widening array of dissertation options reflects, in part, both the diversification of methods in the social sciences over the past half-century and the increased application of social science procedures to the solution of social problems. As the range of acceptable dissertation inquiry has grown, some functions of the proposal are less important for certain kinds of studies, while other functions are more emphasized. We examine this variability in terms of (1) the extent to which the study can be planned in advance (prespecified vs. emergent studies), and (2) the extent to which study findings are intended to have general or more local application (general vs. local findings).

Prespecified vs. Emergent Studies

Some studies are painstakingly planned in advance; others are tailored as the inquiry progresses.

In *prespecified* studies, the questions of interest, arguments supporting the inquiry, and specific procedures of the inquiry are worked out at the beginning of the investigation. Once the design is established, the researcher implements the study, adhering to the original plan as closely as possible. Much of the traditional empirical research in the social sciences is of this kind.

Emergent studies have a long tradition in the humanities and in some branches of the social sciences. In emergent studies, the questions of interest, supporting arguments, and procedural details are worked out as the study proceeds. Such studies are most frequently employed to investigate natural variation, to study phenomena afresh and/or in all their normal complexity, or to explore phenomena to see what can be learned. Emergent designs may also be used because researchers lack prior knowledge of the phenomenon, methodological tools are inappropriate or lacking, or situational control is inadequate to conduct a prespecified study.

Studies need not be one or the other but may blend the two strategies, intentionally or inadvertently. A prespecified study may become more emergent as field controls break down, new information suggests that initial assumptions were incorrect, or unstable conditions demand greater researcher flexibility. Ronnie implemented an experimental study of the impact of a film-editing course on students' spatial visualization abilities. When the pretest measures showed that the control group was already scoring higher than the treatment group, instead of both groups starting out equally, Ronnie responded by making his design more investigative. He included additional data collection points and qualitative impact measures.

Other studies intentionally start as emergent and exploratory and then become increasingly prespecified as background investigations and pilot testing clarify which specific questions are most meaningful, important, and feasible to study. Laura's study of the professional development of medical personnel followed this latter approach. After months of emergent fieldwork and study of prior research, she accumulated sufficient understanding of the important issues and methodological constraints to develop a focused, prespecified design.

The nature of the phenomenon being examined also influences whether a more prespecified or more emergent strategy is the best choice. Suppose you were interested in knowing more about how different personality types respond to chronic stress. You might choose as your dissertation to conduct a meta-analysis (combining results of comparable studies into a single index) of the considerable empirical literature that relates elevated blood pressure to such personality characteristics as level of affect expression and defensiveness. A prespecified design that summarized the extent of the available literature, specified the criteria for selecting studies for review, and stated the analytic procedures to be used would provide a strong proposal and an efficient work plan. Instead, you might choose to study the psychological and physical effects of prolonged unemployment. In this case, a more emergent design of following selected individuals through extended periods of unemployment might be more revealing. The kinds of data collected would depend, in part, on what the individuals in the study were experiencing.

Note that the prespecified vs. emergent distinction is not synonymous with the common division of qualitative (e.g., interpretivist, naturalistic, ethnographic) vs. quantitative (e.g., behaviorist, postpositivist, experimental, statistical) approaches. Some ethnographic and systematic qualitative studies employ relatively prespecified designs, while some single-subject and investigative quantitative studies use relatively more emergent designs. Although qualitative studies most frequently employ emergent designs and quantitative studies most commonly use prespecified designs, there are numerous examples of the converse.

Functions of the Proposal in Prespecified and Emergent Studies

Proposals function differently between prespecified and emergent studies. Because of greater detail on specific tasks, time lines, and budgets, prespecified proposals are better suited to provide an argument for the anticipated results and to serve as a work plan, as a basis for contractual commitments, and as an evaluative criterion. Proposals for emergent studies allow greater responsiveness to changes in the study context and incremental understanding of the phenomenon of interest. Both types of proposals serve the functions of providing evidence of the student's ability and of soliciting commitment. Differences across prespecified and emergent studies are summarized in Table 2.1 on the next page.

General vs. Local Findings

Some studies emphasize production of findings that generalize beyond the instance and circumstances in which the study was done—generalizable findings. Other studies emphasize the solution of problems in a particular setting—local findings. Let us examine the nature of such studies and implications for functions of the proposal, beginning with those seeking generalizable findings.

TABLE 2.1

**A Summary of How the Functions of a Proposal Are the
Same and Different for Prespecified and Emergent Studies**

Proposal Function	Prespecified Studies	Emergent Studies
Provides an argument for conducting the study.	Yes, fully elaborated argument is expected.	Yes, but argument also emerges as study is completed. Includes as much as is feasible at time of approval (with pilot study, it may be fairly complete).
Describes a work plan.	Yes, usually with detailed timeline, and resource analysis.	Yes, but includes only general purpose, approach, boundaries, rules for proceeding, possible outcomes, and maximum resource expenditure.
Provides evidence of student's ability.	Yes, quality work must be demonstrated.	Yes, quality work must be demonstrated.
Serves as a request for commitment.	Yes, and may also request field entry, data-site approvals, or financial aid.	Yes, and may also request field entry, data-site approvals, or financial aid.
Serves as a contract.	Yes, extensive detail provides strong basis for monitoring work.	No, or only weakly, since only general boundaries and parameters are specified.
Serves as an evaluative criterion.	Yes, for both process and product.	No, or only weakly, since few design details are specified.
Provides partial dissertation draft.	Possibly, if extensive detail provided initially and few subsequent changes made.	No, initial statement is insufficient and subject to considerable change.

Studies Emphasizing Generalizable Findings

Empirical Studies	*Conceptual Studies*
Sample Survey	Philosophical
Experimental	Historical
Case Study	Methodological

What is considered acceptable dissertation inquiry differs by discipline, institution, department, and dissertation committee. In many doctoral programs that prepare researchers to work in academic settings, the dissertation is to be a form of research, resulting in *generalizable* findings. These are findings that apply to (and therefore could be replicated with) other persons, situations or contexts, treatments, observations or measures, study methods or designs, and times. Further, in the social sciences it is often expected that most dissertations will be *empirical,* that is, gathering data from or about persons. They typically employ such methods as sample survey designs; experimental/quasi-experimental designs; longitudinal designs; case study/single-subject designs; qualitative designs; meta-analytic/secondary data analysis designs; and so on.

An example of an empirical study seeking generalizable knowledge was described earlier—Dana's investigation of whether the use of study outlines helps students understand philosophy.

In contrast, some forms of dissertation research employ *conceptual* methods to investigate philosophical, historical, methodological, or theoretical topics, but are still concerned with producing generalizable findings. In these doctoral programs, dissertations are judged according to the established canons of social science or the humanities relevant to each particular domain. Although topics for dissertations of this type are often more abstract and narrowly focused on issues of academic importance, the proposal must still show the student's familiarity with prior research and research method.

> David had a full fellowship for the last year of his dissertation, and he spent almost the entire year reading, studying, and writing. He seldom left his apartment except to shop, exercise, and socialize with a few close friends. He met with his dissertation advisor whenever possible. David's dissertation task was to clarify the forms of reasoning that could be used in making evaluative judgments about social and educational programs. In his proposal, he had to convince colleagues in a narrow professional area that his problem had substantial intellectual merit and that he was capable of making a significant contribution to the problem's solution. Although he was seeking generalizable knowledge, few individuals outside this narrow area could judge the importance of the problem or its likely solution (certainly no one in David's family could understand why he chose to spend so much time studying such an arcane issue).

Consider, for the moment, how the faculty viewed these respective proposals of conceptual and empirical research designed to produce generalizable results. Since David was doing conceptual analysis, his proposal had no plan for empirical data collection and only a very modest method statement. His proposal was accepted late in the dissertation process. It consisted primarily of his progress to date, offered as evidence of his ability to work on the problem. Neither David nor the faculty knew how long the study might take or whether an acceptable solution would be found. (By the way, David published a major portion of his research within one year after defending his dissertation!)

Similar to David's work, only a few of Dana's fellow researchers were capable of assessing her arguments based on prior research in cognitive psychology and instructional design. Her ability to conduct her proposed research had already been established, however, through collaborative studies she had done with faculty and her pilot study experience. In reviewing her proposal, her committee members were most concerned with the strength of her study design, the quality of the measurement instruments, and the logistics of actually collecting the data in the field.

Functions of the Proposal in Studies Emphasizing Generalizable Findings

Generalizable findings may be located by both prespecified and emergent studies. The nature of the generalities found by the strategies may differ, however, with those from the prespecified tending to be abstract and more independent of context whereas emergent study findings often are heavily context dependent. Indeed, in emergent studies, the extent of generality is often left to the interpretation of the reader, with descriptions rather than conclusions resulting from the study.

The functions played by the proposal are largely determined by whether it more closely resembles prespecified or emergent. Prespecified empirical studies are usually expected to result in generalizable findings. Experiments and sample surveys have been common approaches, with proposals expected to be fully developed statements serving all the functions described above. In emergent studies, the function of the proposal as argument, work plan, contract, and evaluative criterion is weak or nonexistent. Therefore, the functions of giving evidence of ability and requesting commitment on the part of faculty become more critical.

Studies Emphasizing Local Findings—Application Studies

Development Studies	*Problem-Solving Studies*
Measuring Instruments	Cost Analysis
Curriculum	Evaluation
Software	Diffusion

Many doctoral programs prepare practitioners who are more concerned with the *application* of knowledge in specific contexts. In these programs, the dissertation is often a process of *development* resulting in a needed product with demonstrated effectiveness, such as a measurement instrument, a piece of equipment, a curriculum, computer software, a policy, or a program or intervention. Such studies tend to be prespecified so that all the functions of the proposal are important.

Some application dissertations are explicitly *problem solving* in nature—for example, action-oriented studies, evaluations, need assessments, diffusion studies, and cost analysis studies. Application dissertations may be as broad as the development and testing of a new K–12 mathematics curriculum or as narrow as the evaluation of a local substance abuse program. Application dissertation proposals are expected to emphasize social relevance and utility and the use of existing knowledge to address a practical problem. They must show familiarity with the practical issues involved and give evidence of the student's interpersonal and managerial skills that are often as important as technical and analytic skills in doing such studies.

Functions of the Proposal in Application Studies

Proposals for application studies are likely to emphasize the functions of request for commitment, giving evidence of ability, and describing the evaluative criteria against which the problem solution should be judged.

> Philip worked in the human resource development area of a large utility company. His dissertation involved the development and testing of a training intervention designed to encourage employees to take greater responsibility for their own professional development. There was little question of Philip's ability to do the study he proposed, since he had been a corporate trainer for many years and planned to conduct the study in a setting he knew well—the corporation where he currently worked. Further, his study was based on a major theory of adult learning of which his dissertation chairperson was a nationally known proponent.

> Much of the dissertation committee's discussion of Philip's proposal concerned the logistical problems of implementing a complex quasi-experimental design in a practical setting. Because Philip planned to conduct his training intervention with corporate employees taking classes offered by a local college, he had to obtain permissions and protection of human subject clearances from his corporation, the local college, as well as his own university. Initial approvals had to be renegotiated when the corporation became concerned about potential employee union objections and possible conflict-of-interest charges arising from the use of corporate resources to conduct personal (dissertation) research. Dealing with such problems took as much of Philip's time as clarifying his arguments that his intervention would indeed ameliorate the existing staff development problem. Clearly, the functions of request for commitment and evidence of relevant abilities were important for Philip's proposal.

Dissertations may be a blend. For example, constructing a measurement instrument or developing an instructional CD-ROM may be each a dissertation in itself or may be parts of a test of an instructional learning theory. Anna's dissertation proposal involved her in a sequence of tasks, including development of instructional materials, evaluation of a training intervention, research on cultural differences, etc.

The prospect of combining the dissertation study with ongoing job responsibilities has appeal, but two half-time jobs often add up to more than one full-time job—pleasing two (or more) masters simultaneously. The dissertation committee may encourage the student in one direction, the job setting in a different one, usually at a faster pace.

> Janeen left the university for a well-paying job at a research corporation that was doing a study very similar to her approved proposal. She continued with only minor changes, but the intellectual ownership of her results had to be renegotiated since the corporation legally owned the work.

You can see why faculty members pay particular attention to matters of field relationships, time lines, and control of the study when reviewing proposals for application dissertations.

Think about which of the various functions your dissertation proposal will be expected to serve. Worksheet 2.1: Proposal Function Review is provided to help you. Also think about the kind of study you might propose (prespecified vs. emergent) and the kind of findings you hope to produce (general vs. local), and then fill in those sections of the worksheet relevant to your plans. Be sure to review prior accepted proposals similar to the studies you are considering and to discuss expectations about the proposal with your chairperson and committee members.

Since the primary function of every dissertation proposal is to justify the proposed study, we next consider in chapter 3 how viewing the proposal as a chain of reasoning facilitates that task, especially for those studies emphasizing generalizable findings.

WORKSHEET 2.1

Proposal Function Review

What Are Expectations for My Proposal?

For the type(s) of study you expect to propose for your dissertation, describe the extent to which your proposal will be expected to serve each of the functions identified. It may be helpful to consult faculty advisors, more senior dissertation students, and prior local dissertation proposals.

To What Extent Will My Proposal Need To . . . ?
Provide an argument for justifying my study?
Include a work plan?
Provide evidence of my ability to do the study?
Serve as a request for commitment to work with me?
Serve as a contract for how my study is to be conducted?
Be used later to judge the quality of my dissertation work?
Serve as a partial draft of my final dissertation report?

CHAPTER 3

The Proposal as a Chain of Reasoning

CHAPTER CONTENTS

THE PROPOSAL AS A CHAIN OF REASONING

As noted in the previous chapter, not all studies produce findings involving a generalization; some simply describe, leaving the range of application to be supplied by the reader.[1] But, as we will describe in this section, those studies that do seek to generalize, whether the generality is found by prespecified or emergent means, *present their findings as a chain of reasoning.* If the study is prespecified, the initial links of the chain will be developed in the proposal. If the study is emergent, then building as much of the chain as is feasible at the study's outset provides the strongest proposal.

Let us carry this point a bit further. The end goal of research that produces or supports a generalization is the development of a carefully constructed chain of reasoning. Both the write-up of the proposal and the dissertation itself follow a logical, deductive sequence of presentation. The process of doing research, especially in the case of prespecified studies, often follows a similar sequence.

---

1. Some qualitative research, such as Whyte's *Street Corner Society* (1993), results more in description of situations than in generalizations about them. Though the proposal for such a study may be written deductively, the dissertation is not.

But it also may not, and in that instance the process is reconstructed as a logical sequence in the write-up. Even though the logic involved in developing generalizations from emergent studies is inductive rather than deductive (as is most apparent in exploratory research), *research reports presenting findings supportive of a generalization* do so deductively as a chain of reasoning.

The basic logic underlying the chain of reasoning not only applies to studies seeking generalizable findings, but may also be interpreted so as to apply to the developmental and problem-solving efforts described in the previous chapter as local application studies. For example, the production of a new measuring instrument or curriculum, the solving of a local problem, and conducting an evaluation all follow a series of steps comparable to those involved in studies seeking generalizations. Let us first examine how the chain of reasoning applies in the latter case, and we will then take up the former.

THE CHAIN OF REASONING IN STUDIES WITH GENERALIZABLE FINDINGS

Our most beneficial research studies provide results that are generalizable beyond the context in which they were carried out. Figure 3.1 represents the logic underlying the write-up of such studies as a chain of reasoning analogous to a metal chain. Each of the links in the chain successively develops a logical path from the onset of the study to the presentation of findings. This is described in the discussion of each of the links in the following section. It also shows the value of the metal chain analogy. The chain of reasoning logic also underlies the research proposal.

The Links in the Chain

In the presentation of new findings, as well as in beginning to do a study, one usually links back to what was already known about the phenomenon in terms of published work or experience. Thus, the first link in the chain is *Links to Previous Research*. It shows how the idea for this study arose out of this background.

How much background on the intended study already exists determines the nature of the next link, *Explanation, Rationale, Theory, or Point of View*. With little prior knowledge or experience, it leads to a rationale for doing the study and perhaps a point of view about what to study. With more background, one may have an explanation of a phenomenon; with still more, perhaps a theory about a process.

The specificity of the prior link determines the *Questions, Hypotheses, Models* link. With little background, one may pose a *question* describing the initial focus of attention for the study. With an explanation, one may be able to make a prediction that is presented as a *hypothesis*. If there is extensive prior research so the underlying causative variables may be fathomed, this leads to a model in-

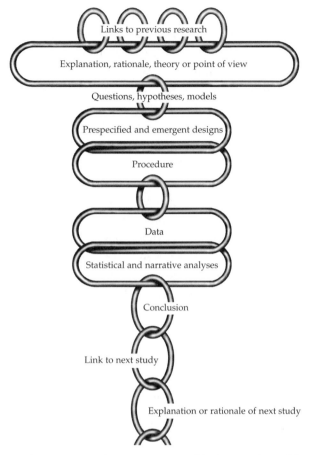

Figure 3.1. The chain of reasoning in the presentation of findings (adapted from Krathwohl, 1998/2004 with suggestions from John T. Behrens).

dicating the interrelation of the variables in a process. The study would then seek data to test that *model*.

The question, hypothesis, or model forms the basis for the *Prespecified and emergent designs* of the study, the next link. With little prior knowledge, an emergent design is usually indicated; you don't know where the "handles" are on the phenomena. The more that is known about the phenomena, the more certainty you can preplan the study. Whereas beginning with a question most likely leads to an emergent study, starting with a hypothesis or model leads to a prespecified study. Some studies begin in an emergent mode, and as more is learned a planned study becomes possible.

Just as the question, hypothesis, or model translates into the choice of emergent or prespecified design, the latter choice determines the *Procedure*. The procedure spells out the who, where, what, when, and how of the study. In an emergent study it will tell who will be studied, what will be the focus, when and how it will be done, etc. In a prespecified study, the nature of a treatment or intervention, the measures of effect, the pattern of treatment and measurement, etc., are decided upon and the details specified of when, how, where, etc., the observations, interviews, measures, treatments, etc., will take place. The link tying *Procedure* to *Data* is detailed below.

Carrying out the design leads to gathering *Data,* the next link. For example, the scores on measures, the observation notes, the recordings or transcripts of interviews, and the results of surveys are the data.

In both emergent and prespecified studies, the data are usually voluminous, more than can be grasped by just looking at them. This requires data reduction using the methods of *Statistical and Narrative Analyses,* the next link. Narrative analysis usually involves finding the significant themes in the observation notes, interviews or documents; statistical analysis, descriptive summary statistics, relationship and pattern-seeking statistics and displays, and singling out findings unlikely to have resulted from chance.

The results of these analyses are summarized in a final section of the report, the *Conclusion.* These conclusions are read by other researchers and lead in turn to continuing the chain of reasoning as these findings are built on by new research. This is indicated in the last two links of the chain, which, although not part of the study report, show each study as part of the continuing research process.

Details of the Links from Procedure to Data

Figure 3.2 provides a more detailed look at the link between *Procedure* and *Data* in the chain. It reveals that instead of a single link, it has been split in order to describe the who, where, what, how, and when of the procedure.[2]

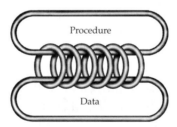

Figure 3.2. Detail of the connections between the *Procedure* and *Data* links.

Figure 3.3 spreads these links out to bridge across the *Procedure* and *Data* links and labels them to indicate the who, where, what, how, and when of procedure that must be described.

More specifically, these six links are:

2. Rudyard Kipling's little ditty usefully describes the elements to describe: "I keep six honest serving men, / They taught me all I knew, / Their names are What and Why and When / And How and Where and Who." We covered *Why* in the *Explanation, rationale* link. The others are covered in *Procedure.*

1. *Who*, the *Participants*—these are all the persons selected for the study or present in the situation being observed.
2. *Where*, the *Situation*—this is the situation and context in which the experiment is carried out, that in which observation is done, that interviewing takes place, etc.
3. *What*, the *Focus(es) of Action*—that is, for experimental research, the independent variable, treatment or experimental variable(s) (cause), the dependent variable (effect), and any control variables (e.g., measures of ability where one wants to rule it out as an alternative cause). For qualitative and nonexperimental research, it is those processes and activities that are the focus of attention.

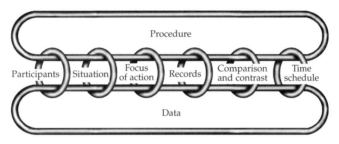

Figure 3.3. The connections in the chain of reasoning between the *Procedure* and *Data* links.

4. Also a *What*, the *Records* from (3) above—these are the data resulting from observations or measures, the field notes and the answers to tests, questionnaires, etc. The latter are scored and interpreted at the next stage.
5. *How*, the *Comparison or Contrast*—in experimental research, that which forms the basis for sensing that the treatment or experimental variable had some effect, or, in nonexperimental research, how things changed as the process or activity continued.
6. And *When*, the *Time Schedule*—when things are done, such as what observations are made, when, where, and of whom, and, if there are measures and treatments, how, where, when, and to whom they were administered.

For example, consider Rowe's (1974) hypothesis. She hypothesized that after posing a question to the class, increasing the amount of time the teacher typically waits before calling on a student would improve the nature of classroom discourse. She found a normal "wait-time" of one second on average could be increased to three to five by training. The six rings translated the above general hypothesis in these ways:

• The *Participants* were the teachers and students in the classrooms where this effect was demonstrated.

- The *Situation* and context were those found in the classrooms. In this instance, as in many, the choice of the "participants and/or informants" determined the "situation."
- The *Focuses of Action* were the treatment, the teacher's increase in "wait-time" (cause), and the change in the students' responses to the treatment (effect). To attain control for variations in what was meant by "delayed wait-time" that might result from embarrassment or discomfort, training of the teachers ensured the "treatment" was administered uniformly and as intended.
- *Records* included measures of effect such as recordings of classroom discourse to determine who talked and what kind of teacher-pupil interchange took place. There were also pre- and posttraining measures of the teacher's wait-time to show that it actually increased.
- The *Comparison and Contrast* involved contrasting measures of both wait-time and classroom discourse prior to teacher training with those after wait-time training.
- Finally, *Time Schedule* involved a procedural plan indicating when and where the training would take place and of whom, and when, and of what, observations would be made.

Were this Rowe's dissertation, her proposal would have provided detail on the links of the chain of reasoning model from the previous literature at the top, down through the six rings of the "procedure" links in Figures 3.1 and 3.3. In addition, it would have included a general description of the data that would be gathered and the methods of analysis of the data.

Rowe's data showed that higher-level thinking appeared in the answers following longer wait-times as well as other positive changes. Note that in figure 3.1 and the next figure, 3.4, Rowe's findings, in turn, link to the beginning of subsequent studies when researchers used her findings to build their studies' chains of reasoning. (To determine the extent to which this occurred, one would look up "Rowe, Mary Budd," in the *Social Science Citation Index*.)

The complete chain of reasoning with the labels attached to the connections between *Procedure* and *Data* is shown in Figure 3.4. This figure may be useful for you to refer to as you read the rest of this book.

FOUR USEFUL CHARACTERISTICS OF THE CHAIN ANALOGY

The chain analogy is useful because many characteristics of a metal chain carry over to research chains of reasoning (Krathwohl, 1998/2004). For example, it is an old truism that a metal chain is only as strong as its weakest link. Similarly, *a research proposal's logical chain of reasoning is only as strong as its weakest link*. If one of the links in the chain is weak—for example, if training is omitted from the

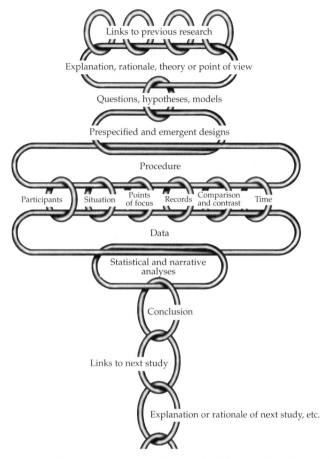

Figure 3.4. The complete chain of reasoning with all the labels (adapted from Krathwohl, 1998/2004 with suggestions from John T. Behrens).

proposal so the teachers do not increase their wait-time—then you can hardly attribute any change to the treatment. Like a metal chain, the research argument is only as strong as the weakest part of it.

A second feature of the analogy, and a corollary of the first, is that each link in the chain should have the same strength. It would make little sense to have one link in a metal chain as thick as that for a ship's anchor and others as thin as sewing thread. Similarly, in planning a project, for the most efficient use of your resources, *each of the links should be the same strength as the others.* Why spend resources refining measures of the effect of a treatment to great sensitivity when resources to ensure that the treatment itself is administered as it should be are not allocated? You should allocate resources to the various links in the chain of reasoning so that each level in the chain can appropriately support the argument.

A third aspect is that just as a chain picks up the load at the beginning and successively transfers it to each link, thereby determining the nature of each successive link in terms of the load it has to carry, the same occurs in the chain of reasoning. *Each link in the chain determines the nature of the next link.* This aspect became apparent as the chain was described: past research leads to the present explanation, that explanation to a hypothesis, question, or model that determines the choice of design that is translated into procedure, and so on.

A final feature of a metal chain is that at any point in the chain where several horizontal links across the chain's breadth serve jointly to connect the links above and below them, each of the horizontal links shares the load. In the research chain of reasoning, this occurs as shown in Figures 3.2 and 3.3 between *Procedure* and *Data.* In a metal chain, where links share the load, one of them may be made stronger in order to compensate for weakness in another in order to carry the load from the levels above to the levels below them. In the same way, *one of the links connecting Procedure and Data may be strengthened to compensate for another facet that is weak.* For instance, assume the "wait-time" effect, even with training, is so small it is hard to notice the change—a thin, weak " comparison and contrast" link. You may compensate by strengthening any or all of several of the other design links. For example, you could strengthen the *Participants* link by both increasing the size of the sample and using especially bright students who are likely to be particularly responsive to the treatment. You could strengthen the *Records* link by using tests or observations especially designed to catch the small changes that are expected to occur. Thus, various design trade-offs can be made to achieve the strongest overall chain, each of these horizontal links compensating for one another.

RELATION OF THE CHAIN ANALOGY TO THE PROPOSAL

As noted in the Rowe example, the report of the study follows the chain of reasoning, and to the extent possible, the proposal should as well. Insofar as the nature of the study can be anticipated before beginning the actual dissertation data collection, the proposal encompasses all of the upper part of Figure 3.4 through the six horizontal rings of the study's procedure. To the extent possible in anticipation of what is expected to occur, it usually also describes the data that will be collected and the process of analysis to be used. The relations of the successive links described above and shown graphically in Figure 3.4 should be reflected in the preparation of the proposal. The problem statement should be built so that the project's hypotheses, questions, or models flow logically from it. The statement of objectives and method of attack should build upon and move beyond the review of past research, showing how this study will add to prior accomplishments, and remedy past failures. These, in turn, will suggest the population and sample and the rest of the research design. The kind of data gathered will determine what analysis, statistical or narrative, is appropriate.

All research studies presenting the case for a generalization are logical chains of reasoning. A strong proposal intended to demonstrate or validate such a generalization reflects this chain by the plan of its structure, by its internal logical consistency, and by the appropriate development of each section. Each section reflects the previous material and carries it a step further in a consistent way. Study details are not overlooked: objectives are not slighted, plans for data collection are not included in the analysis section of the plan, and the like. Resources are properly allocated to strengthen weak aspects, and design trade-offs are appropriately made.

The idea of a proposal as a chain of reasoning underlies the advice given in the next two parts of the book. Part 2 provides general advice about how to develop the core proposal components of the problem statement and method statement. Part 3 deals with adapting the core proposal to fit particular types of inquiry approaches. So both parts should be consulted, part 2 in its entirety and such chapters of part 3 as seem relevant to what you plan to do.

THE CHAIN OF REASONING IN DEVELOPMENT
AND PROBLEM-SOLVING STUDIES

Earlier, we noted that the chain of reasoning analogy usefully applies as well to local application studies, whether development studies such as those creating a product (e.g., an instrument or curriculum) or problem-solving studies such as performing an evaluation or conducting a cost analysis. When such studies are described in a formal report, they also follow a chain of reasoning sequence, and the chain analogy, together with its applicable properties (strong as its weakest link, etc.), also applies. The interpretation of each of the steps in the conceptualized chain, however, must be adjusted to fit the context—development or problem solving—of the study. Table 3.1 suggests for each of the links in the chain how it may be interpreted for development and problem-solving studies. In some instances, entries are examples of what would represent that link in a particular kind of study.

Most of the entries in the table are self-explanatory, but a word might be said about the data and analysis steps and formative and summative evaluation. What occurs at these steps depends on how quickly you complete the development or problem-solving process, succeeding on the first attempt or requiring several trials. If a prototype or trial, at the data link, you may seek diagnostic information intended to help learn how the product, intervention, or process can be improved. Since you are seeking diagnostic capability, the instruments or measures used may be different from those used once past this stage. And if the data indicate improvement is needed or possible, you may then cycle back through the earlier stages. How far back depends on whether you must start from scratch or are on the right track and satisfaction lies in adjustment. If the evaluation of the prototype or trial yields data that look as though only a bit of tweaking is needed, or if it has been developed as far as you

TABLE 3.1

The Chain of Reasoning in Development and Problem Solving Studies

	How Successive Links in the Chain May Be:	
Links in the Chain	**Interpreted for Development Studies**	**Interpreted for Problem Solving Studies**
Links to previous studies	Lessons learned in previous, similar studies	Analysis of strengths and weaknesses of previous solutions or alternative processes
Explanation, rationale, theory, or point of view	Problem solving rationale, development models	Intervention strategies, diffusion theory, cost-analysis models
Questions, hypothesis, models	Criteria which product must meet	Criteria which solution or process must satisfy
Planned and/or emergent design	Plan for product development	Plan for development of solution or application of process
Procedure		
Participants	Persons used in tryouts	Defined by locale of problem
Situation	Defined by location of persons used in tryouts	Defined by locale of problem
Focus of action	Variables involved in development of product	Variables involved in solution or process
Records	Measures or instruments used to evaluate product	Measures or instruments used to evaluate solution or process
Comparison and contrast	Basis used to determine improvement	Basis used to determine improvement or success of process
Time schedule	Procedural steps involved in developing product and its evaluation	Procedural steps involved in solution or in process and evaluation of outcomes
Data	Prototype product and formative evaluation Or Product and summative evaluation	Trial intervention or process and formative evaluation Or Implementation of intervention or process and summative evaluation data
Statistical and narrative analysis	Analyses appropriate to data gathered	Analyses appropriate to data gathered
Conclusion	Description of product, its uses, advantages, weaknesses, and limitations	Description of solution or process, other possible uses, advantages and weaknesses

intend to take it, or you are satisfied, then you proceed to the summative evaluation. It leads to the conclusion and wrap-up of the project.

A variation for problem-solving studies should be noted. Once you have solved a problem at the local level, even though that is all you intended at the outset, you may realize that the solution or process has more general implications. This may result in cycling back to the design and procedure links of the chain and making new choices in the six aspects of procedure. This would allow you to determine how well the intervention or process works in other situations, with other persons—whether, as they say, "it has legs" and is generalizable.

Worksheet 3.1: Chain of Reasoning Analysis is provided here to give you practice in analyzing how well a dissertation proposal builds a chain of reasoning. Use Worksheet 3.1 to review the chain of reasoning in chapter 11, one of the annotated proposals included in this book. Then, once you have a draft of your own proposal, come back to this worksheet to review the strength of its chain of reasoning so you can make the most convincing case for conducting your study.

Chain of Reasoning Analysis

How Strong Is My Proposal's Chain of Reasoning?

In reviewing your proposal's argument for the study proposed, first describe each element in the proposal's chain of reasoning, and then review its strengths, weaknesses, ways to correct those weaknesses, and, finally, how well it follows from prior elements and contributes to subsequent elements in building a convincing overall argument.

Chain of Reasoning Levels	Description (Comprehensive? Concise? Convincing?)	Strengths?	Weaknesses?	Ways to Correct For Weaknesses?	Follows Well From Prior Links?	Leads Well to Following Links?
Links to Previous Studies						
Explanation, Rationale, Theory, Point of View						
Questions, Hypotheses, Models						
Pre-planned or Emergent Design						
Procedure *Participants* *Situations* *Points of Focus* *Records* *Comparison & Contrast* *Time Schedule*						
Data						
Statistical & Narrative Analysis						
Conclusion						

Advice Common to Most Proposals

This part gets down to the nuts and bolts of writing a proposal and making it hold together as a logically integrated chain of reasoning (the chain of reasoning analogy was described in the previous chapter; pick it up if you missed it). Although it gives advice that will apply to most proposals, the advice is described in terms that may make it appear to apply primarily to prespecified proposals (the prespecified/emergent distinction is described in chapter 2; go back and pick it up too if you missed it). This is necessary in order to make it specific enough to be helpful. But wherever advice for an emergent or qualitative dissertation would differ from the advice given, that is noted in this part's chapters and then is further developed in appropriate sections of part 3. Part 2 consists of three chapters that cover successive sections of the proposal, the four topmost rings of the chain of reasoning.

Chapter 4 describes how to present the problem and foreshadows the rest of the proposal. It shows how the review of literature develops and refines the problem statement as well as suggesting appropriate refinements in method. The refined problem statement leads to a question, hypothesis, or model, depending on how advanced the state of knowledge is in the area being studied, or leads to a more detailed description of the phenomenon to be focused upon, in the case of emergent studies.

Chapter 5 describes how to present your research method or process in sufficient detail that gatekeepers will be comfortable in approving the proposal as a basis for proceeding with the dissertation.

Chapter 6 describes what kind of additional evidence may be helpful in presenting your case and how this may be marshaled so as to be convincing to gatekeepers.

CHAPTER 4

The Description of the Problem

CHAPTER CONTENTS

Your first task is to describe your problem in terms so enticing as to make the reviewer eager to examine the rest of your proposal. This job falls especially to the introduction and initial problem statement, but is shared with two other sections described in this chapter, the literature review and the questions, hypotheses, and models sections. The introductory section typically develops understanding of the problem by describing its significance in relation to the large, important problems already of concern to the reviewer and by showing the problem in the perspective of the field in which it is embedded.

    This leads into a section on related research (the literature review), which further develops problem understanding and appreciation by showing specifically how the problem is solidly grounded in the previous work of the field and how this project will take a significant step beyond what has already been done.

This makes it possible at the end of the literature review for the problem to be restated in a more precise and detailed fashion with greater understanding. And from that problem statement are teased the research questions, hypotheses of the project, or, if enough is known of the causal factors, a model of how the phenomenon occurs. These are stated in such a way that their translation into project procedure, the topic of the next chapter, is natural and easy.

But first, there is the matter of choosing a topic, a matter that could consume the rest of the book. Instead, we begin the chapter by noting one of the most difficult aspects of selecting a research topic—balancing the trade-offs between the importance of the problem chosen and the feasibility of effectively addressing it.

THE PROBLEM OF THE PROBLEM

The problem of balancing problem importance with dissertation is nicely illustrated in Kathy Beissner's proposal.

> The topic in the dissertation proposal by Kathy Beissner, which is reproduced beginning in chapter 12, is a study of the *Effectiveness of Concept Mapping in Improving Problem Solving*. In many ways, her choice of this topic is typical of the way such dissertation decisions are made. Undoubtedly, Kathy had a personal interest in this topic, an "itch to scratch." Since the improvement of problem solving is central to the work she does as a trainer of physical therapists, why not tackle it in her doctoral dissertation? One must give her credit for undertaking a difficult problem central to her work. Further, where researchers so often work on abstract problems primarily of interest to other researchers, Kathy's problem is for those on the therapist-training front line.

> Now comes the "but." An individual's problem-solving skill is developed over a lifetime; in the case of Kathy's students, over the past eighteen to nineteen years. Her intervention, by the constraints on her own time and resources, must be comparatively small. Eisner (1984) noted that the length of the experimental interventions reported in the 1981 *American Educational Research Journal* averaged only seventy-two minutes. We might expect Kathy's intervention to be of similar length or perhaps a bit longer. But this is an infinitesimally small amount of time in comparison with that involved in the habits built into problem solving over years of school. From just the title, we don't yet know the length or the exact nature of the intervention. But Kathy has already set the problem in such a broad context—a common tendency for graduate students—that it presents difficulties in designing a study sufficiently sensitive to show any effect at all, let alone one that would have any practical significance in training physical therapists.

> Kathy's choice reflects the trade-offs both the graduate student and her faculty face: how does she define a topic with enough "bite" to be satisfying and interesting, to be

more than an exercise by having practical ramifications, to keep within the scope of her own skills and resources, and to avoid areas where even top researchers have not yet found a satisfactory approach? Kathy has chosen to err on the side of possible practical significance—assuming that even a small intervention effect could later be developed into something worthwhile. Her faculty chair and committee, in approving this proposal, apparently decided they could live with this choice as well.

Each doctoral student must balance these trade-offs: finding a problem within his competencies with a reasonable and feasible approach, yet significant enough that he is not just content to work on it, but sufficiently committed to follow it through to the end. Then he must convince his committee of this choice as well. As we noted earlier, if you are still uncertain about your dissertation topic, consult appropriate readings, such as chapter 5, "Finding a Problem," in Krathwohl (1998/2004). Use Worksheet 4.1: Characteristics of a Good Dissertation Topic at the end of this chapter to review how strong your current topic is.

PROBLEM STATEMENT

First impressions are important! The sentences with which you open suggest to the reader whether this proposal will be creative and interesting or just routine. Come back after you have a complete draft and rework your opening so that it invites the reviewer to read further. Because your initial problem description is so important, we provide the following eight guidelines to help you create a focused and effective opening statement.

Show the problem's importance. The opening statement should convince the reviewer that the project is important. For example:

> Just as overseas adaptations of the United States' social-psychological discoveries have contributed to their industrial success, so our failure to use that knowledge has compounded our problems in competing with foreign goods. This project seeks modifications in the use of this knowledge that will be effective in our culture. The reason I think this is possible is . . .

or

> A universal problem at federal, state, and local levels is ensuring that funds intended for a program are used to enhance it rather than merely substituted for program funds already allocated. Accountants are extremely resourceful at moving money around to defeat legislative provisions intended to ensure enhancement. This project will search for successful legislative practices, both here and abroad, that accountants haven't been able to defeat.

Contrast these brief examples with the opening statements in Warters's paragraph 1 in chapter 11, which gets to the problem in the third sentence. But even Warters could be sharpened; consider this alternative first sentence: "If therapists who treat men who batter their wives view their problem differently from the batterers themselves, clearly the effectiveness of treatment is likely to be affected."

Show the problem in the perspective of the larger field in which it is embedded— management practices as a part of our lagging in international economic competition, accounting procedures as a facet of making government intervention effective. Warters does this in his tenth paragraph.

Show the problem's generality. Although the dissertation's place in the graduate program has become that of a learning experience, it was originally conceived that it should be a contribution to knowledge. And many dissertations still are. If you think yours is or could be, indicate the generality of the problem and the generalizability of the research. A good way of doing this is to point to the project's contribution to theory and to knowledge of the phenomenon. Indicate how the project builds on previous theory or contributes new aspects. Relate it to the large, important problems of the field. If you can, describe the value of some concrete applications of the knowledge as well as the potential importance of these applications.

Note, however, that a generalizable project does not necessarily require a national sample. The sample's characteristics must be known, however, in order to show how and to whom the findings might be transferred. Similarly, the research situation must have enough characteristics in common with other situations that locations to which the findings might transfer can be recognized.

> Look at Warters' statement of significance beginning with paragraph 2 as an example of how one embeds the problem in a larger context and shows the generality of the problem.

Limit the problem. Learning to focus a study is a skill. Novices often believe that only by encompassing large pieces of a problem can they avoid triviality. Doctoral dissertation proposals are often rejected three or four times as the project is successively reduced in scope; yet it is only by focusing on the manageable, on the critically important aspects of problems, that progress can be made.

Don't dwell on the obvious. One of us recently read a proposal that used its first eight pages to convince the reader that research in the field was necessary. If the reader were not already aware of this, he would not have been asked to be a reviewer or should not have agreed to be when asked. Assume your reader's interest in research in the area.

Find the balance between completeness and brevity. Some researchers are too brief, taking too much for granted concerning the reviewer's knowledge of the topic (e.g., knowledge of the job market for technicians in a technician employment survey). Conversely, one may make this initial problem statement extra long on the assumption that if one sells the reviewer on the importance of the project, flaws in the remainder of the proposal may be overlooked in order to get something going in this field—that isn't likely. In this section of the proposal, as in several others, find the balance between completeness and brevity; adjust the length of this section to correspond to the way the rest of the proposal is developed.

Give the reader perspective on the whole proposal. Include a two—or three-sentence sketch of the approach you are planning to use. Also, briefly point out the merit of this approach. Foreshadowing what is to come can be used throughout the proposal to good effect, serving to integrate it. In this and other sections that tend to be lengthy and unbroken by headings or subsections, it is especially important to help the reviewer find a succinct statement that summarizes the points being made. Underlining and paragraphing are especially useful.

Here again, take a look at the first paragraph of Warters's proposal, chapter 11.

Set the frame of reference. The problem section establishes the frame of reference and the set of expectations that the reviewer will carry throughout the proposal; be sure they are the correct ones. Unfamiliar terms or words used in unusual ways may cause problems. If such terms cannot be avoided, work their definitions into the presentation early and prominently so that the reader learns them.

RELATED RESEARCH

The related research section of the proposal builds further understanding of the problem by showing that the proposal is solidly anchored in past work yet moves beyond that work in important ways. *It is an excellent place for you to give an indication of your scholarly competence: Writing this section well is a sign of professional maturity. It indicates your grasp of the field and your methodological sophistication in critiquing others' research. It shows the breadth and depth of your reading.*

Qualitative and emergent dissertations may differ in the way they handle the literature review from what is described below, particularly if they are oriented toward "It is best not to be influenced by the past literature until I know what is of significance in the situation I want to study." Those of you adopting this point of view will still find this section of value, since you will do a review of the literature during the dissertation research, if not for the proposal. Discussion of qualitative proposals and the place of the literature review in them are included in chapter 7.

What to Include

No project starts de novo. The extent to which the researcher builds the project upon what has already been done shows command of the current state of the field and the extent to which the proposed project moves the field ahead in some significant manner. Some section of the proposal should, therefore, deal with how the project contributes to this forward movement. The section on related research provides such an opportunity.

In writing this section you should:

- survey a select group of studies that provide a foundation for the proposed project,
- discuss these studies in detail sufficient to provide an understanding of their relevance,
- describe how they contribute to this study, and
- indicate how this study moves beyond them.

Beissner's literature review, paragraphs 19 and 20, is an example of citing apparently relevant literature, but then she doesn't make the connection to her study. This is a common error.

Obviously, the review should encompass the best and most recent literature in *both* content and method; an outdated review hardly adds to the impression of scholarliness. Similarly, dependence on secondary sources such as other literature reviews may be appropriate, but the scholar must review key pieces of the original literature *herself.* Work in your original findings from the basic literature to indicate this.

In discussing studies, *point out their technical and methodological flaws* and show how these pitfalls will be avoided in your work. State whether the authors correctly interpreted the findings of their studies and how their findings impact your study.

If there is a *theoretical base* for your study, be sure to discuss it here. Science is a systematically accumulated body of knowledge. Theories interrelate individual findings and permit greater generalization. This section is an excellent place to convey your grasp of how theory is currently being developed and tested in your area and to critique the solidity of the structure being erected.

See Warters's section on theoretical issues beginning with paragraph 26 as an example.

Be highly selective in this section, citing only those studies that form the base from which your study is building. More is not necessarily better. *The most common error is including too many references and doing too little with them.* Proposals are often submitted with lengthy bibliographies on the research topic rather than selected references that relate directly to the proposal. Such a comprehensive list does little to convince the reader that the researcher has any skills other than the ability to use an index.

It is what you do with the references that is the basis for judging this section. The skill shown in selection, the technical competence used in evaluating contributions, and, above all, the originality displayed in realistically and constructively synthesizing the conceptual bases of past and proposed work are what will impress readers.

Don't give up and say that the literature is too large to summarize easily; this is another point in the proposal where you must find the balance between the extremes of being too broad and too narrow.

Except for studies you are sure your readers will be familiar with, summarize the pertinent information needed to understand the study's contribution to the work being proposed. Do not expect readers to go to the library to look up references.

> Warters's paragraph 6 is an example of citing relevant material but not going far enough with it nor showing its relevance to the study.

Become aware of relevant literature from disciplines other than your own. It is surprising how often researchers who could benefit from learning what each other is doing proceed on parallel tracks in different fields completely unaware of each other's work. Review research in related disciplines using bibliographic sources that extend broadly, such as the *Social Science Citation Index.* Discuss your proposal with colleagues from other disciplines. Use of colleagues in other fields alerts you not only to relevant literature, but also to the jargon these fields use to discuss your problem, thus helping you use journal indexes much more successfully.

If possible, *include studies currently under way* that are likely to overlap your project. Knowing what is currently being investigated in one's field is another sign of competence. Show how your project differs from such studies and/or meshes with them in a constructive way. The various government agencies have set up Web sites (you can access them from http://www.firstgov.gov [accessed September 29, 2004]) on the Internet and usually post newly funded projects there. *The Chronicle of Philanthropy* Web site (http://www.philanthropy.com [accessed September 29, 2004]) also lists grants by foundations and individuals and is searchable.

Sometimes the literature review section is an afterthought. After the "fresh, new idea" has been developed into a project, one may go to the library to complete the sole remaining section—related research. Such a practice makes it difficult to reconcile past research with the "new" project. If past studies are taken into account during the planning stage, the project is much stronger.

Being human, researchers naturally want their ideas to be their own, to claim them as original, unrelated to what others have done. However, research programs cannot go on "rediscovering America" to satisfy the egos of individual investigators. All too often readers will encounter the statement that this is a "new idea" and that "nothing has been written" that bears on the problem. This is a red flag! Your chairperson and committee members know that few projects start from scratch, and they know how often the "wheel has been reinvented" by someone who did not do the proper background research. They are likely to feel challenged to search their memories for relevant studies. If they find some, they may be inclined to question the thoroughness of your scholarship and, perhaps, your technical competence as an investigator. Therefore, *if you state that "no research bearing on the problem exists," cite the closest research you found and show how it falls short.* Also indicate under what headings and in which references checks were made.

Although various fields have their own conventions, most use the *Publication Manual of the American Psychological Association*'s (2001) format of author and date of publication in parenthesis—for example, (Smith, 1981)—to identify reference sources in the text. That is the method used in this book. Accompany it with an alphabetical list of the references. In contrast to numbering the references, this saves flipping pages back and forth to see who was referred to. Reference list format should also follow the format used in your field. Again, this book uses the *Publication Manual of the American Psychological Association* format (American Psychological Association, 2001; also see http://www.psywww.com/resource/apacrib.htm [accessed September 29, 2004]).

If you refer to an obscure or difficult to obtain reference that is very important to your argument or research method, it may be helpful to your chairperson and committee to supply copies in an appendix.

SEARCH STRATEGIES AND INFORMATION SOURCES

Figure 4.1 is a diagram that summarizes the information sources that are discussed below. Refer to it to see where you are in your literature search and to suggest sources not yet used.

Cooper (1998) is an excellent updated compendium of the earlier very thorough reference on the skills of literature search in the third section of Cooper and Hedges (1994). In the latter, White (1994) discusses different search strategies, Reed and Baxter (1994) review the use of reference indexes and abstracts, and M. L. Rosenthal (1994) covers how to find fugitive literature.

Use of the Internet and World Wide Web

The Internet has changed searching forever and is likely one of the first sources to which the computer literate student turns. Using search engines (browsers such as Microsoft Explorer, Netscape, Safari, or Opera), you can use key terms to search for relevant material on such postings as faculty and methodology

SOURCES OF INFORMATION IN A LITERATURE SEARCH AND THEIR CONNECTIONS TO OTHER SOURCES IN POSSIBLE FOLLOWUPS

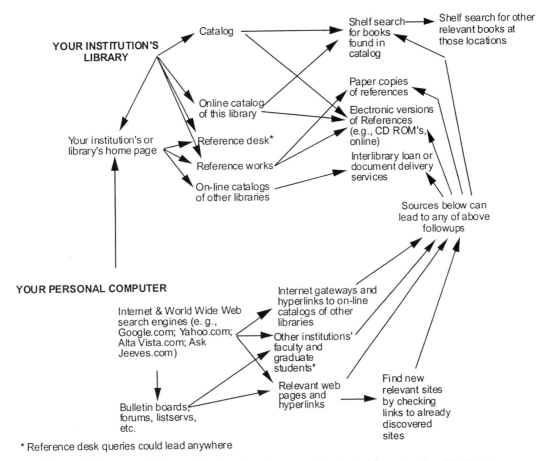

* Reference desk queries could lead anywhere

Figure 4.1. Sources of information in a literature search (adapted from Krathwohl 1988).

Web sites, online syllabi, archives, and conference proceedings, wherever the search engine has indexed the Web. Among widely used engines are: AltaVista.com, AskJeeves.com, Google.com, and Yahoo.com. There are also meta search engines like Alltheweb.com, Dogpile.com, and Metacrawler.com that simultaneously submit your query to multiple search engines. Depending on the search engine, you can find relevant sites not only in your own country but in others as well, and many engines have a translation facility. As you make these searches, you learn the terminology of the field and therefore are in a much better position to benefit from the variety of abstracting and indexing services.

It is important to realize that search engines don't run out and search the Internet each time you enter a query. It is much faster and more efficient for them to search a proprietary index of the Internet created by software that continuously roams it looking for new sites and changed ones. But variances in how they do that may result in different responses for the same query from unlike search engines. These differences arise primarily from three sources:

1. *The interface provided you to describe your query.* Engines may interpret the same query differently and/or use unique codes for advanced searches. Soople provides an interface for Google.com that makes it easier to access some of Google's advanced features (http://www.soople.com [accessed September 29, 2004]).
2. *Their use of different indexes.* Some use proprietary software to create their index; some contract for one. Indexes can differ in what sites they index and what they harvest from each site. Boardreader.com, for instance, indexes only message boards on the Web. A number of such specialty search engines exist; see http://www.searchenginewatch.com/links/article.php/2156351 (accessed September 29, 2004).
3. *The proprietary software used to evaluate matches, rank, and present responses.* Even search engines using the same index may present different responses depending on their selection, ranking, and presentation procedures.

Clearly, with queries for which there may be more than one recognizably right answer, consult multiple search engines or use a metasearch engine like Vivisimo.com.

Learn to use special search features (called "advanced searches" in some; go to http://www.searchenginewatch.com/facts [accessed September 29, 2004] and see "Power Searching for Anyone"]. Type "search engine reviews" into a search engine to learn about new ones, to learn what a particular one does, or to find comparative reviews. One-click access to a variety of specialized information sources is available at http://www.extremesearcher.com/ [accessed September 29, 2004].

Research Strategies Before the Internet

The Internet is useful, but suffices in only rare cases because some of the best indexing and abstracting services are proprietary. The traditionally used sources are still needed, though most can now be accessed through the Internet. According to White (1994, where he cites Cooper, 1985, 1987, 1989; and Wilson, 1992), here are the strategies experienced authors found most useful and widely used in searches before the advent of the Internet:

- consultation,
- traditional indexing and abstracting services, and
- "footnote chasing" (tracking down the cited references in articles on the topic of interest)

Browsing through library shelves and citation indexes were more helpful but less widely used.

Consultation

Cooper (1985) had reviewers rate sources for their centrality (significance or centrality of references found) and utility (number of references yielded). When one combines these two ratings, the most helpful, widely used strategy involved consulting others: persons who regularly share information with you, contacts at conventions and with other students (highest combined utility and centrality), and formal requests to those active in the field. White (1994) quotes a noted author on scientific communication: "If you have to search the literature before undertaking research, you are not the person to do the research" (p. 48). That is much, much too strong, but his point, as White notes, is "you may read to get to a research front, but you cannot stay there waiting for new publications to appear; you should be in personal communication with the creators of the literature and other key informants" (White, 1994).

Once you have located who these persons are, you can contact them through phone, e-mail, or correspondence. You may find contacting information in the directories of professional organizations. Many of them are available online. Such individuals will almost always be willing to send you references, possibly reprints of prior publications, and usually new manuscripts (return the favor for the latter by sending them helpful comments).

As White (1994) notes, in consultations, one is searching the bibliographies in persons' heads. That means you are tapping into their information network, as wide or limited as that may be. Experienced researchers quickly learn who is working in their field, and they tend to communicate with them and be influenced by them (what is called the "invisible college," those in regular communication in a field). Thus, all may come to use similar references and be familiar with roughly the same literature. You need to be aware of this limitation when using consultation and, if possible, also tap those who lie on the periphery or in related fields as well.

Indexing and Abstracting Services

The next most useful strategy that Cooper (1998) identified was a hand or computer search of indexing and abstracting services such as *ERIC, Psychological Abstracts, Sociological Abstracts, Social Science Citation Index*, and the other citation indexes. Traditional abstracting services were widely used, but citation indexing, though it had a higher combined rating of utility and centrality, was used by only a quarter as many of the reviewers. Old habits die hard, but you, as the new generation, need not be bound by them. Citation indexing is discussed further below.

Abstracting and indexing services are currently largely limited to the journal literature, although *PsychINFO* has a separate service that indexes chapters in edited books. An advantage of these services is that their collections are in-clusive of everything in the journals they regularly cover. One is not limited by the subscriptions of a library. M. L. Rosenthal's (1994) chapter on fugitive liter-ature lists a number of sources of conference proceedings (pp. 90–91). Many university libraries subscribe to the online versions of various abstracting and indexing services, making them available with passwords to their faculty and students. *PsychINFO* is available on the Internet to anyone for a fee. Alterna-tively, it is easy to search a wide variety of indexes on compact disc at univer-sity libraries, including the heavily used *PsychINFO (Psychological Abstracts)*, *Sociofile (Sociological Abstracts)*, and *Social Scisearch (Social Science Citation Index)*. Note, especially, that you can search these abstracts for not only terms that would typically appear in an index, but also, in *PsychINFO* and *Sociofile*, much rarer ones that would usually appear only in an abstract. (In *Social Scisearch*, the words would have to appear in a title.) For example, this allows you to find studies that employ certain methodology, software, or equipment where that fact might be abstracted but not typically indexed.

Browsing the Library Shelves

Although used by only a quarter of the reviewers in Cooper's study, browsing the library shelves had a higher combined rating than any of the above! The usefulness of browsing depends: (1) whether you are working so close to the re-search frontier that the research has not yet had time to get into the books, or the literature is still mainly in journals, and (2) whether books on your topic are lo-cated together on the shelves or spread all over the collection. When they are scattered, inefficient use of time is added to the already present luck-of-the-draw character of browsing—much search time results in only a few "hits."

As with consultation, the particular library collection you are browsing represents the selections of a particular librarian and/or faculty. Depending on the arrangements your library has with others, and/or your skill in attaining access on the Internet, you can browse by Library of Congress catalog number in the online catalogs of some of the best research libraries in the country. Books not in your institution's library then may be available via interlibrary loan.

Citation Indexing

Citation indexes result from copying all the references cited in each article of the journals covered and merging them into a single list ordered alphabetically by the person cited. Thus, if you look up an author and title of an article in the citation index, you can find the journal articles that included it in their refer-ences. Then, in the same set of volumes, by looking up the citing article's author in what is called the "source index," you can see all the references the author cited in that article. From those and the title, you can usually discern if it is an article worth pursuing.

Using citation indexing, you can find who has built on a given article, since in doing so they will cite it. You can therefore trace the development of ideas forward in time. This is something, at best, only imperfectly done by subject indexing. Starting with some of the pioneering or recently important papers in your topic of interest, you can find who has developed those ideas to create new work in the same area.

Though used by about only 9 percent of searchers (Cooper, 1985), the citation index is an especially valuable tool, since it is likely to retrieve items not found by other search methods. Citation referencing is independent of the language used in an article. Therefore, unusual terminology, the terminology of another field, or inadvertent omission by indexers is corrected by the links the author made to other articles. Such referencing reflects the greater expertise of the author than the indexer. Further, because of the multidisciplinary nature of citation indexes, references are more likely to cross academic lines.

Published by the Institute for Scientific Information (ISI), Inc., the *Science Citation Index* thoroughly covers the current literature in more than one hundred fields of science and technology. The *Social Science Citation Index* covers the social and behavioral sciences literature thoroughly and broadly from 1960 on. In 1977, the *Arts and Humanities Citation Index* began as well. Among the three of them, they cover most of the journal literature one would be interested in searching. Since current articles refer to past work, the significant past literature rapidly becomes mapped as well.

Staying Abreast of Current Literature

There is an easy way to find what one should read to stay abreast of developments in one's field, especially if it is spread across a variety of journals. Also published by ISI, *Current Contents: Social and Behavioral Sciences* collects and indexes the most recent tables of contents from the major journals in the behavioral sciences. It is available online to subscribers and in CD-ROM format.

Obtaining Journal Articles not Locally Available

Sometimes your library may not have a journal article, paper, etc., that is needed for your research. First, try your interlibrary loan office. Alternatively, or if you are in a hurry, use *ISI Document Solution.* Order from the Internet at http://www.isinet.com/products/docdelivery/ids/ (accessed September 29, 2004). There is a significant fee. Delivery is prompt and can be made by fax. Articles in journals published by the American Psychological Association are available from their Full-Text Document Delivery Service. Their Web site has a list of services that may be able to locate articles not published by the association (see http://www.apa.org/psycinfo/about/fulltext.html [accessed September 29, 2004]).

Relevant Information Sources Appropriate to Successively Specific Stages of Problem Definition

Table 4.1 suggests different starting points depending on where you are in the conceptualization of your problem. It suggests appropriate reference sources, some or all of which you may consult, as your problem develops.

A useful source for additional reading on literature searching is Reed and Baxter (2003).

Save Steps and Time with Your Computer—An Example

Susan was interested in the impact of cognitive styles on online instruction. For her literature search, she thought of using one of the search engines like AltaVista.com on the Internet from her home computer. "Cognitive styles" yielded too many responses that were irrelevant, and she wasn't sure how to refine her search. She had heard the name of a professor who might have written in the area, but could only guess at how to spell his name. She typed in her approximation of it using a wildcard, the asterisk (*), to substitute for the letters she wasn't sure of (some search engines use a question mark) but was unable to find a lead.

Her library, however, made a large number of databases available to its students through its subscription to *OCLC FirstSearch* (a database is a compilation of information; in this case, the databases were indexing and abstracting services [e.g., *Sociological Abstracts*], statistical facts, texts of journal articles, etc.). So she tapped into it from home, using her student number and name to gain access, and found that it included *PsycINFO,* an abstracting journal that has followed the psychological literature since 1894. Searching its database, she turned up a number of relevant articles. One, a dissertation, she could order from her library's interlibrary loan office on its Web site.

She had noticed that there was an entry that read "More like this" on the *First Search* record of the dissertation. Clicking on it opened a form where she could refine her search by checking several of the search terms offered. This led her to a number of new journal articles. Now that she knew the best search terms, she tried the meta search engine DogPile.com that queries several search engines at once. Where a query required more than one term to describe what she wanted, she placed plus signs between them (e.g., qualitative+analysis+software). (If she had wanted the three words to show up as an exact phrase, she would have put them in quotation marks instead of joining with plus signs.) She turned up a number of relevant sites to check. When she found relevant references on the sites, she entered the references (or, in the case of library entries, downloaded) the entries into bibliographic software. The software would format them into proper APA or MLS format and save her a lot of time.

Susan noticed that one faculty member's work at another institution was particularly relevant. She put his name in Google.com, found his Web site, and

TABLE 4.1

Relevant References and Reference Sources at Entry Points in the Literature Search That Are Increasingly Close to a Specified Problem.

Entry Points	Purpose	Sources to Consult
A general problem area	To find the important sources of information in an area—encyclopedias, handbooks, reviews of research	General guides to reference books such as *Guide to Reference Books* (Balay, 1998). Reference guides specific to a field like Reed and Baxter (1992). To find online sources, consult your institution's website for the databases available to students and faculty. Try a metasearch engine like www.vivisimo.com (accessed 9/30/04) that clusters results and ranks the clusters to provide a view of the terrain.
A specific problem area	To learn what research has been done, what terminology is being used, where the frontier is, what keywords to pursue in journal literature, dissertations of others in the area	A library's subject index or on-line catalog for relevant bibliographies, books and other materials (Find one centrally relevant book; try clicking on its call number to bring up the list of books shelved with this one; browse! Or do a call number search.) Compilations such as handbooks (*Handbook of Research on Teaching, Handbook of Social Psychology*) and research reviews (*Annual Review of Anthropology, Annual Review of Psychology, Annual Review of Sociology, Review of Educational Research, Encyclopedia of Educational Research, Encyclopedia of Psychology*) Most dissertations can be searched at www.umi.com/dissertations (accessed 9/30/04); on-line dissertations are at: oai.dlib.vt.edu/~etdunion/cgi-bin/index.pl (accessed 9/30/04) Thesauri (*Thesaurus of Psychological Index Terms*) and the *Cross-Reference Index* show what terms to search.
A specific problem	To find recent research, learn how terminology is changing, identify new fields related to the problem, explore current methodological approaches, determine the current frontier To identify the major aspects of a topic and prolific writers in the area	Appropriate indexes and abstracting services, such as *Psychological Abstracts* and *Sociological Abstracts; ERIC* and its *Current Index to Journals in Education (CIJE) and Research in Education (RIE); Education Index; Dissertation Abstracts International;* Permuterm Index of *Social Science Citation Index, Science Citation Index,* and *Arts and Humanities Citation Index* (particularly good for searching current jargon, but requires knowledge of vernacular of the time for older references)

TABLE 4.1 *(cont.)*

Entry Points	Purpose	Sources to Consult
Finding research studies basic to the problem	To find out which scholars followed up on this research and what they did with it To find the most cited authors in an area of work and the basic references to which other authors in the field refer To trace the historical development of an area by tracing back to who was cited first in an area, who cited this work, and who, in turn, cited that work, and so on	Citation Index of the *Social Science Citation Index, Science Citation Index,* and *Arts and Humanities Citation Index*
Latest terminology for a problem or the names of persons doing extensive work in the area	To locate the most recent work in an area, including ongoing work	For latest published work, *Current Contents: Social and Behavioral Science* Find relevant electronic bulletin boards and forums on the Internet. Often these are sponsored by divisions or interest groups of professional organizations and can be found from the associations' home pages. For a roster of listservs see www.lsoft.com/catalist.html (accessed 9/30/04) and www.topica.com/dir/?cid=841 (accessed 9/30/04). Participate in the dialogue and post requests for help. For ongoing research, search the Internet, especially for sites listing funded projects of government agencies [e.g. www.firstgov.gov (accessed 9/30/04) or specific sites if known like nsf.gov/home/sbe (accessed nsf.gov/home/sbe 9/30/04). For private funding, the *Journal of Philanthropy* [www.philanthropy.com (accessed 9/30/04)]. Convention programs of professional associations are often posted and increasingly searchable. Write to researchers working in the area (addresses are in convention programs or in membership directories of professional societies).

noted his publications. There she located a particularly useful book. Finding it checked out in the online catalog of her library, she placed a recall on it using the library Web site; she would be notified by e-mail when it became available. She also checked to see what sites were linked to the faculty member's by placing his Web site's uniform resource locator (URL) after the word link followed by a colon in the Google search form. This led to a list of Web sites interested in the same things he was, some of which appeared to be relevant and could be followed up. The URL for one site turned up a "not found" message; she trimmed successive pieces from the complex URL (e.g., from http://www. nova.edu/ssss/QR/QR5–1/pifer.html, she trimmed to http://www.nova. edu/ssss/QR/ and then to http://www.nova.edu/) until she found one that worked. From that she was able to trace where the one she sought had been moved.

Susan noted that this author had also been an officer in an interest group of the American Educational Research Association. From Yahoo.com she found the association's Web site and, in turn, the interest group's Web site. It indicated that the group sponsored a listserv that she could receive via e-mail. The listserv records the free-floating conversation on topics listserv members raise for discussion. It had an archive of the previous discussions, and she searched it and found some interesting material on her topic. She also noted persons actively contributing to the site on her topic and checked for their Web sites and publications. A little bashful about asking a question on the listserv, she did e-mail one of these contributors who had no Web site, asking where his publications might be available. His e-mail address was available on the university's Web site under faculty and staff directories.

While Susan was at the library picking up the book, she checked the *Social Science Citation Index* to see who had cited the book she was picking up and who was citing this author's work. She looked at the titles of these works and found some that appeared to be building on that faculty member's work. She also looked at the other books on the shelf where the book she was picking up had been shelved to see if there were other relevant materials. (Note that she also could have done a shelf scan from home by entering the call number in the library's catalog search software.)

One of the difficult problems of an extensive literature search is keeping track of interrelated points in your notes. Susan had taken a lot of notes on these various materials, and it was time to organize them. Using a word processor's table function, or a spreadsheet program, she entered the notes in rows of the table, putting the notes on a topic in one column and an easily recognized code for the source in a second. Then assigning key words to the notes, she broke up the notes into themes or salient points to confine those in a row to a main topic. She described that topic with a keyword in a separate column in the row and, if it was needed, a second keyword using another column for these secondary descriptors. Using the sort function, she brought together first the rows for the same secondary descriptor, then sorted on the primary descriptors. This moved into successive rows notes with the same descriptors. She then considered how she might outline the material she had. This brought to her attention the areas where the notes were thin and those where they were ample. This would provide a road map guiding her further literature searching.

She could have organized the notes more elegantly using qualitative analysis software ATLASti, NVivo, NUD*IST, and winMAX (free downloadable demonstration software at their Web sites—locatable with a search engine—but results cannot be saved) that allow you to code notes, interrelate codes, and organize them. Di Gregorio shows how to use NVivo for the literature search (http://www.sdgassociates.com/training.html; look for "Using NVivo for Your Literature Search" [accessed September 30, 2004]). Some software provides a graphical depiction of the interrelation of codes. Two listings of such software are the Web sites of Content Analysis Resources (http://www.car.ua.edu [accessed September 30, 2004])—click on software—and the Computer Assisted Qualitative Data Analysis Networking Project (http://www.qualita-tiveresearch.uga.edu/QualPage [accessed September 30, 2004]); the latter includes hotlinks to software sites. Also listed at the first site are the increasingly sophisticated software available to computer analyze text to show its important themes; it may help you determine whether to take the time to read it.

Quantitative Literature Summaries

If you are researching an area where there are a number of prior quantitative studies, consider doing a quantitative literature summary. Some of the summary methods, such as tabulating pro and con studies, are relatively simple. Other methods that compute an effect size may require getting statistical help if you don't have the statistical skills.

Traditionally, literature reviews analyze the positive and negative findings of studies relevant to a proposition. But to draw an overall conclusion, the authors find it difficult to know which studies to weight most heavily—the largest, the best experimental design, the most representative sample, the most valid and reliable instruments? Rarely does each in a set of studies satisfy all these criteria, so there are difficult trade-offs to consider. Further, where the results of studies are mostly in the expected direction but were not statistically significant, should these be counted as positive evidence or, as the statistical purist would suggest, as merely chance aberrations? Because of these problems, most traditional reviews conclude with ambiguous generalizations that call for more research. This contributes to the impression that the social and behavioral sciences have a weak knowledge base.

Meta-analysis is a way not only of taking into account a series of near misses but also of summarizing a series of conflicting studies. Cooper and Hedges (1994) describe a variety of ways of doing quantitative summaries:

- Counting the positive, neutral, and negative results and comparing these with what would be expected by chance (Bushman, 1994). If one counts only statistical significance as positives, because so many studies have too small samples to be sufficiently sensitive to real differences, positives will likely be underrepresented and result in biased findings.
- Combining the results of individual studies into a single test of significance (Becker, 1994).
- Developing something resembling a standard score estimate of the average strength of treatment across all studies. This is called the "treatment effect size" or just "effect size" (R. Rosenthal, 1994; Fleiss, 1994; Shadish and Haddock, 1994).

When doing a meta-analytic study, it is often a good idea to show the results several ways such as comparing the effect sizes: (1) when each sample contributes only one estimate to the combined average vs. where there were multiple measures of the effect in a given study, allowing all of these to enter the combined average, (2) with and without corrections for restriction in range, and/or (3) when the best studies are separated from those poorly designed and executed.

Should you include a meta-analysis in your review? The first question to ask yourself is whether there are enough comparable quantitative studies to supply the raw data. A pilot study of the literature will provide an estimate. If the pool of studies is very large, the meta-analysis could possibly become the dissertation in and of itself.

When the task is beyond suitable proposal development effort, not suitable as the dissertation, but doable and desired, add it to the proposal as a first stage of the study and describe the magnitude of the pool of studies. Because this leaves open the impact of the meta-analysis results on the study, base the proposal on the most likely outcome of the literature search. Also, discuss likely alternative results and how they would affect the direction of the study. This serves notice to your readers that you have given this matter consideration.

Combining a meta-analytic study with traditional judgments of the quality of the studies is particularly useful for small pools. Meta-analyses have their advantages, but traditional reviews can take into account the individual circumstances and problems of particular studies in a way that quantitative reviews don't. Such a proposal section provides good evidence not only that you are on top of the literature, but also that you really do understand how to write technically and judgmentally sound literature reviews—clearly, things you wish to demonstrate in this section of the proposal.

Literature reviews can be conducted to summarize and assess knowledge in order to *answer* a research question. A thoughtful, comprehensive review can be, itself, an important research contribution, and may serve as the entire dissertation or be published independently. Meta-analysis studies (chapter 8) are examples of such dissertations. Generally, however, the purpose of the literature review in a dissertation is not only to answer a question of what is known about a given problem, but also to support the argument *posing* the research questions to be further investigated. In doing such a literature review, then, you will be looking for what is already known about your research problem, what methods have been used successfully (or not) to study the problem, and other resources that might support your work, such as names of key researchers, relevant instruments, existing data bases, etc. See Worksheet 4.2: Topics of Interest in Reviewing Literature for a Dissertation at the end of this chapter for a list of items to keep in mind as you review the literature for your dissertation.

QUESTIONS, HYPOTHESES, OR MODELS?

So far in the problem statement, you have described the problem in general terms, shown its importance, and set it in a larger context. In the related research section, you described what previous work has been done and alluded to how you are going to build on it: going beyond previous accomplishments, opening new territory, redoing a study a new and better way, possibly replicating a study to show the generality of its findings, and so forth. This section, which then follows, further shows the study emerging from the background of previous thinking and theory. Like every link in the chain of reasoning, this section forms a basis for judging the remainder of the proposal. It sets the stage for showing how one intends to solve or contribute to the solution of the problem set out in the first sections. Just how specific this section can be depends on what you have said in the previous sections, and what turned up in the review of literature:

- The less you have found out about the area, the more likely this section will be devoted to questions or descriptions of where to look.
- If you have some ideas about at least certain aspects, you may have hunches to test to see if they are true. This section will set forth those hunches as hypotheses.
- If you have a good idea about how things work, you may be able to construct a model of how various variables are related to each other. This section then describes the model you would like to test.

Because this section comes early in the proposal, you may still be in an expansive frame of mind and desirous of solving a problem of "major" significance. As a result, you may cast the problem more broadly than is possible to address once the procedure section is completed. Therefore, after the proposal is completed, reread it to ensure that this section flows smoothly from the preceding problem statement, and that the next section, that on procedure, adequately encompasses all that is covered in this section.

The most frequent error made in writing this section is that it becomes a set of vague generalities rather than clear-cut criteria against which the rest of the project can be judged.

Another error is that instead of setting forth specific research objectives, they are imbedded, usually by implication rather than explicit statement, in a running description of the project. Your readers must then tease them out, trying to infer what you are implying and to place emphasis on different ones as can be "guesstimated" from contextual clues. Obviously, the readers' accuracy in doing this is critical. Rather than run the risk of misinterpretation, you will fare better by making the objectives clear and explicit in this section.

Descriptions of Where to Look and Questions

Questions, or descriptions of where to look and at what to look, are most appropriate where the study is an emergent one, where the research is exploratory, or where the study is seeking certain facts or descriptions. The specificity of the questions or descriptions shows how carefully the problem has been thought through and/or studied through previous research. For example, consider a study of the effects of female teachers on male students.

> You would not gain the impression that the researcher has a grasp of his problem if he merely lists the question "What is the effect of the female teacher on male students?" But if the researcher poses the question "Which of these is the dominant effect of female teachers on male students?" and then follows with a list of the possible dominant effects and explanations, it is clear that he has thought through the possible alternatives and is prepared to investigate at least these particular ones.

> Alternatively, the researcher, believing that previous research has not adequately compiled the important effects, may be searching for new ones. Instead of specifying questions, the proposal can present an argument as to why there are significant ones yet to be found and how they might be identified.

So, if your literature search was futile, and you have little basis for constructing hypotheses, state questions or describe areas to be explored and indicate:

- Why these are the important questions to ask or areas to be explored.
- What their potential implications are for moving your field ahead.
- Why other reasonable questions that might be asked or areas of exploration are not of interest and will not be addressed.
- What the implications of addressing and possibly answering these particular questions or exploring these areas may be.

Warters's proposal embeds the description of the goal of the study and the focus of attention in the first paragraph in the second from the last sentence: "To assist in . . ." instead of making it a separate statement, paragraph, or section. This works well in this particular proposal because it provides an early foreshadowing for the reader that is then amplified by statements in paragraph 5, especially in paragraphs 8 and the end of 9 where research questions are specified.

Suppose that, in order to come to your own conclusions about what is significant, as some qualitative researchers do, you are refraining from reading previous research. Then this section will mainly state questions or indicate areas on which to focus. Describe the kinds of questions or what areas will initially guide your observations or your inquiries, and why you are starting with these instead of other possibilities. If you are a "purist" about starting de novo in the situation, this will be a very short section. But as indicated in chapter 7, this gives your chair and your committee very little to go on, and you'll want to develop this section further as described there.

Hypotheses

You may find it helpful to phrase your objectives as hypotheses that are to be tested. If at all possible, hypotheses should be related to a theoretical base. If the theoretical base was not introduced in the previous sections, state it here, then refine and extend it to show how the study's objectives are derived from it, carefully building the bridge from theory to study so that the relation is clear. For instance, a study of the effects of a vocational education program would be strengthened if the choices that the student must make in the program were related to the developing theory that describes why and how students go through stages of vocational choice.

Hypotheses as objectives must be stated in such a way that they are *testable*. That is, they can be translated into the research operations that will give evidence of their truth or falsity.

The topic may be chosen because it is judged to be important, but the objectives should not themselves be stated as value judgments (e.g., "All sixth-grade boys should learn to play a musical instrument."). Research can indicate the extent of popular support for such a value statement (e.g., "A large majority of our town [two-thirds or more] believe that all sixth grade boys . . ."); or it can indicate the consequences of an action (e.g., "If all sixth-grade boys play musical instruments, they will attend more concerts outside school."). But humans must judge how much value to attach to these consequences or to the extent of popular support.

Directional hypotheses should be used wherever there is a basis for prediction. There will be such a basis if the study has a theoretical underpinning. State hypotheses as succinct predictions of the expected outcomes and findings rather than in the null form. For instance, say: "Students who receive the experimental treatment will have more differentiated interests than those who do not," rather than "There will be no difference in interest patterns between the experimental and control groups." The latter statement is an important part of the logic of the statistical test, but it does not belong in the objectives section and leaves an amateurish impression with experienced researchers.

One would expect hypotheses in a prespecified study such as Beissner's. There they are, in paragraph 15, in a section of their own. Further, note that they are all directional; the theoretical rationale for the study has provided a basis for predicting the direction of the outcomes.

Similarly one would expect hypotheses in the Phelan proposal, but paragraph 9 is titled "The Research Question." As one reads it, however, his hypothesis is clearly there. But, after stating it verbally, he restates it in null form and does not capture the centrality of motivation he stated earlier. Note how the null form not only adds nothing to the description, but actually detracts from the argument.

Models

When one is concerned with a larger picture than the relationship between two variables, and begins to look at the interrelationships among a set of variables, one is into the construction of models. Usually, these are built upon previous research. In an effort to synthesize disparate pieces of a larger picture, you construct a representation of how each variable influences and/or is influenced by other variables. Usually, this results in the construction of a diagram with arrows indicating the direction of influence. The task of the study is to provide evidence that the relationships exist, confirm the directions of influence, and estimate their size. Most such dissertation models are relatively simple; confirming complex relationships requires large-scale studies unlikely to be undertaken by graduate students.

In the literature review section of the proposal, show the basis in previous research for the proposed model. Indicate where you have gone beyond previous work and how this study contributes new knowledge to the field. Describe the model both graphically and narratively and indicate the parts of it that are well confirmed by previous research and those that are more tenuous. If there are alternative conceptualizations of the relationships, indicate them and give the basis for each. If you believe that one is more likely to be supported by the data, indicate that as well.

Since the study of models is only recently appearing in dissertations, there are no examples of such studies in this book. But linear equation modeling is increasingly an important statistical tool, as is apparent from numerous federally funded behavioral studies. So modeling studies will no doubt become more common in dissertations.

As you draft and revise your proposal problem statement, it is helpful to periodically review its strong points and shortcomings. Worksheet 4.3: Characteristics of a Good Proposal Problem Statement is provided here to help you check your progress.

Characteristics of a Good Dissertation Topic

How Strong Is My Current Dissertation Topic?

A dissertation topic is continually developed and refined as you move toward a specific study design. Briefly describe your topic below as you currently understand it, and then use the following list of criteria to see how well it measures up. You might also use this worksheet to have other researchers or your dissertation chairperson rate your topic and then offer suggestions for next steps. You will probably need to return to this worksheet several times as you reconceptualize and reshape your interests into a strong dissertation topic.

Current Topic Description:

Review Criteria	Strong	Acceptable	Weak	Don't Know Yet	Not Applicable
Topic Importance					
Is relevant to a larger, significant problem, but is conceptually bounded.					
Is focused, but not trivial.					
Reflects a creative or original perspective.					
Has important practical implications.					
Has important theoretical implications.					
Has important methodological implications.					
Is acceptable within my academic or professional field.					
Personal Match					
Reflects a strong personal interest.					
Will promote my academic and career interests.					

(Continued on next page)

Review Criteria	Strong	Acceptable	Weak	Don't Know Yet	Not Applicable
Is of interest to potential dissertation chairpersons and committee members.					
Is acceptable within my academic department and school.					
Operational Feasibility					
Is a good fit with the knowledge and skills I have or can acquire.					
Is a good fit with the resources I have or can acquire.					
Can effectively build on prior theory, knowledge, and personal experience with the topic.					
Can effectively build on prior personal and professional experience with possible methods.					
Can be developed into a manageable study.					
Can be investigated in an ethical manner.					

What to Look for in Reviewing Literature for a Dissertation

What I Should Look For as I Begin Searching the Literature

As you review the literature, you should seek to understand more fully the nature of the problem you are investigating, how best to study it, and what relevant resources are available. The following is a checklist of items to look for as you review the literature.

Topics	Key References
Research Phenomena of Interest	
Problems: nature, incidence, significance	
Contexts: historical, social, political, economic, geographic, psychological	
Conceptualizations: values, perspectives, philosophies	
Terms/Concepts: definitions, ambiguities, operationalizations	
Theories: descriptive, explanatory, causal models	
Facts: confirmed, generally accepted, hypothesized	
Solutions: tried, successes, failures, problems, shortcomings	
Questions/Concerns: unknowns, uncertainties, unconfirmed aspects or issues	
Research Inquiry Methods	
World Views: perspectives, purposes of inquiry, epistemologies	
Queries: questions, variables, hypotheses, models	
Designs: design logics, inquiry methods	
Techniques/Procedures: field conditions, interventions, controls; measures, information sources, data collection; data analysis, modes of interpretation; study management	

(Continued on next page)

Topics	Key References
State of the Art: successes, problems, limitations	
Dissertation Resources	
Professional Groups: associations, societies, agencies, departments, institutes (re: policy, research, method, practice)	
Special Interest Groups: commercial firms, non-profits, advocacy groups	
Fund Sources: foundations, private sector, government agencies	
Key Individuals: policy makers, researchers, methodologists, national figures, local and regional experts, practitioners	
Study Resources: data bases, instrumentation, measurement collections, hardware, software, courseware, multimedia	
Information Sources: publishers, libraries, journals, newsletters, websites, online publications, listservs, bulletin boards, chat rooms, distribution lists	
Skill Development Resources: courses, workshops, training materials, mentors, tutors, consultants, collaborators	

Characteristics of a Good Proposal Problem Statement

How Strong Is My Proposal Problem Statement?

Since it usually takes many iterations to produce a strong, convincing problem statement, you will want to refer to this worksheet repeatedly as you refine your proposal. For assistance with weak points that need improvement, refer back to the relevant sections of this chapter and to the annotated proposal examples in chapters 11, 12, and 13. Also consider having others review your working drafts using this worksheet.

Current Problem Statement:

How Well Have I . . . ?	Strong	Acceptable	Weak– Improvements Needed	Not Applicable
Problem Statement				
Begun the statement with a strong, interest generating opening?				
Clearly stated and described the problem?				
Demonstrated the problem's importance?				
Shown the problem's generality?				
Appropriately limited the problem's scope?				
Adequately balanced completeness and brevity?				
Provided a perspective on the entire proposal?				
Set a proper frame of reference?				
Literature Review				
Selected the most appropriate studies to support the proposed research?				

(Continued on next page)

How Well Have I . . . ?	Strong	Acceptable	Weak–Improvements Needed	Not Applicable
Carefully evaluated the strengths and weaknesses of prior research and thought?				
Explained how the essential details of each study are relevant to the problem to be studied?				
Critically, yet succinctly, summarized current substantive knowledge about the problem?				
Critically analyzed relevant theoretical positions related to the problem?				
Critically assessed methodological alternatives for studying the problem?				
Demonstrated awareness of relevant work both in progress and in other disciplines?				
Stated an explicit set of goals for my research to accomplish and how they will be achieved?				
Convincingly argued why my study will appropriately address questions, hypotheses, or models?				
Clearly shown how my study will both build upon, and go beyond, prior research, substantively and methodologically?				

CHAPTER 5

The Method Section

CHAPTER CONTENTS

The method section, which describes the procedures that will be used, translates the problem section developed in the previous chapter into project activities. *This is usually the most carefully read section of the whole proposal.* Up to this point, you may have told in glowing terms and appealing generalities what you hope to do and what this will mean to your field. The section on method brings this down to earth in operational terms. Frequently, proposals that sound as though they will revolutionize a field appear much more mundane in the method section; the techniques proposed for attacking the problem may fall far short of what was implied when the earlier sections were written. Obviously, the method section should fulfill the expectations created by the foregoing sections.

The following material assumes that you have a reasonably clear idea of what you wish to study and how you wish to study it. The term *design* is used to describe the latter, both here and in the chain of reasoning. So the study's design is described in the method section. Obviously, that term *design* applies quite loosely to studies with emergent topics.

Our discussion of the method section is in two parts: In Section 1 we discuss general points to take into consideration in developing and describing method. Section 2 is a detailed discussion of each of the subsections of design that together, typically, are required to describe the method.

SECTION 1: GENERAL CONSIDERATIONS

Adapt the Material on Method to Your Study

Of all the proposal parts, the method section is the most dependent on the nature of your study. Some of the material in this chapter may be irrelevant to your kind of study. Consider what is important in your study and adapt it. For example:

> If the study is a sample survey, elaborate on the sampling section. If it is an emergent study, collapse the sections on the links in design into a single description of how and where data will be gathered and the initial focus of attention. Suppose you plan to examine the educational and medical records of late-nineteenth-century Italian immigrants to determine how they differed from nonimmigrants. Describe where you are going to study the records, what you expect to find there, how you will get access, what information will be gathered and how, and what analyses will be performed.

Further discussion of how to adapt this section is given in chapters 7, 8, and 9, addressing the special requirements of various kinds of proposals.

The Method Section Flows from the "Questions, Hypotheses, or Models" Section

Considering a project as a chain of reasoning, the "design" link in the chain is logically derived from the previous links, specifically the "questions, hypotheses, or models" link. The design specifies the operations by which you will investigate whatever you chose at the questions-hypotheses-or-models link. If it is a question, it will indicate where, how, and when you will seek an answer to it. If it is a hypothesis or a model, it will describe how you will provide evidence in support of the prediction and relate it to the underlying explanation of the phenomena that resulted in the prediction. Also, it will indicate how relevant alternative explanations can be ruled out.

The process is usually one of a direct translation of the concepts in the question, hypothesis, or model into the choice of:

1. participants,
2. situation,
3. focus of action—the core variables such as treatment and effect,
4. records—measures and observations,
5. comparison and contrast (basis for sensing attributes and changes)—the basis on which the change due to an independent variable or experimental treatment or whatever happens at the focus of attention will be sensed (e.g., pre/post comparison or comparison with another group), and
6. time schedule—the study's procedures and the schedule of the various activities involved. These may involve observations, sensing the presence and strength of the independent variable, administering an experimental treatment, and/or measuring and observing any effect.

For example:

Consider this hypothesis: "Up to some reasonable point, the more time African American students spend studying African American history, the stronger their self-concept." This hypothesis suggests that increasing levels of study of African American history will result in gains in self-concept up to some point. To develop the design, decisions will have to be made about how to translate into operational terms all the concepts in the hypothesis:

The researcher must specify what is meant by "African American students" in terms of age, grade, and whether such variables as socioeconomic class or urban/rural background are important.

What does "study African American history" mean? Will any African American history curriculum do, or does it need to be one that stresses African American accomplishments?

Is there a measure of self-concept that is valid for African American students at the age chosen? The easily available measures for college students are not appropriate for elementary pupils.

What design will determine whether the variables change together as hypothesized? For example, one design might involve groups of students who are comparable except for the time they have studied African American history. You could compare self-concept change for those who have studied it for short vs. longer times. Alternatively, a longitudinal design might be developed that follows the changes in a group exposed to a lengthy study of African American history.

For many of the decisions (e.g., choice of age and grade or use of comparable groups vs. longitudinal designs) you must choose among alternative translations. Thus, a variety of interpretations can result when a hypothesis is translated into operational terms. The same process is involved in translating questions and models.

Some terms seem to immediately translate into design features. Here are some examples:

Long-term retention vs. immediate recall	Requires multiple posttests. Note that even here there are alternatives: the same group can be tested several times, or, to eliminate the effect of retesting, use different groups—one tested immediately, others for different lengths of retention.
Cumulative treatment effect	Requires multiple posttests. Again these could all be of the same group or of different groups, each tested after a different length of treatment.
Anticipatory effect (e.g., effect of studying sculptures on enjoying paintings)	Pre—and posttesting. One group before exposure to sculpture as well as before and after paintings exposure; one group before and after paintings exposure only.
Enhancing or interactive effect of a variable with treatment (e.g., printing the words that are key to understanding a text in a contrasting color in a reading test)	Separate treatment groups with and without the presence of the interactive variable conditions.

Operationalizing Terms May Result in New Conceptualizations

As terms are operationalized, you often come to a different understanding of the study from when it was initially conceptualized. Terms take on new meaning, and often the initial conceptualization has to be sharpened and modified as the problem becomes better understood.

> Suppose that you start out to study the relation of per pupil expenditures to achievement across a set of public school districts. In operationally defining per pupil expenditures (determining their dollar value), you find that different districts include different costs.

> In an effort to get comparable data across districts, you adjust each district to include a common set of basic costs. But at that point, the study begins changing. There isn't much variability in these basic costs across districts; the variability is in the nonbasics, the discretionary money available to a school's principal to improve instruction. So that becomes the focus of the study, forcing you to go back and change the whole front end of the proposal to fit this new conceptualization of the problem.

Some researchers argue that you really come to understand the problem only in operationalizing the study. However, operationalization may never be completely satisfactory when you are dealing with constructs that can't be concretized so as to satisfy everyone (e.g., personality characteristics such as likableness, monetary estimates of the value of good health, etc.). Remember this if you are dissatisfied with your study and/or the redevelopment of the method section seems never-ending. A compromise operationalization may be the only way to study your problem but, also, the source of your dissatisfaction.

Sometimes, when the questions, hypotheses, or models are given operational translations, it becomes immediately apparent that the problem is too large or too complex. In the per pupil expenditure example above, an attempt to estimate *all* the discretionary resources available in a given classroom might put the project beyond the realm of feasibility (parent volunteer time, laptop computers brought into the class by students, etc.). Yet these might be important inputs to the classroom in certain circumstances. First attempts at problem definition are particularly susceptible to impracticality where the student insists on doing "something significant."

Refocusing and delimiting the problem to restore feasibility are the answers. But, sometimes, even after the problem has been refocused, certain requirements may still be too great. Consider whether these may be handled by alternative design choices. For example, if there are too few cases to establish both a control and an experimental group, the participants may be used as their own control with pre—and posttests.

Development of the design is an iterative process. The researcher sets an initial set of pieces in place, but changing one sets off a cycle of resulting changes. That may in turn result in a reconceptualization, further changes, and so on, until all the pieces fit together and are feasible. The new curriculum takes too long, so it must be reduced to its essentials. That is likely to result in weaker learning, which in turn requires the size of the sample be increased in order to detect it. To get a larger sample you must include atypical persons. Now you must find a comparison group that includes similar atypical persons. And so it goes.

Often you must go all the way back to the beginning and redesign the study on a different basis. Many cycles may take place before a satisfactory solution is reached.

Restrain the Design to Realistic Limits

Even as the design is first being considered, you must make tentative decisions on what level of resources you can practically employ. Take into account your own time and what access and cooperation you can expect from other institutions, participants, etc. These estimates are important for making methodological decisions: the possible number of participants, number and location of study settings, and so on. Indeed, the limits may rule out certain methods that take too long, such as a longitudinal study. Getting parents' consent to test children may be difficult or impossible. The most desirable and cooperative institutions may be too distant.

Some of the limits are easy to estimate, others more difficult, but some reasonable determination must be made for all of them if development of the design is to proceed realistically. Further, just as other parts of the design are successively adapted, so initial limits may have to be adjusted as the plan develops. Since many of these judgments are based on practical experience, seek the advice of your chairperson, committee members, and other researchers who have conducted similar studies and learned what is realistic through hard experience.

Resource Limits

As soon as you begin to translate the study into operational terms, the question immediately arises, "How big shall I make it?" Although it need not be answered precisely at the outset, some working estimates must be set. A key one is how long you can afford to work on your dissertation. Here again, seek the opinions of others: ask more senior graduate students how long the various pieces of their dissertation research are taking them.

Institutional Limits

When other institutions or agencies are involved, either as collaborators or as sources of data collection, support, etc., their perspective must be considered to ensure that requests made of them are reasonable. Most institutions operate by trying to do too much, for too many, with too little time and resources, and so may limit access to participants, facilities, equipment, or personnel. Further, they tend to resist changes in routines that interfere with "business as usual."

Ethical Limits

Ethical limits must be considered in developing the design. Any federally funded research involving human participants must be approved by a Committee on the Protection of Human Subjects concerned with the ethical implications of the study. Federal regulations prescribe the composition of the committee, which includes individuals outside the university. Although approval is required only for federally funded projects, nearly every university extends that requirement to all other research involving human participants, *including dissertations.* If clearance has already been routinely obtained, note it in the discussion of method. If not yet obtained, or expected not to be routine, it may require a section of its own along with other assurances. Committee on the Protection of Human Subjects clearances are further discussed in the next chapter (p. 110–11).

Time Limits on Proposal Development

It seems you ought to be able to control your schedule. But pressures to get your degree in a reasonable time, to gather data before certain natural breaks in institutional schedules, faculty unavailability due to trips and sabbaticals, and other scheduling difficulties may impinge on your timetable. Circumstances may, for example, require completion and approval of your proposal by an early date, enforce a particular schedule on data collection, or compel use of nonpreferred sites for data collection.

Consider the trade-offs involved in rushing to meet the immediate deadline or, if there is one, waiting for a later one when some of these problems could be more successfully resolved. A several-month delay in proposal approval might pay handsome dividends in more cooperative site conditions as the staff of these institutions and agencies are given a chance to contribute to the research plan and feel it is partly theirs. Considering that this may make for a more cooperative milieu and possibly better data, the delay may be worthwhile. But other considerations such as the availability of your own or a key person's time may be overriding.

Sort out those things that can be done satisfactorily in the time available for proposal development from those that are unwise to attempt or, perhaps, cannot be done even if tried. Attempting too much usually results in a proposal that shows it, as does similar haste in data collection and analysis in the dissertation. As in sewing, "find a pattern that fits the cloth available," or as in sports, "find a league in which you can comfortably play."

Eliminate Plausible Alternative Explanations

Whatever the methodology, all studies concerned with setting forth an explanation for a relationship must be concerned with the elimination of competing plausible explanations. Whether experimental, qualitative, survey, or whatever, if the design is not adequate to ensure the integrity of the study's chain of reasoning against plausible alternative explanations, readers may prefer an alternative to the explanation that the study is intended to support. The proposal should describe how the design so structures the study that plausible alternative explanations are ruled out as significant explanatory factors. Here's an example.

> In a study comparing the effect of two different curricula, the researcher would be concerned that any initial differences in the groups might be reflected in their after-treatment performance. Otherwise, such after-treatment differences might be attributed as well to the initial differences as to the effect of the curricula. In this situation, the researcher might be expected to control such potentially contaminating factors as the beginning level of competence, general academic ability, and/or motivation.

The term *design* seems to go with *experimental* as in *experimental design*. You might be tempted, therefore, to assume that this discussion is of little importance to other than experimental studies, to a qualitative study, for example. Nothing could be further from the truth! A qualitative study observer, for example, must protect against a variety of alternative explanations; to name just a few:

- the possible effect of the observer's prevailing attitudes and values as they affect observations,
- the possible choice of individuals and times to observe which are "atypical" samples,
- the possible effect of "dropouts"—persons present at the start of the observations but not as they progress (usually referred to by the name *mortality*),
- the possibility of going "native" and perceiving things differently as observations progress.

Clearly, when we refer to *design* in qualitative studies, we are using the term to refer to such investigator decisions as whom to study, what persons or situations to contrast, what instances in time to compare, and similar judgments.

Control of Alternative Explanations

How do you control for possible alternative explanations that might equally plausibly be considered the cause of what you are studying? We have three ways: (1) elimination, (2) adjusting, and (3) spreading their effect equally across whatever groups or individuals are being compared (if all units are equally affected, then differences must be due to something else, presumably what you are studying). This last method is used in the two-curricula comparison. Individuals are ranked on achievement (assuming that achievement is a reflection of both ability and motivation so it controls for both), and persons with even-numbered ranks are assigned to one curriculum group, those with odd-numbered ranks the other.

Clearly, one of your tasks in writing the proposal is to *identify potentially serious plausible alternative explanations and discuss which ones to control and how to control them.* That is, you must:

- decide which alternatives are the most serious threats to the study,
- decide how they can be controlled,
- determine how controls for the set of the most serious threats can be combined into a design, and finally
- determine whether the design is feasible, adjusting it until it is.

This requires asking such questions as:

- How likely is each of these alternative explanations to appear?
- In your estimation, therefore, how critical is it that each of them be controlled?
- If there are several requiring control, how will you prioritize their relative importance?
- Will your chairperson, committee, and intended audience likely agree with your priority order?
- How, taking your own and these other opinions into account, shall these alternatives be prioritized in their claim on your resources?
- Which design best controls the top-priority alternative explanations?
- Is that design feasible? If not, how can it be modified so it is?
- Given the other claims on resources, what design is preferable?

The final decision must depend on the particular circumstances of each study, but a general principle is to find the design configuration that provides the best possible use of available resources at the same time that it:

1. Gives priority to the most serious alternative causes of the effect, taking into account their likelihood, and
2. Control by elimination if that is possible; by adjustment as a second choice if a good method is available; or, where it is not, as a third choice, by building them equally into the groups being compared.

Control for as many variables as are important and as can feasibly be accommodated. This is one of many areas subject to your good judgment for which no set of foolproof rules can be provided. *Every study is a compromise between what it is realistically possible to control and those variables that would be nice to control in the most perfect of all possible worlds.*

Unfortunately, not all judges will weigh the desirability of controlling possible contaminating factors the same way. Their "most acceptable compromise" may differ from yours. Once again, this is a place to demonstrate your mastery of the problem. Nobody knows better than you do the multiple sources of contamination that might affect your study. Therefore, in your proposal, convincingly indicate:

- The nature and basis of the particular compromise being proposed,
- The reasons for accepting it,
- The reasons for choosing to control the variables selected,
- The reasons for ignoring certain others, and
- How the design realistically controls the critical variables without sacrificing the integrity of the study.

Where do you place this explanation of elimination of alternative explanations in the proposal? Usually, you will find it in the discussion of one of the links of the design, especially the comparison and contrast—the basis-for-sensing-attributes-and-changes link. But it can be covered anywhere it fits; the important thing is be sure it is included.

It is possible that you can do the study only in a laboratory-like situation if your design becomes sufficiently complex. This markedly reduces the generality of the findings. Such a consideration is obviously more of a worry in an applied or developmental study than in one dealing with basic research. But even in doing basic research, the need for generality may force consideration of other design choices.

Avoid expediency as a reason for failing to control a factor if reasonable effort and/or expense would permit doing so. For less critical variables, experienced faculty will recognize the reality of expediency as a good and sufficient basis.

Which alternative explanations are likely to be most troublesome varies with methodology and the study's circumstances. The most thorough delineation of alternative explanations has been in the context of experimental studies where they are termed *threats to validity* (see Campbell and Stanley, 1963; Cook and Campbell, 1979; Krathwohl, 1998/2004, pp. 526–531; Shadish, Cook, and Campbell, 2002; thirty-three of them are listed in Wortman, 1994). But there are also lists for qualitative studies (see Krathwohl, 1998/2004, pp. 317–320).

Some Illustrative Common Alternative Explanations to Be Eliminated or Controlled

For purposes of illustration, some examples that plague a variety of types of studies are briefly described below.

Reactivity. The effect of special attention is a reaction to the perception that there is something special about this situation. It usually elicits "I'd better do what is right" or "I'd better be good" behavior. One looks for reactive effects where obtrusiveness tips the situation from normal to special:

- The presence of an observer can change normal behavior—a teacher better controls her temper; the children are on their "good behavior."
- The treatment obtrusively stands out from the normal sequence of events—the experimental group is taken from the classroom to the computer cluster.
- Measurement of effect is obtrusive—students spot the video camera that is recording their use of reference books in the library.

Obviously, reactivity is eliminated or at least reduced when things proceed naturally, or as much so as possible. Concealing the observer by providing him a social role in the group being observed and allowing time for him to become a normal part of the situation may control for reactivity. Having the usual classroom teacher, social worker, or other professional administer a special treatment, instead of the researcher, may do so as well. Further, that person may be the best one to decide how and when to introduce a treatment into the situation. Where measurement is a problem, see Webb, Campbell, Schwartz, and Sechrest (1981) and Lee (2000), books on unobtrusive measurement and methods as ways of reducing reactive behavior.

Researcher Expectancy and Placebo Effects. A very closely related influence is the expectation of the researcher that influences result in the direction the researcher hopes to see. It refers both to the elicitation of such behavior from those studied as well as to faulty or self-deceiving perceptions by those recording the study's results. Researchers or their assistants may inadvertently tip the scales in favor of preferred results in a variety of ways: Participant observers may give inadvertent cues to desired behavior. Participants typically try to fathom the purpose of the study and give the responses they perceive as wanted. Ambiguous situations may be recorded as instances of the study's expected outcome. Errors in recording, observation, or measurement procedure may unintentionally favor the expected outcome (when totaling your checking account register, why do errors usually favor you instead of the bank?).

Use of "double-blind" procedures, where neither observer, measurer, nor subject knows the intended outcome of the study, eliminate expectancy effect. Treatments appear as identical as possible, but participants are coded so some uninvolved party can separate comparison groups after treatment. The control treatment is referred to as a "placebo" or "placebo treatment" after the inert pill that is used to mimic an experimental drug. Double-blind procedures cannot be used when: (1) the participant's knowledge of treatment is part of the treatment itself, (2) it is obvious which treatment is to be favored from merely observing the treatment or being exposed to it, (3) the treatment can be readily identified from side effects, or (4) withholding a more favorable treatment would have ethical consequences.

Selection and Mortality Effects. Selection and mortality are opposite sides of a coin. Selection adds an alternative explanation by affecting the composition of the group through the nature of the persons selected for study, mortality by those leaving the study as it progresses.

The alternative explanation comes about because the persons selected are distinguished from those not studied by a factor that may also cause the desired effect. If unrecognized, it can lead to the wrong conclusion, like assuming that, generally, bottles are discarded in the ocean with their caps on, because they predominate along the shoreline. Rather, the others sank—these are the survivors. Similarly, high school graduates and college and graduate students are "survivors." Volunteering is a common selective factor. Alternative explanations arise from the fact that those who volunteer are different from nonvolunteers (usually brighter, better educated, higher in social status, more sociable, have a higher need for social approval, etc. [Rosenthal and Rosnow, 1975]).

"Mortality" as an alternative explanation is not the death of an individual, but the change in group composition resulting from their leaving. "Leavers" depart for a reason—uncomfortable, bored, afraid to fail, etc. Because this modifies the average characteristics of the study group, their leaving should be noted and taken into account. Their having left can be easily overlooked when concentrating on others in the group.

Instrument Decay. Changes in the measuring instrument over time might cause one to conclude an effect occurred when it was the recording standards that were changing. In qualitative studies, since the observer is the "instrument," changes may occur as she becomes more familiar with those studied and/or the situation. Where measuring equipment is concerned, as in hearing or other discrimination tests, lack of calibration may cause the effect. Where essay tests are involved, the first ones graded may be held to a different standard than the last. Instrument decay can take many forms.

A General Strategy. The important thing is to be aware of possible alternative explanations, to describe the likely ones in the proposal, to tell how they will be handled, or if they won't, why not. Show in the description how well you have analyzed the design and how familiar you are with the literature on this topic so that you have recognized and adequately taken into account the relevant threats to your study.

Design Efficiency

At some point, *determine whether the design is maximally efficient.* For example, can better use can be made of participants or informants; data collection points be reduced; more data collected at each visit, measurement, or observation;

persons be scheduled more efficiently; and so on? The development of the work plan, discussed in the next chapter, is especially helpful in showing where economies can be made in scheduling (your time is the major resource to allocate for a dissertation). If feasible, considerable savings in resources can result from combining your study with that of other researchers so as to use the same participants, situations, and/or data.

Give Special Care to Those Sections Critical to Your Research Method

As noted at the beginning of this section, the nature of your study affects what parts of the proposal are critical and therefore need special attention. But, regardless of the kind of study, the design aspects of the method section deserve special attention because within any research method, there are a variety of ways to proceed.

Choice of design is still an art. A design's strengths in one aspect may result in a weakness elsewhere. Choice requires assessing the gains and losses involved in various alternatives. Unfortunately, they are rarely known accurately in advance; good estimates come from knowing one's field and having worked with it long enough to have learned which options yield gains, which losses, and their frequency and seriousness. As a new researcher you may not have the experience to weigh all these variables as your chairperson and committee will, but use all the resources you can to develop the best possible design. Talk with other graduate students and particularly with those faculty members who frequently serve as design consultants. Then rely on your chairperson and committee to point out problems and solutions that you may have overlooked.

Because choice of design is an art, reasonable persons may differ as to the best design for a given problem. Your initial choice may not be that which springs to the mind of your chairperson or committee members. But they may be thinking in stereotypes, and your approach may indeed be best. Help readers follow your line of reasoning so that they, too, may see your design choice rationale—your reasons for so choosing and why this choice over alternatives. *Creating a strong proposal is also a matter of knowing your audiences and being able to adequately anticipate and meet their concerns.* There is more on this point in the material that follows.

SECTION 2: DEVELOPING THE SUBSECTIONS OF METHOD

The method section describes the structure of the investigation: the way participants or situations will be studied; how groups will be organized; if there is a treatment, when and how it will be administered; when observations will be made, of whom, when, and, if known, of what; the protection against alternative explanations; and the like. Begin the write-up of this section with a one-paragraph summary or overview of the method to be used.

Then, in whatever order seems most appropriate for what you plan to do, cover the six links of design in the chain of reasoning so as to describe these various aspects of method:

1. Participants—population and sample
2. Situation
3. Focus of action—the core variables such as treatment and effect,
4. Records—instrumentation and data collection,
5. Comparison and contrast (basis for sensing attributes and changes)—the basis on which the change due to an independent variable or experimental treatment or whatever happens at the focus of the study will be sensed (e.g., pre/post comparison or comparison with another group), and
6. Time schedule—the procedure.

Having described your data gathering plan, next describe your

- analysis plan and
- expected end product.

Although one can use the six links in design as an organizing framework, most proposals will not have a subsection for each of them. This is apparent in the annotated proposals in part 5 of this book, and they are typical. But the information describing all six links is somewhere accounted for. Be sure to adapt your proposal format to best describe your study. The following discussion specifies what is typically included to describe each link, examples of where this appears in the proposal, suggestions for writing it, and some of the common, and/or most serious, errors.

Participants—Population and Sample

For all studies involving gathering data from people, a description of who they are is essential to determining the potential generalizability of the study findings. The characteristics of the population to which the sample studied belongs define the group to whom the study's results may transfer. Obviously, this generality should be consistent with the generality claimed in the problem statement and objectives sections. The representativeness of the sample indicates how confidently we can generalize from sample to population.

While random sampling provides *on average* a sample that is representative in every respect—even some characteristics we don't care about, like length of one's little toe—*there is no guarantee that any given sample will be representative of those characteristics crucial to our study.* Therefore, we often take steps to ensure that the sample is representative with respect to key variables. There are a number of ways of doing this such as stratified and cluster sampling with random selection within strata or clusters.

For studies concerned mainly with description, characterizing the nature of the participants allows readers to determine what, if any, parallels exist to their own experiences, thus allowing a determination of whether the results "ring true" and, if they do, what, if any, implications the study might have.

Therefore, regardless of how those studied were or will be selected, be sure to describe that process in detail, giving a rationale for why that process is the best of those available. If you seek findings that generalize, indicate the variables that will be used as the basis for ensuring representativeness—e.g., the basis of stratified and cluster sampling, the significance of those variables for the study, and why they were chosen over others. Indicate where the data on the variables used to stratify or cluster individuals will be obtained. If there is any reason to believe the database from which they are to be selected is not error free, give some indication of the anticipated error's extent and its likely impact on the study.

To study a proposition that is presumed to be universally applicable, you can use anyone or any situation except where the choice of participant or situation might favor or disfavor it. Any random sample of the world's population will do. We often substitute a convenience sample such as graduate or undergraduate students for such an unbiased sample. But if one or more characteristics of university students would normally be expected to affect the study's outcome, you must explain why you believe this will not be so for your study. It is important to anticipate such concerns.

Sample size is another important decision. Giving a good rationale is more impressive than picking an arbitrary number or using whatever size convenience sample is available. Power analyses provide such a rationale by providing a design basis such that if the expected result does appear, the study will be sensitive enough to show it as statistically significant. Increasingly, studies intended for publication must be designed using such analyses. They require making some decisions about:

1. How precise must the estimate be? Put another way, how small a difference is to be sensed? Other things being equal, the greater the precision required and the smaller the difference to be sensed, the larger the sample required.

2. How different are individuals with respect to the characteristic being estimated; how much variability is there? If everybody is about the same, other things being equal, you can estimate from a few cases. But if people differ greatly, that is, there is high variability from person to person, more cases will be needed.

3. How much certainty is required of the estimate? This is another way of asking whether you want to use the 1 percent level of significance, 5 percent level, 10 percent level, and so on. At the 5 percent level, your confidence that the

population value is bracketed by the confidence interval is expressed by odds of 19 to 1. Again, other things being equal, the greater the certainty required (e.g., the 1 percent rather than 5 percent level, the smaller the confidence interval), the larger the sample required.

Where does the information come from to determine sample size? For questions 1 and 2 above, from your pilot studies, from other researchers' use of the same instruments with comparable participants, or, failing these, from "guesstimates" made on the best basis you can command. With such estimates and a decision on question 3, any good statistics book or Cohen (1988) or Lipsey (1989) will show how to calculate a sample size such that if an event of interest occurs, the odds heavily favor that it will be statistically significant. For an interactive statistical power analysis site on the Web, try http://www.stat.uiowa.edu/~rlenth/Power/index.html (accessed October 1, 2004). To create the tilde (~), press "Shift" and the key to the left of "1." Alternatively, after "link:" copy and paste its URL into Google.com to find similar sites (e.g., link:www.stat.uiowa.edu/~rlenth/Power/index.html).

Occasionally a student will propose using the total population, which, though large, is presumably manageable. In such instances, even though feasible, it may be preferable to work more intensively or carefully with a sample than to use the same resources trying to cover the entire population. Indeed, if a power analysis indicates a sample instead of a census can satisfactorily be employed, the resources required to canvass an entire population when concentrated on a sample may result in better and deeper information or the same information obtained more cheaply. However, if your research is intended to convince lay policy makers, there may be no substitute for a census. How best to employ your resources is determined by the sophistication of your intended audience and the purposes of your study.

Situation

In many instances, the situation or the setting in which you will gather your data is determined by the sample, so one has already described it in the previous section. But where that is not the case, such description indicates where the design will be implemented. It helps readers determine the possible applicability of findings to comparable situations. Though typically covered in the population and sample section, description of the situation may be covered in other sections of the proposal.

See for example, Beissner's paragraph 48, which is in the "Procedure" section.

Focus of Action—Treatment(s), Independent and Dependent Variable(s)

Here is where you describe what it is you are studying—the effect of one or more treatments, the effect of one or more independent variables, or whatever one is focusing attention on, such as what results when certain conditions occur.

Warters, for instance, specifies his focus of action early in his proposal as he is citing literature to indicate the importance of his study in paragraphs 8 and 9.

Except in emergent studies, description of the treatment and variables is most often put in cause and effect terms where the causes are treatments or independent variables and the effects are the dependent variables—that is, they are dependent upon the presence, and often the strength, of the independent variable. In some instances, this information is covered in the instrumentation or measurement section.

Beissner, for example, describes the independent (paragraphs 40–47) and dependent (paragraphs 28–39) variables within the section titled "Instruments." Note especially in Beissner that she also describes independent variables that might cause the same effect as the treatment—level of factual knowledge, critical thinking ability, and the processes by which one relates new knowledge to old (measured by her "Inventory of Learning Processes"). If one is to claim an effect has a particular cause, one must eliminate such alternative causes as plausible.

In an experimental study, one normally finds a careful description of the treatment.

Beissner assumes the readers are familiar with concept mapping and with Novak and Gowin (1984) (see her paragraph 14) and so describes only the scores that will be produced (see paragraph 46, the section "Instruments"). In contrast, although omitted in this cut-down version, Phelan provided detail regarding his treatment—a workshop on self-directed learning—in an appendix (see paragraph 26). Placement in the appendix is a common practice.

So it is clear, the specifications of the treatment and variables in the study, the focuses of action, need to be explicitly spelled out somewhere in the proposal, but they need not have a section of their own. They are frequently specified and described in the course of completing other sections of the proposal.

Records—Instrumentation and Observations

In this section, records—the measures and observations—to be made in gathering data should be detailed and their appropriateness for the task convincingly described. Instruments may be unnecessary in a case study with few individuals. They may be inappropriate for exploratory and emergent studies, where to start by using instruments would presuppose you already knew what you were seeking to study. But they are both appropriate and necessary for the many studies that are confirmatory in nature, highly structured in their approach, concerned with cross-case comparisons (individuals, programs, sites, etc.), or combinations of structured and/or exploratory-confirmatory designs. In all of these instances, some forethought about instrumentation at the proposal stage will help reduce data collection and analysis problems and facilitate and enhance comparisons within cases and across them.

Instrumentation may range from those with very light structure—categories of behavior or phenomena to count—through increasingly structured data gathering: observation scales, rating scales, interview guides, interview schedules, conventional questionnaires, computer-adapted branched questionnaires, individually administered tests and measures, computer-adapted tests, and group tests. Which of these, if any, are appropriate will depend on the study, what is already available, and the trade-off of expending time and energy early in instrument construction in order to save time and energy at the analysis end. Whatever your choice, indicate it and describe its supporting rationale in the proposal.

The Observer as Instrument

As noted under "Instrument Decay," studies using observation have their own set of problems. The discussion of them and safeguards against them will typically appear under a section title like "Research Method" rather than "Instrumentation." This is discussed more extensively in part 3.

Measures

Some variables—time or distance measures, for instance—present little problem. But most studies in the behavioral sciences involve constructs that must be translated into behaviors that can be sensed in order for us to assess them. When we meet people, we cannot directly sense their intelligence, for instance, but we judge it by their behavior. Sometimes we do this by exposing them to a standard set of problems, an intelligence test. This permits comparison of their behavior with other persons on a common scale. Psychological, sociological, and economic constructs such as anxiety, socioeconomic class, and marginal utility require interpretation into characteristics that can be sensed and measured. The instrumentation section is where that translation is described and the case made for its adequacy.

This is another section in which the expansive rhetoric of the problem description may be reduced to mundane terms when the reader sees what the problem has become in measurement terms. If the realities of measurement are modest, keep the early rhetoric modest too.

Often the translation process helps to sharpen your understanding of the study's constructs as you are forced to choose among alternatives that represent different operational definitions.

> "Anxiety" may be undefined in the hypothesis, but one will find many possibilities when one comes to choosing a measure. They range from self-report of one's "state" of anxiety to self-perceptions of it as a persistent "trait" to physiological measures (galvanic skin response or heart and breathing rate). Are these interchangeable definitions

of the same characteristic? The problem definition and explanation should provide sufficient guidance to choose among the possibilities; if they do not, they need further refining.

When it is impossible to find totally satisfactory measures, describe the problem and justify, as well as possible, the measure that comes closest, indicating why it will be adequate for your study.

Be sure that all the terms critical to the questions, hypotheses, or models are discussed in this section. Variables mentioned earlier and then dropped leave ends dangling that are sure to be noticed by your chairperson or committee. And it is hoped that they do, since attending to them at the proposal stage may save you a real crisis later. In addition, dropping variables leaves the impression that you are not paying sufficient attention to important details and suggests there may be other carelessness in the proposal.

The interpretability of commonly used instruments may be well established for the purposes you intend. For new or experimental tests, however, your audience will expect empirical evidence of the test's quality and meaning. If it is not available from use of the test by others, make provisions in the proposal for establishing that the test has appropriate characteristics (if possible, before the data are collected. For an example, see Beissner's paragraph 39, regarding her plans to gather evidence of validity for the test she developed.). Here, as elsewhere, do not assume that the reader will rush to the library to look up missing reliability and validity information. If there is any doubt that the reader is likely to know it, supply it.

Validity. Construct validity provides evidence that forms the basis for intended score interpretation and serves as a unifying framework for other validity evidence. Evidence based on relations with other variables shows, for instance, that the test correlates with an already accepted measure of the variable. It correlates with measures it ought to be related to and does not correlate with those it should not. Look at an example in paragraphs 28–31 and 45 of Beissner's proposal.

Validity evidence based on content, also called "content" or "curricular validity," provides a comparison of the test items with specifications of what subject matter content and skills the test is supposed to cover. Predictive and concurrent validity evidence shows the measure predicts or is correlated with work or academic performance. Evidence of validity is usually found in a test's manual or in such references as Buros's *Mental Measurements Yearbooks*. Cite evidence for those kinds of validity needed for the problem posed.

Although not usually considered part of construct validity, "face validity"—that the test looks as though it measured what it was intended to measure—is very important when the study's acceptance is determined by policy makers, parents, and others with little or no professional background. Treat it in the validity discussion if it is likely to be a factor in your study.

Reliability. Just as there are various kinds of evidence for validity, there are also for reliability: stability reliability—the test scores are stable over time; internal consistency reliability (homogeneity)—the various test items measure the same characteristic so the scores are interpretable; and equivalence reliability—different test forms are comparable. Which reliabilities are required depends on the design. For example, test results compared over a substantial period of time require evidence of stability reliability and internal consistency reliability (for an example, see paragraphs 41 and 44 of Beissner's proposal). If the retest used a different form of the same test, equivalence reliability would be required as well. Again, such evidence is usually given in a test's manual.

Objectivity. Observation scales, in particular, require that all observers in a study use them the same way so that they agree when rating the same phenomenon; this is objectivity. Observers often train by rating the same videotapes, continuing until all observers respond to events the same way. Describe any planned training and what level of agreement among observers will be sought. Remember that a correlation coefficient will show agreement on relative but not exact position on the score scale; it does not detect that one person is a tougher grader than another, for instance. Use the intraclass correlation to show exact correspondence of judgment.

Objectivity is also a problem for multiple raters of essay or similar material.

Beissner's scoring of concept maps is an instance of this; see her paragraph 47 and the related annotation.

Sources of Instruments. If you are looking for available instrumentation, be sure to use the considerable resources for finding both established and experimental ones. At one time the sole source of information about tests was Oscar Buros's *Mental Measurements Yearbook,* published at irregular intervals since 1938. Information on commercially available tests is available from the Buros Web site, http://www.unl.edu/buros (accessed October 1, 2004); reviews on the most heavily used tests can be downloaded for a fee. In addition, there are now a number of compilations of instruments (Backer, 1977; Goldman and Mitchell, 1995–2003; Fabiano and O'Brien, 1987; Educational Testing [ETS] Service's TestLink—http://www.ets.org/testcoll/index.html [accessed October 1, 2004]).

The Internet is continually changing, so check for new sources, but these sources, which include ETS TestLink's more than twenty thousand tests, should go a long way toward pointing you in possible directions. Pursue them in databases like the *Social Science Citation Index, PsychINFO,* or *Sociofile.* In these, one may be able to find instances where a specific instrument has been used, its strengths and weaknesses noted, and sometimes an improved version.

Constructing and validating new instruments is both difficult and expen-

sive. Established instruments may not be quite as close to the desired operational definition as new or experimental ones, but usually are better validated
and more easily and widely understood by one's audience. However, a specially designed instrument may result in a more on-target study. Which to
choose? Consider such factors as: How much difference in validity would be
gained with new construction? What are the odds the construction effort will
be successful? How feasible is it? Must the results be accepted by a lay audience
who might better accept the established instrument? Can data be obtained that
document the new instrument to your audience's satisfaction?

If you lean toward constructing a new instrument, consider it carefully
with your chairperson and committee. Developing an instrument can be a dissertation in itself. They won't want you to overcommit yourself by undertaking
more than is reasonable in a dissertation, any more than you do. But they may
have a better idea of the time and effort involved. So, lay it all out for them to
consider. (Remember as indicated at the outset, approval of your proposal is a
"shared decision-making situation"—see chapter 1, pp. 3–5. If given a green
light, describe how the test will be developed and lay out a development plan.
Display sample items in an appendix. Such plans will be found in many measurement books (e.g., Gronlund, 2001; Hopkins, 1998).

Comparison and Contrast—The Basis for Sensing Attributes or Changes

This link in the design serves two purposes that are most easily seen in experimental studies. The first purpose is providing a basis on which one can say that
a treatment had an effect. This might be by comparison with an untreated experimental group as in the Beissner study. (Beissner describes the difference in
treatment of the two groups in her "Procedure" section, paragraphs 48 and 49,
and examines the effect of the treatment in her "Data Analysis" section, paragraph 50.) As with previous links, in those sections of the proposal where it is
relevant—the procedure section being a common one—show how you will
sense attributes or changes.

The second purpose is the elimination of alternative explanations, as discussed earlier in this chapter.

> Beissner eliminates the alternative explanations of differences in prior knowledge, in
> critical thinking ability, and in learning style. The assessment of these variables is noted
> in Beissner's "Instrument" section (paragraph 41 and 43) and their effect in the "Analy-
> sis" section (paragraph 50).

Although it is less obvious in nonexperimental research studies that seek
explanations and generalizable findings, this link serves the same two purposes: noting attributes and changes and protecting against alternative
explanations.

For instance, Warters is seeking attributes of effective programs. In paragraph 17, he notes how, using theory-based sampling procedures, he will select individuals for interview from three or four different treatment programs to allow "the opportunity for some comparison of treatment modalities" and to identify "specific aspects of group process thought useful by the men themselves in eliminating abuse."

In terms of protecting against alternative explanations, Warters notes in paragraph 31 that he is "currently functioning as an advocate of social intervention to reduce men's domestic violence," and that "This perspective will most certainly affect my interpretation of events and discussion during the course of my study." He then indicates in paragraph 32 how he hopes to overcome this concern on the part of his audience.

So, regardless of study method, if one is advancing a generalizable explanation, somewhere in the description of design, one needs to note how these two functions of this link will be attended.

Time Schedule—The Specification of the Procedure

The description of the procedure is a narration of the plan for data collection over time. It indicates what observations or measurements will be made, when, where, and of whom, and, if there is a treatment, how, where, when, and to whom it will be administered. It is usually the place where a reader can get the clearest idea of exactly what you plan to do and how and when you plan to do it. Usually, it is a verbal account, with the actual schedule with dates, which is described in the next chapter, forming a later section. It often contains a graphic of the work plan. Obviously, the procedural narrative and activities in the work plan or schedule should be coordinated so they tell the same story. Because of this relationship, you may wish to lay out the work plan or schedule section first and then describe it in the method or procedure section. Alternatively, constructing your work plan or schedule from the procedure section provides a test of its adequacy.

Usually the account is labeled "Procedure," as it is in Beissner, where it begins with paragraph 48. But it sometimes appears, as in Warters, under the heading "Methods," where it starts with paragraph 11, or "Research Methods," as in Phelan, where it starts with paragraph 10. In all three instances, readers can get quite a clear picture of what the researcher plans to do from these sections.

Problems in Data Collection

Indicate your provisions for handling potential problems that may arise in the course of gathering data.

Beissner, for instance, fearing that students may communicate so that the control group may learn how to do concept mapping, indicates that "the participants will be advised not to discuss the content of their sessions with other study participants" (paragraph 49).

The social-psychological aspects of studies are all too often ignored. Use of middle-class Caucasian interviewers in an economically depressed African American or Puerto Rican community is an example. Active opposition by teachers threatened by a study of their teaching methods is another. In both instances, the social dynamics of the data collection situation, if ignored, may destroy a study's validity. Project TALENT, a large longitudinal study, found this out the hard way when parents at one data collection location gleefully made a bonfire of all their children's answer sheets because they believed the information sought was too personal. The contingencies are too numerous to cover, but the following examples may sensitize you to some concerns.

A most serious problem occurs when those familiar with an experiment are concerned that an untreated or unobserved group is being discriminated against. This can be especially serious with therapy, remedial, accelerated, or enriched treatments where administrators, other professionals, or parents may become upset when control or unselected groups are not also helped. This can often be handled by setting up a waiting list of individuals who can be used as a control group and then treated later.

For most studies, the more normal the situation, the more generalizable the results. Show your good training in field method by avoiding periods immediately preceding or following holidays, a big athletic or social event, etc.

The more your planned activities will disturb normal routine, the fewer institutions or organizations likely to be willing to cooperate. Further, those sites that do may well be atypical, so generality of findings may be reduced. Include letters in the appendix from persons in authority indicating intent to cooperate with the study so your committee learns who is involved and can assess any implications.

If you are studying a controversial topic such as sexual attitudes or other highly personal matters, obtaining permission may be difficult. Even such apparently innocuous topics as school achievement may present problems if it is a sensitive issue. Anticipate these problems and show how you plan to handle them.

Whenever data are gathered from more than one group, or in several situations, describe the provisions made to ensure that the circumstances for data collection are comparable.

Using an observer, tape recorder, or television camera may markedly influence a situation or create an artificial one. Describe the steps to be taken with respect to this problem, such as concealment of the camera, special rooms with provisions for concealed observation, or an adaptation period. Kounin (1970) left a box in the classroom throughout the year. Participants never knew whether it contained an active video camera and came to ignore it. Of course, the ethical implications of such possibly deceptive practices have to be dealt with in your proposal and ultimately approved by your local Committee on the Protection of Human Subjects.

Analysis

The method of analysis must be consistent with the objectives and design. For instance, when the study calls for finding the extent of a relationship, some measure of the size of relations such as a correlation coefficient is in order. Too often, we find instead a contrast of high with low groups to compute a difference statistic such as a *t* test. A statistically significant *t* test would indicate that had a correlation been computed, it would be significantly different from zero. But the extent of statistical significance does not indicate the size of the relationship; it could be so low as to be, practically speaking, insignificant. That a difference is statistically significant at some extremely small percentage level may be testimony more to the statistical power of the study than to the strength of the relationship. Without knowing the size of the correlation, you don't know whether the relationship is strong enough to permit any kind of reasonable prediction and, therefore, any practical application.

The assumptions of the statistics should fit the data. If they seem not to, describe the corrections that can be made. For instance, analysis of variance assumes normally distributed populations, but corrections in the level of significance can easily be made for nonnormal data.

A description of how missing data and/or unequal cell frequencies of a complex design are to be handled displays a sophistication that is comforting to the reader.

When new statistical techniques, computer programs, or other unfamiliar analytic tools are to be used, adequately describe them and show their advantages over current methods so the reader may be assured of their appropriateness.

It is not always possible to completely anticipate in advance the nature of the analysis that will be called for; it may depend on the nature of the data collected. This is especially true of content analysis procedures, but it may also be true of statistical methods. As is probably obvious by now, the best strategy is to *reveal the depths to which these problems have been anticipated and describe the projected solution in sufficient detail as to clearly convey its nature. At the same time, show awareness of where anticipated departures from plan may occur.* Before leaving this section, check to make sure the analytic procedures will handle all the relevant data that will be gathered and will yield evidence bearing on all the questions, hypotheses, and model aspects proposed for investigation.

Expected End Product

This section will not appear in all proposals, but is a good section to include if there are products in addition to the usual report of results or if the report of results is other than routine. Tests, evaluation instruments, curriculum materials, videotapes, audiotapes, films, pamphlets, and the like, even though they may be but by-products of the project, are sometimes more important and more enduring than the project results. Describe them and their possible use outside the project.

One possible very important end product is your dissertation formatted as an article ready to publish! Read how next to achieve that.

AN ALTERNATIVE DISSERTATION FORMAT: ARTICLES READY FOR PUBLICATION

If you are serious about obtaining a position in higher education, consider writing your dissertation as an article ready for publication in an appropriate journal. Nearly all institutions will allow this, even though it is a rarely chosen route in the social and behavioral sciences. Some encourage it; it is more common in the sciences than the social sciences, but ought to become more common over time. See Krathwohl (1994) and Duke and Beck (1999).

Having the dissertation ready to send off for publication will net you an early career publication and save you from trying to cut your dissertation to journal size at the same time that you are adjusting to your postdoctoral situation. After all, a new job, learning the ropes in a new institution, planning courses and writing teaching materials, starting a research program, and learning how to advise students, to say nothing of all the non-higher education problems of relocating, provide a full plate. You don't need, in addition, a dissertation that you may possibly have grown tired of hanging around your neck.

Publication will require that you use the format of the particular journal to which you intend to submit. The length of their typical article will unquestionably be less than dissertation length, requiring a significant departure from dissertation format. Depending on your chairperson and committee, and the typical procedure at your institution, you may be required to put considerable work in an appendix so that your committee and the external readers at the final oral examination can understand what you did. The literature review may need to be prepared as a separate article for a different journal than the main body of the study.

If you plan to use the dissertation-as-article format, share this idea early with your chairperson and committee. Be sure they will cooperate with you in this endeavor. Then make your intent regarding writing format a part of the proposal compact. This makes clear to everyone what to expect.

If there is likely to be any question regarding "how much is enough," that is, when your committee is willing to agree that you have fulfilled your "contract," read the last section of chapter 7. It is discussed there because it is a common problem with qualitative proposals, but can be for other kinds of studies as well.

Finally, since the description of your study methods may be the most closely read section of your proposal, it is important to produce a carefully thought-out statement. Use Worksheet 5.1: Study Methods Review to assess and improve your methods statement.

Study Methods Review

How Strong Are My Study's Methods?

As you develop your proposal, periodically review how strong your study's methods are, and where they need to be strengthened.

In Decribing My Study's Methods Overall, How Well Have I . . . ?	Strong	Acceptable	Weak– Improvements Needed	Not Applicable
Selected procedures that address the expectations created in prior chapters?				
Adapted my procedures statement to the specific methods of my study?				
Clearly shown the connection between my method and the questions, hypotheses, or models I have chosen to study?				
Constructed a design that is a relevant, feasible, and internally coherent operationalization of the concepts being examined?				
Appropriately considered resource limits, institutional limits, ethical limits, and time limits?				
Identified and eliminated or controlled each major alternative explanation of the results I might obtain?				
Anticipated and accommodated possible study problems?				
Outlined appropriate analysis procedures?				

(Continued on next page)

In reviewing specific aspects of my method, how well have I selected and described . . . ?	Strong	Acceptable	Weak– Improvements Needed	Not Applicable
In Decribing My Study Methods Overall, How Well Have I . . . ?				
Study participants, including population(s) and sample(s)?				
Study situation?				
Study focus of attention, including treatments or interventions, if any, and study variables?				
Study records, including observations, measures, and instrumentation, and their technical quality?				
Study comparisons or contrasts for sensing attributes or change?				
Study time frame and procedures?				

CHAPTER 6

Ensuring Feasibility
and Other Proposal Parts

CHAPTER CONTENTS

This chapter is about giving assurances. Your chairperson and committee may agree that yours is a good problem and you have described a reasonable procedure. But before giving you the green light to proceed with their blessing, they want to be assured you will be able to complete your project. Their concerns typically involve questions like:

- Can you do the project in a reasonable time frame, especially in relation to when you expect to get your degree and move on? What would such a time schedule look like? (Answered by a work plan section.)
- Have you the competencies to do the project? If not, how will you obtain

them? By taking courses? Cooperating with others? Obtaining consultants? (Answered by a section on past experiences, pilot studies, training
you plan to get, available assistance, or the like.)

- Can you get access to the persons you plan to study? Administrative
  and/or institutional approval? Will the study leave a situation that can be
  used by other researchers? (Answered by a section on access.)
- Can you get approval from the Committee on the Protection of Human
  Subjects? (Answered by a section on clearances.)
- Do you have, or can you obtain, the resources needed to complete your
  study? Computers? Observers? Test copies? Equipment? Should the proposal be submitted somewhere for funding? (Answered by a section on
  budget.)

These parts of the proposal therefore provide assurances that you have the
time, competencies, access, clearances, and resources. There are also other parts
of the proposal we will consider: the appendixes, the abstract, and your title
page. Finally, there is the editing and rewriting of the draft and duplication of
copies. These topics form the organization of this chapter.

TIME SCHEDULE OR WORK PLAN

Not every dissertation chairperson will require a work plan as part of the proposal. Unless you do it to submit the proposal for funding, if you do a work
plan, it may be primarily for you! You may think that it is a lot of work when it
isn't required, and that's right. For the structured project, however, and especially for the complex one, a carefully developed work plan may save you making mistakes as you proceed, mistakes that can sometimes be costly in time and
sometimes result in loss of valuable data.

For an emergent project where the topic is found as you proceed, about all
you can do is give rough estimates of anticipated time in the field, for analyzing
data, for interpreting, and for writing. But even this much provides some
guidance so that when you exceed those dates, you become aware that you
have a problem if you are to complete your degree as expected. Then you can
take steps to resolve it before it is too late and major life adjustments must be
made.

But even if your project isn't complex, and could be carried out with a general scheme of where you want to go in your head, a work plan has advantages:

- It forces you to think through each activity so you are aware of what it
  entails. This uncovers steps that:
    are dependent on prior activities and so will be held up until their
    completion,

> can be undertaken concurrently and can thus shorten the overall time, and
>
> take too long and threaten the project's feasibility.

- It sets goals for you and deadlines for reaching them. For many of us, initial motivation lags once the initial thrill wears off; then "milestones," as they are often called, provide stimulation toward progress.

- In contrast to the enormity of the project as a whole, it breaks the process into steps so that the next one seems quite doable. Plan to give yourself some kind of a reward when you reach a milestone. Go out to dinner or take in a special concert, play, or movie—whatever gives you pleasure. Then take aim for the next one.

- It provides a panorama of the project as a whole. Some readers turn to it first to get an overall perspective on the project. In other instances, a reviewer who is having difficulty understanding the flow of the procedure turns to the time schedule for the first real understanding of what the researcher intends to do.

- It is a sign to readers of how carefully and realistically the project has been developed.

It follows, of course, that the work schedule should give a *consistent and comprehensive presentation of the preceding material.* Omission of segments of the study makes projections of its length unreliable at best and indicates either carelessness or disorganization, characteristics you don't want applied to your work.

Depending on the complexity of the project, various formats may be used to describe the work plan. A simple table giving a time schedule will suffice for most. Simply list the dates for the start and completion of various activities.

Such a list is provided in paragraph 27 of the Phelan proposal under the heading "Management Plan." This time schedule appears to be a mixture of starting and ending dates, depending on the activity description. It might have been improved by including both starting and ending dates, but it includes all the major steps in the project.

It also makes clear that he intends to write his dissertation report as the project progresses so he can do the writing while the activities and his thinking about them are still fresh. This is good practice for a lengthy project or one being done along with a full-time job. This contrasts with the more common plan of leaving all the writing to the end in the hope that one can reconstruct one's thinking and link it all together. In making time estimates, allow extra time for phases not under your direct control. Data collection is often the most seriously underestimated phase, especially where contact with the field is involved. Control of subjects usually rests with parents and/or the institution rather than the investigator. The priority they give research is usually lower than other time demands. Follow-up of dropouts and incompletes, to avoid selectivity (see p. 86), may take as long as the original data collection. Waiting for clearances of all kinds and awaiting the return of questionnaires are examples of other important variables beyond your control. Plan these phases realistically. In general, required time increases with greater complexity, magnitude, and difficulty, and as control decreases.

Similarly, analysis and interpretation of the data and writing the dissertation tend to be underestimated. Authors frequently end the time schedule at the point where they have a complete draft, ignoring the editorial phases. It has been well said, "there is no good writing, only good *rewriting*." Allow for it.

Graphic Depictions of the Work Plan

Figure 6.1 is a simple time chart that describes the steps in a sample survey. Called a "Gantt Chart" after its inventor, its detail would suffice for most projects. Each significant activity occupies a separate row, and the line in the row indicates the activity's duration in terms of the calendar time scale across the bottom of the chart. Important events that mark the end of a phase of the study are called "milestones" and are marked by triangles.

Computer-Generated Flowcharts and Diagrams

For complex projects, consider graphically laid-out flowcharts or diagrams. Most graphic techniques use some form of *Program Evaluation Review Technique*, usually referred to by its initials, PERT, or its many modifications. These displays result in a flow diagram showing the sequence of the various activities and their interdependence in terms of completion dates. In a sense, they pro-

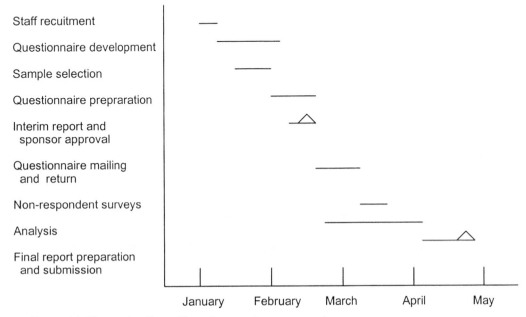

Figure 6.1. Illustrative Gantt Chart for sample survey study.

vide a road map to a destination and show the intermediate points and dis-
tances between them.

They are a better way than a Gantt Chart of indicating the sequence of
work, since they make it possible to show the interrelationships among the
parts of the study and demonstrate more clearly the relative length of various
phases. They have a number of advantages:

1. Each step gets analyzed in sufficient detail (very helpful for the procedure section!) so that difficulties are uncovered that might have remained hidden in a less clearly specified proposal (only to arise later and bedevil you after
the proposal is approved).

2. They require you to explore the interrelationships among activities. They
indicate where there are dependencies such that later stages can't proceed until
an earlier one is completed.

3. You are forced to estimate the time required to meet the criteria appropriate for each activity (e.g., how long will it take to get a 65 percent questionnaire
return?), giving a more reliable estimate of the total time required for the work.

4. They can serve as a basis for resource allocation of personnel time to various parts of the proposal.

5. They provide a basis for administrative control of the project.

6. Since they more clearly show the implications of any change for the total
operation, they provide a better foundation for making informed decisions
when changes are required, both in planning and as the work proceeds.

7. Using calendars for specific dates, the effect of holidays, vacations, and
other problems can be anticipated.

An Example of a Computer-Generated Flowchart

Figure 6.2 is an example of a flowchart that displays the steps in a typical sample survey project. Each box indicates a step in the project. Such charts usually
are first laid out in terms of gross activities and then successively refined. There
is considerable project scheduling software available, but Microsoft Word's
drawing toolbar has the templates needed for most dissertations.

As indicated in the caption, Figure 6.2 was prepared in Microsoft Word,
which, though not as comprehensive as software designed solely for project
management purposes, will serve the purpose for most dissertations. The example illustrates several conventions. The double line connecting the boxes is
what is known as the critical path. The critical path is that line continuously
connecting the events whose total is the longest required to finish the interim
events and, therefore, is the minimum time in which the project can be completed. (For steps to take to shorten the critical path see Krathwohl [1988]. See
also the sections on workload analysis that compares personnel demands with
available staff.) The numbers at the top of each box show the estimated days required to accomplish the task. The dates below the text are the starting and ending dates. Boxes with rounded corners are milestones.

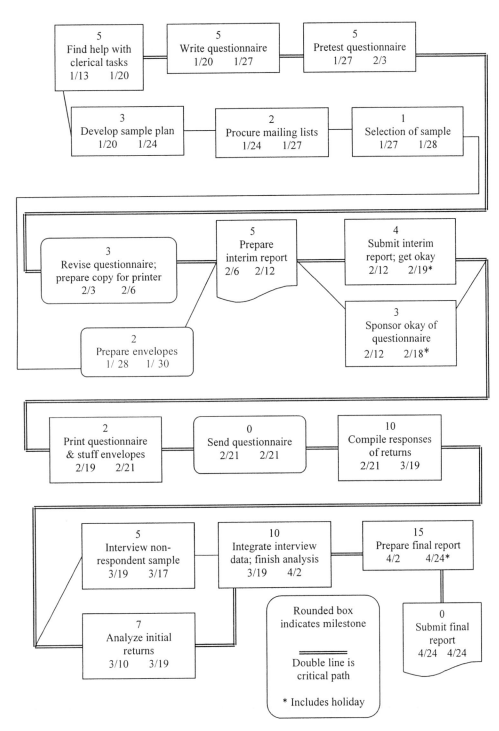

Figure 6.2. A sample survey's work plan created in Microsft Word using flowchart form from Autoshapes in the Drawing toolbar with text inserted by control (Macintosh, for PC, right) clicking it and choosing "add text" from the pop-up menu (graphic adapted from Krathwohl, 1988, p. 76).

If your project is complex and you are thinking about submitting your proposal for funding, look into borrowing project management software. Most are expensive, but will be available at the grant facilitation office of your institution. In many of them, inserting the beginning and ending calendar dates for the whole project together with the time required for each activity provides enough information for the program to generate all the interim dates automatically, a tremendous time saving. Since the programs use calendars for specific years, the effect of holidays, vacations, and other problems can be anticipated. They not only facilitate preparation of the work plan but also tie together the work plan and the budget so that budget totals can be created simultaneously. As one inserts activities into the work plan, one is helped to estimate their costs as well, and the data are then placed appropriately in attached spreadsheets. The better software make it possible to generate several kinds of displays of the project tasks and financial data. The effects of various trade-offs between project duration and cost can then be explored. Flowcharts apply sophisticated common sense and, with the more complex software, statistics and computerization to the tasks of planning, controlling progress, and resource allocation.

ASSURANCE OF COMPETENCE

Your chairperson and committee want to be assured that you have the competencies to successfully carry through your plans or, if you don't have them now, that your plans include their acquisition. Sections labeled "Prior Experiences," "Pilot Studies," "Planned Skills Training," "Methodological Competence," or the like can set your readers at ease.

> Note paragraphs 31 and 32 of the Warters proposal where he describes "The Qualifications of the Researcher." Such a section is particularly important in emergent proposals where the student is being turned loose to search using his "seat of the pants" for a guide. Warters backs up the qualifications section with two additional ones: "Summary of Progress Toward Completion of Dissertation Research, 1/24/91" (paragraphs 34–41) and "Background Research Activities" (paragraphs 42–43). These show significant progress on the dissertation activities and how he has worked at developing his skills since his initial training. Detailing prior experience showing you cannot just survive, but can thrive in such circumstances is reassuring to your doctoral committee.

Indicating how prior prejudices will be handled in emergent studies is important.

> Warters does this by describing his point of view in paragraphs 29 and 30 under "Theoretical Issues." He also tells how by "continuing to read historical accounts of the wide variation in ways that social problems get dealt with, and by maintaining a critical

stance toward my own current work," he will keep some perspective on his own "ideological and practice assumptions."

What if your study requires expertise beyond your own and that of your chairperson and committee, thus calling for the assistance of consultants—other faculty at your institution or at other institutions? Proper use of consultants may satisfy reviewers' concerns about your shortcomings in background and/or experience and increases the probability of a successful project (e.g., help with sampling plans, medical advice, and software selection). Where such a relationship has been established, the nature of the cooperation should be made clear. Where it has not, this section becomes a plea for your committee to help locate missing competencies.

Spell out for your committee any special facilities and/or equipment that will be needed and their availability. Where relevant, mention special strengths available to you that you will draw on as well, such as pertinent special data-processing or computer facilities, statistical consulting services, a survey research center, special equipment, especially relevant library holdings, test or research collections, advantageous building arrangements, established networks of relationships with schools or clinics, available panels of respondents, working arrangements with interviewers, and similar items. Again, if this is needed but not available, it becomes an item your chairperson and committee can help you with.

If your study, like Anna's (p. 15–16), is part of a larger project such as your chairperson's or that of another faculty member, you have no doubt noted this fact considerably earlier. But this is a good section in which to indicate how the availability of personnel, equipment, and facilities of the larger project strengthens yours and makes yours more likely to succeed. If you have not done so already, note here the relationship of your project to the overall goal, your areas of responsibility, and how your study facilitates attainment of that goal.

ASSURANCE OF ACCESS

Can you gain access to the persons you plan to study? If you have not discussed your access situation in the procedure section, a section labeled "Permissions," "Steps Taken to Obtain Access," or the like may be warranted.

Your committee is assured of access if you include letters from persons in a position to grant permission for you to do the study in their facility, with their class, etc. It is even better if the letter shows enough understanding of what you plan to do that this is clearly informed consent, not just a simple "okay." Such letters are usually included in an appendix and alluded to in the text of the proposal.

Some universities maintain good relations with local agencies, which could be overburdened with research requests, requiring a university clearance before they are approached. This also ensures priority access for especially deserving projects. In addition, schools, counseling centers, mental health clinics, social agencies, and other institutions often erect their own "fences," establishing approval committees as well. Failure to observe the procedures required by those committees may result in snarls that take many, many times the initial clearance effort to unravel—if, indeed, they can be unraveled after the fact. Often a project site is lost not only for this project but also for any research for a period of time by individuals who, thinking they have an "in," fail to follow the established routine. Use your "in" advantage if you wish, but provide the cover of following the established route as well.

If possible, obtain approvals in advance of submitting the proposal. Do so even though you'll feel more confident of what you are doing after you are ready to start the project. It makes those involved feel they are a part of the effort, and they are more likely to be cooperative. To approach them afterward makes their concerns an afterthought. If they want to change things or make a suggestion for improvement, the needed flexibility may be lost.

Can you do your study in such a way that others who follow you are not penalized because you were there? While gaining immediate access is mainly of concern to you, continuing access is of concern to your chairperson and committee. They may well have other students seeking to use the same circumstances. It is important that you not ruin access for others.

Keeping the site and/or situation amenable to future research is much harder to assess from the proposal. If problems arise, they usually occur during the study's implementation. But the proposal can indicate what you plan to do to ensure that you leave the study situation at least as amenable to cooperation with researchers as when you found it. This may involve going back to those involved and sharing findings or possibly performing some service as partial recompense for their cooperation. Whatever is planned, pointing this out in the proposal indicates your awareness of the problem and willingness to help solve it.

ASSURANCE OF OBSERVANCE OF ETHICAL CONSIDERATIONS

The federal government has specified a Committee on the Protection of Human Subjects procedure to ensure that projects it helps fund meet ethical and moral standards. Federal regulations prescribe the composition of the committee, which includes individuals outside the institution. The committee's task is to ensure that you will do no physical or emotional harm to those involved nor subject them to unwarranted stress. If your project might, they must decide whether the value of the knowledge potentially gained outweighs the study's negative aspects. Most universities require this committee's approval of *all* projects at their institutions, not only federally funded ones. Thus, in nearly all doctoral-granting institutions, dissertation projects involving humans or animals require this clearance.

Most dissertation proposals will be cleared in a short time by the chairperson of the Committee on the Protection of Human Subjects, who consults other members only where there is some question. But if your topic is controversial, schedule extra time for clearance just in case it is needed. For projects where clearance is projected to be (or, better still, was) routine, mention it in the procedure section. If nonroutine, discuss your situation in a separate "Human Subjects Clearance" section.

> Warters's section "Protection of Subjects," paragraphs 45–52, is an excellent example of providing assurances for a proposal that would probably be considered nonroutine by a human subjects protection committee. Note that he starts off by assuring his chairperson and committee that he has already obtained the committee's approval. But he then proceeds to provide details of how his subjects will be protected: confidentially of data, right of refusal, protection of subjects' victims, program staff as backup, and benefits to subjects. This is a thorough catalog of concerns that might occur to his chairperson and committee and probably did to the human-subjects committee when he submitted an earlier version of his proposal.

Appropriate comments throughout the proposal indicating concern for those you plan to study are the most convincing evidence of a real concern with this issue. See the annotation of paragraph 13 of Warters's proposal.

If you are seeking federal or state funding, there are other clearances to obtain. Discuss this with your campus's office of sponsored programs (see the following section).

BUDGET AND/OR SOURCES OF FINANCIAL SUPPORT

Typically only those students planning to seek university or external funding prepare a budget for their proposals. However, especially if your project is an extensive one, your chairperson and your committee may be concerned about the adequacy of your resources. Alternative to a budget, a section indicating how you will support yourself and pay dissertation expenses provides the necessary assurances.

> Warters does this in paragraphs 53–58 in a section titled "Other Support." There he indicates he will process his own data and seek university support for minor expenses. In addition, he cites other sources of possible support and fellowships. The latter will tempt his chairperson and committee to suggest other sources. Further, knowing he will be applying, it invites them to put in a good word for him where they think it might help.

If you are preparing a budget for submission for funding, be sure to draw upon your office of sponsored programs for help (on state campuses, they are often called foundations). Since funds are given to the university rather than the individual submitting, every university has an office through which proposals to off-campus agencies must be submitted. Such offices know the required certifications for federally sponsored projects and check to make sure that the appropriate clearances have been obtained. They also have persons skilled in budget preparation who can help estimate costs. Since it is in the university's interest for you to complete your project, they will want to ensure that you ask for adequate funds.

Depending on how much help your office of sponsored programs is willing to give you, and where your project proposal is to be submitted, doing a work plan with computer project-planning software helps with budgeting. Besides strengthening your proposal, a work plan is usually an expected part of federal proposals.

OTHER PARTS OF THE PROPOSAL

Appendix

Not all proposals need an appendix; none of our annotated ones did. But the appendix can be a very useful section, not just an afterthought. Consider putting in an appendix:

- Anything that gets in the way of the logic of the proposal as it flows from paragraph to paragraph and section to section.
- Material that provides detail but is too bulky to include in the copy.
- Supplementary comments on literature you read, or on difficulty in finding material and where you looked for it. This challenges your committee to come up with other suggestions.
- Copies of new or unfamiliar tests or questionnaires, as well as technical information on validity and other aspects crucial to the success of the study (e.g., ease of administration).
- Sample questions for instruments or interview schedules you plan to construct and samples of new item formats.
- Explanations of statistics that may not be familiar to the chairperson and committee.
- Letters from institutional administrators or other relevant persons indicating you have access.
- Charts that will be referred to repeatedly; tab them for easy access.
- Samples of intended products.
- Any other item about which your chairperson or committee might raise a question and ask for further information. Anticipating such requests is always good practice—it saves their time and therefore yours, shows you

are attempting to communicate thoroughly, and indicates thoughtfulness regarding their concerns.

Abstract

The abstract briefly describes the objectives of the study and the procedure. First impressions are important, and the abstract is the very first part read by nearly everyone. As Reif-Lehrer (1995, p. 25) notes, "You never get a second chance to make a first impression." Don't slight preparation of the abstract!

There are two points of view on when the abstract should be written: (1) at the outset of proposal preparation (a succinct and accurate abstract may be doable when one has the project well in mind from the beginning) or (2) as a last step. Most projects seem to change considerably during the proposal development process; therefore, the abstract is usually formulated after the main text of the proposal is completed. Even if you write the abstract at the outset, carefully review it at the end to be sure it is faithful to the proposal as fully developed.

All proposals should include an abstract: it provides a succinct initial overview of the intent and direction of the proposal. It orients the reader to what will be presented and why. Emergent or nontraditional proposals especially need an abstract to alert the reader that what follows will not be a highly detailed, prespecified plan. Since the dissertation itself will require one, it is good practice to start developing the abstract at the same time you do the proposal. Then it will be at least partially developed in good form when the final must be completed. Bear in mind that your abstract, just as you wrote it, as well as the first twenty-four pages of your dissertation, will be posted on the Web at the UMI ProQuest Web site (http://www.il.proquest.com/umi/dissertations [accessed October 1, 2004]) for the entire world to see. (Still more will be available if yours is one of the institutions publishing their dissertations online.) Your graduate school or departmental office will have the requirements that your abstract must meet.

Developing the abstract early gives many chances to revise it so you will be pleased with its ultimate form, especially important if your dissertation is your first publication! In writing the proposal abstract:

- Paraphrase the objectives and procedure using broad but accurate strokes and keep parts in proper perspective with appropriate emphasis.
- Include key terms that are likely to be commonly used for indexing projects in your field.
- Employ the key terms used in the body of the material so as to prepare the reader for them.
- Write so as to communicate to persons who are not specialists in the field.
- Indicate in positive terms what you will do, not what you will "try to do."

Title

The title serves many of the same purposes as the abstract in an even briefer way. In some information systems, *only* the title is entered and indexed. Keep the title short but descriptive even for the casual reader. In general, avoid jargon, inappropriate double entendres, and flippancy.

LAST STEPS BEFORE SUBMITTING FOR APPROVAL

A Final Check and Review

Fine, the draft is finished. Now you can check to make sure that the proposal is a consistent chain of reasoning. Each section should reflect the previous material and carry it a step further in a consistent and coherent way. Make sure that ends are not dropped, objectives are not slighted, data to be collected are identified but no analysis plan is given, and so on.

It almost goes without saying in these days of word processing that you will use spelling and grammar checkers to get rid of gaffs. You don't want it to look as though you don't care enough about your proposal to send in well-written copy.

Even the best writers benefit from having someone not familiar with the write-up criticize it. Don't be embarrassed to ask one or more friends to read it; choose ones that will be frank, but only if that is what is *honestly* wanted.

If you have the time, put the draft aside and then come back to it afresh after a long enough period to look at it in perspective. You'll be amazed at what you find.

Preparing the Final Copy

How important is the appearance of the proposal? Some students do a very artful job of putting the proposal in attractive form. We cannot say that the reader will be unimpressed by this. But the major emphasis should be on legibility, lucidity, and clarity of presentation. For a long or complex proposal, tabs readily convey the organization, and colored paper will distinguish sections. Place the color code in a prominent and accessible place (front cover, table of contents, or first pages). Don't use paper so dark it makes reading difficult.

Carefully proofreading a document requires time; your word processor will not catch an improper but correctly spelled word. When errors make enough sense that they are not immediately spotted as typos, the reader must slow down to decipher your meaning. Only time-consuming, careful proofreading eliminates such problems. Most of us who read a lot are so used to skipping past errors that we are terrible proofreaders. If possible, find someone who is good at finding errors and treasure that person. Usually, the less familiar the proofreader is with the proposal, the better.

And if you find yourself pressed for time in getting the final copy duplicated (and who doesn't?), consider this version of Murphy's law, which appears over our photocopying machine:

Warning

This machine is subject to breakdowns during periods of critical need. A special circuit in the machine called a "critical detector" senses the operator's emotional state in terms of how desperate he or she is to use the machine. The critical detector then creates a malfunction proportional to the desperation of the operator. Threatening the machine with violence only aggravates the situation. Likewise attempts to use another machine may cause it to also malfunction. They belong to the same union. Keep cool and say nice things to the machine. Nothing else seems to work. Never let anything mechanical know you are in a hurry.

FUNDING

Many of you may need additional resources in order to complete your degree. Consider submitting your proposal for funding. If you have followed the previous advice, you have a solid proposal that should merit support if you can interest a funder. In addition, you will gain valuable experience managing a budget, just as you would later if you seek a position in higher education or in some institutions. Did you know that many funders allow you to budget support for yourself as a graduate assistant or whatever title your university's budget office allows? See chapter 14 for suggestion on submitting for funding. In addition, besides Krathwohl (1988), several of the references in the "Additional Readings" section at the end of this book will be of considerable assistance; look at their abstracts (pp. 275–77).

WRITING THE PROPOSAL AFTER YOU ARE WELL INTO THE STUDY

This option applies to any study where the design of the study is essentially emergent rather than known in detail beforehand or when preparation of the proposal can be preceded by a pilot study. It has purposely been placed at this part's end since it isn't possible in all institutions, and even where it is, it isn't the best course for every student to follow.

The foregoing sections of the chapter have assumed that your faculty or institution insists that a proposal be completed and approved before you begin your dissertation. But, especially if you do a pilot study, it is difficult to define precisely when the dissertation is begun. Pilot data are frequently merged with data collected after the dissertation proposal is approved. And as we have noted, in many qualitative dissertations, the problem emerges as the study progresses. Sometimes the real target of the study emerges early, sometimes not until one is well into data collection.

If you can delay doing the proposal until its target has been identified, it may save you considerable labor as well as the anxiety and uncertainty of trying to frame a proposal when you haven't yet identified the target of your study. In some instances, this will mean risking the time and energy of data collection (or, in the case of a philosophical dissertation, countless hours of reading, thinking, and discussing) on the assumption that the target will emerge.

Sometimes, nothing satisfying does emerge! Some faculty may insist that research is like that—it doesn't always pay off; if it did, it wouldn't be research. So, if nothing turned up, you have just learned your first lesson about research and may still be held to doing a satisfactory study! That is the risk one takes. It is also why other faculty, before letting you loose on your study, tend to insist on a proposal that serves as a kind of contract between themselves and you that you both agree this is a project worth pursuing. If that turns out not to be the case, then both having been wrong, the student is not to be penalized by withholding the degree until a satisfactory study is done. The study is written up with as much of a focus and conclusion as can be salvaged.

In most institutions, however, at the doctoral level, even more than previously, you are allowed considerable freedom and treated as an adult. Faculty members leave it to you to determine when you do the proposal and when you consider it ready to submit for approval. If you want to take the risk of embarking on your dissertation and submitting your proposal quite late in the process, that is your prerogative. For secure students, confident of their abilities, and willing to take some risks, this may indeed be the best course. We have had some excellent students submit the proposal almost at the same time as the dissertation. We have not only permitted it, but also, considering the study they were pursuing, thought it a wise course and encouraged it.

But not all faculty will agree to this, and not all institutions will permit it. Indeed, many faculty consider it an inappropriate laissez-faire attitude toward an inexperienced student researcher who isn't in a position to know any better. This is especially true when the student has come to expect much protection against doing the wrong thing—so many of the courses are prescribed, the sequence of experiences is largely set, etc.

If the university regulations are such that an approved proposal is required early in the process, that settles the matter. But otherwise, before proceeding to do a proposal late in the process, clarify feelings on this matter with your chairperson and committee. Further, you need something in writing to ensure that it is permitted! There may be personnel changes in your chairperson and/or committee before you are finished. A record doesn't bind new members, but it helps persuade them as to what is reasonable. So after discussing it with your chairperson and committee and obtaining their consent, write them a note summarizing your discussion with them and indicating your understanding of the ultimate decision. Try to get a written response from the chairperson that this summary is accurate. If they do not write you back rejecting your understanding of the discussions, they at least have been informed. While it isn't without risk, this forms a tacit agreement for you to proceed.

Finally, use Worksheet 6.1: Assurances Review to make sure you have responded to anticipated concerns and justified faculty confidence that you can successfully accomplish the proposed study.

Assurances Review

How Well Does My Proposal Provide Assurances of a Feasible, High Quality Study?

It is important to convince your chairperson, committee members, and other participants in your research, that they can count on you to conduct a strong, well thought out study. Use the following to ensure you have provided all needed assurances of that.

How Well Have I Described . . . ?	Strong	Acceptable	Weak– Improvements Needed	Not Applicable
A detailed work plan of timelines, activities, and milestones?				
A summary of needed financial and other resources, and how they will be acquired? (See, e.g., Worksheet 1.2)				
An analysis of competencies needed to do the study, those that are currently available, and how others will be acquired? (See e.g., Worksheet 1.1)				
Arrangements and permissions for gaining access to people, facilities, or situations?				
Procedures and approvals related to human subjects protection, protection of research animals, and other issues of conducting ethical research?				

PART THREE

Advice Specific to Particular Kinds of Studies

Part 2 has supplied information general to the proposal, but it cannot cover all possibilities—especially since each of the different social science research methods places different demands on the proposal writer. This is also true of certain kinds of problems, such as those involved in evaluation, demonstration, and action projects. Topics such as the latter ones may be acceptable as dissertation topics in certain departments of some institutions. The intent of this section is to help you avoid errors of omission or commission with respect to the special requirements of your particular research problem.

Just how to organize this section to best fit your needs has been something of a puzzle. There are so many ways of categorizing research problems—basic-applied, exploratory-descriptive-validating-predictive, process-product, etc. Each of these would emphasize and de-emphasize certain parts of the proposal. We listened to faculty and graduate students talk about their studies and considered the differences in what is included in the proposal depending on how the study is characterized.

As a result, we decided to organize two of the chapters around research methods—chapter 7, "Qualitative Methods," and chapter 8, "Quantitative Methods." We pick up other study types—survey, evaluation, development, demonstration—in the third, chapter 9.

Because certain disciplines develop dominant research traditions, one chapter may be more relevant to your study than the others. However, it is hoped that you will find sections close enough to what you plan to do to be helpful in preparing your proposal.

CHAPTER 7

The Special Requirements of Proposals Using Qualitative Approaches

Emergent, Qualitative, Philosophical, Historical

CHAPTER CONTENTS

This chapter is divided into two sections. Section 1 takes up proposals for studies using qualitative methods, and section 2 those involving historical and philosophical problems. Each section describes proposal format, structure, and aspects requiring special attention. Because Warters's annotated proposal (chapter 11) is used as an example at a number of points in this chapter, we suggest that you read it before reading this chapter or while studying it.

None of the types of proposals discussed here necessarily follows a set format as typically do experimental, statistical, and measurement-oriented studies. The lack of a specific format frees you to adapt your proposal to your study's particular demands. But this in turn requires that you present your case in such an integrated and logical fashion that it is easy for a reader to find desired information even without a standard format to fall back on.

If you have never written a proposal, you may prefer a template to fill in. The lack of it may give you almost too much freedom before you have the experience to handle it, and too many choices before you know which format would best fit the project. By presenting a checklist among the material that follows, we try to allay your anxiety with some structure without making you feel constricted by our suggestions.

SECTION 1: QUALITATIVE METHOD STUDIES

This discussion of qualitative method studies is more oriented toward those doing emergent studies than prespecified ones. Those doing the latter will benefit from reading both this and the first part of the next chapter, which focuses on important aspects of prespecified studies, even though that discussion is oriented toward studies comparing and contrasting conditions.

The Special Problems of Emergent Study Proposals

An Element of Risk

Emergent dissertations have an exciting element of risk. They are like going fishing, or bargain hunting in stores; the element of chance is an important part of it. Just engaging in such activities can be exciting, and especially so if you get a bite, or find a real bargain. If you get enough of a handle on something significant, it is fun, like working a "fish" with whatever tackle you have and "reeling" it in. Of course, you may not find something where you started looking, but wind up somewhere else with something quite different. You may or may not bring anything home. You may or may not have a story worth telling about your efforts. Unless you bring something home, at least a good story, the trip isn't usually considered a success.

The parallel to emergent studies isn't exact, but you can see many elements of similarity. For example, when you start out, you can't always be sure you'll be able to do the study you intended. You may find something else much more interesting and significant. If you aren't successful in completing the study you set out to do or finding something else, there isn't much to write about that makes a dissertation. Not everyone enjoys taking risks; emergent studies are not for everyone.

How Can an Emergent Study Be Described Ahead of Time?

It may seem a contradiction in terms to suppose that a study, the focus of which is expected to emerge from data collection, could be the subject of a proposal. Preparing a proposal for qualitative method studies (including participant observation and ethnographic studies) requires more than just describing the method to be used. Yet, for those who want to begin their entry into the study situation with a clean slate, a proposal anticipating what they will be looking for seems to violate a basic premise of the method.

However, to satisfy your chairperson and committee that you have a viable dissertation topic, to show them that you know how to go about it, to satisfy need-to-know gatekeepers who control your entry in their institutions, to have a document that presents your study appropriately in case you seek funding (a good idea! see pp. 265–71), and, sometimes, just to get clear in your own mind what you are about, a proposal is in order.

What is a qualitative researcher to do? As Guba (personal communication) notes: "The apparent looseness and fluidity . . . should not be mistaken for lack of discipline." Yin (1984) makes the same point another way:

> When Christopher Columbus went to Queen Isabella to ask for support for his "exploration" of the New World, he had to have some reasons for asking for three ships (why not one? why not five?), and he had some rationale for going westward (why not north? why not south?). He also had some criteria for recognizing the New World when he actually encountered it. In short, his exploration began with some rationale and direction, even if his initial assumptions might later have been proved wrong. This same degree of rationale and direction should underlie even an exploratory case study. (p. 30)

And Miles and Huberman (1994) note:

> At the proposal stage: many design decisions are being made—some explicitly and precisely, some implicitly, some unknowingly and some by default. . . . [D]esign decisions can . . . be seen as . . . a sort of *anticipatory data reduction* because they constrain later analysis by ruling out certain variables and relationships and attending to others. Design decisions also permit and support later analysis; they prefigure your analytic moves. (p. 16; emphasis in original)

Qualitative proposals can range from the lightly structured proposal that is basically a hunting license, to the structured and detailed proposal that matches a quantitative study in its anticipatory nature. Only if you work in certain qualitative traditions is the amount of structure in the proposal constrained.

Few doctoral dissertation proposals are at the completely unstructured extreme since probably no committee will approve a proposal describing solely method and devoid of a content focus and rationale. But just how much structure they will require depends on a variety of factors: the nature of the committee, the worthiness of the previous qualitative research experience of the student, the trust the committee members have in the student, the persuasiveness of the rationale for the study, and the case that can be made that pilot studies are unnecessary or impossible.

A Checklist for Qualitative Method Study Proposals

Instead of suggesting a format, we specify below a checklist of those points that should be included in any qualitative method proposal.[1] Their ordering provides a logical progression and that is the order in which they frequently appear in qualitative proposals. See Table 7.1.

The paragraph numbers following each of the items in the checklist show where each of these items was covered in the annotated Warters qualitative proposal, chapter 11. Consulting that proposal will help you understand how that proposal covered each topic.

If you examine the order of the paragraph numbers from topic to topic, you will see that:

1. It does not appear that the logical ordering exhibited by the checklist was followed in that proposal. Yet, for the most part, the proposal seems to flow fairly well. The exception is the material at the end that was added without rewriting the earlier material.

2. Evidence bearing on a topic appears to be scattered throughout the proposal, and worked in wherever the writer deemed it was relevant. Often the same paragraph will give evidence on several points.

Both are in large part a function of the fact that topics are foreshadowed so that the reader gets an early perspective on the proposal as a whole and knows what to anticipate. They are then dealt with in detail at a later point where it is appropriate to do so. Examine, however, the ordering of the asterisked paragraphs, which designate the paragraphs devoted to the first major treatment of a topic and its immediate development. You will see that the topics are not as much out of the logical checklist order as they at first appear, although a topic is also often returned to and further detailed in later context where it is relevant. Both the foreshadowing and the further development in another context are good practices!

As demonstrated by the Warters proposal, you may cover the items in the checklist in whatever order and wherever in the proposal that they best fit your study. However, check to ensure that you include each of them somewhere or, if not, there is good reason for the omission. The ordering of the checklist provides some guidance as you gain experience with this format. Table 7.1 shows the seven topics and their subtopics.

Let us discuss each of the sections one might find in a qualitative proposal: (1) focus or question and rationale, (2) sample of persons and sites, (3) the qual-

---

1. A revision of Nick Smith's adaptation of material from Egon Guba (personal communication).

TABLE 7.1

A Checklist of Topics and Subtopics That Should Be Included in a Qualitative Method Proposal Together With Where Examples of the Items May Be Found in the Warters' Proposal, Chapter 11. Asterisks Indicate the First Major Treatment of a Topic.

Topics	Subtopics	Paragraph numbers of where they appear in the Warters' proposal (Chapter 11)
1) An initial focus or question that provides boundaries for your inquiry and a rationale for doing the study which includes:		
	—its potential significance	2–5*, 33, 50–52
	—its base in theory, and previous literature, if any	6, 7–10*, 14, 23, 26–28
	—why a qualitative approach seems most appropriate	
	—appropriate kinds of persons, sites, situations, etc	5*, 13*
	—sensitizing concepts that orient your study at the outset (what kinds of things you will pay special attention to—you can't take in everything	14*
2) Who will be studied and what they represent and what contexts will be studied and what they represent		17, 20–21*, 36–38, 42–43, 48, 13*, 20
3) The approach used such as symbolic interactionism, ethnography, etc.		12*, 29–30, 46
4) Your qualifications and experience with this approach		24, 29, 31–32*, 35, 37–38, 40–42
5) The methods of data collection		11*, 13–17*, 25, 37–38, 45–48
	—anticipated entry problems, if any	
	—instrumentation, if any	15–16*, 17, 22, 36
6) The methods of data analysis		18–19*
	—at minimum, a rough time schedule for data collection and analysis	
	—anticipated research quality concerns and how they will be handled	13, 18–19, 24-25*, 32
7) Anticipated ethical problems and how they will be handled		13, 34, 45, 47*, 49*, 52*

itative orientation used, (4) your qualifications for using it, (5) the methods of data gathering, (6) methods of data analysis, including time schedule and means for ensuring research quality, and (7) ethical problems.

The Focus or Question and Its Rationale

Whether loosely or tightly structured, all studies will require a rationale for what is to be done. It will describe the focus or central question and the rationale for choosing it. Most researchers will base that rationale on previous theory or literature in the area, some on their own experiences. Typically, this section will also foreshadow what actions will be taken to gather data, analyze it, and draw conclusions.

Basically, this section is the pitch that Columbus gave Queen Isabella for sponsoring his trip to the New World. Here, you are convincing your chairperson and committee that your dissertation topic is worth looking into.

> I want to study these families on welfare to get an idea of how they view receiving money from others. Is it a game? Have they learned to "work the system"? Do they feel it is owed them? Unless we learn how they view it, we won't know how to help them get off welfare.

The rationale not only establishes what is of interest, but it begins to set the boundaries of the study. This is very important, especially when you are just beginning to do research. All researchers have the problem of balancing breadth and depth. You can use your resources (time, energy, etc.) to explore broadly, but then can do so only thinly. Is that better than more limited exploration in some depth? It is a trade-off, but a decision that must be faced at some point, usually the earlier the better for the beginning researcher.

The rationale is often tied to a theoretical position. Basing your understanding on a theoretical position tests the limits of the position's application, gives greater depth of understanding to its usefulness, and provides a framework into which the data can be organized, thus simplifying analysis.

> From a Marxian viewpoint, one might look at how well the understandings of the welfare families can be explained in terms of power and control. From a psychological standpoint, one may see how well Maslow's hierarchical set of needs explains the differential responses of families, and/or members of families, to welfare.

Undeniably, especially for the beginner, using such a framework makes both proposal development and data collection and analysis simpler.

But at the same time, one of the real strengths of qualitative research is that it is inductive in its exploratory logic and so is a source of new grounded theory—theory grounded in the data. By using the lens of a previous theory to bound the gathering of data and provide a framework for analyzing it, except as the data do not fit and you must modify or invent new conceptualizations, you considerably reduce the likelihood that new theory will be an outcome. Like the breadth and depth problem, it is a trade-off, one that should be faced and discussed in the proposal.

Review of Related Research

As noted briefly in chapter 3, the review of related research may be a part of the proposal or may be delayed until you have a much better idea of what will be significant. You may wait until you have formulated your own ideas and are now ready to consider what others have found and how others may have conceptualized it. Researchers quite justifiably differ in their view of whether delay is the best practice. There is no question but that one enters a situation afresh only once. If that is critical to your study, then the review of literature is best delayed. But make this point of view and your rationale for it explicit in the proposal.

But if your study is one of further developing a theoretical point of view, testing its applicability, or a similarly structured inquiry, then include a review of previous research in the proposal. Indicate how you enter the problem with a "well-prepared mind." It has been demonstrated that discovery favors a prepared mind, one that brings useful background to the situation. Indicate that you have such background by suggesting the applicable theories, analogous situations, points of view, and hypotheses in the proposal. This will not only better prepare you for entrance into the field, but as Wax and Wax (1979) note, prior preparation

> is a mark of respect to the hosts, as it demonstrates that one considers their affairs of sufficient importance to learn whatever one can about them before formal introduction. Preparation is also a mark of respect to the scholars who have studied the community in the past. True, when one enters the field, one may be hampered by inaccurate ideas gained from prior studies, [but] the researcher will always be entering with some freight of expectations. It is better that these be grounded in past scholarship, rather than in what passes for conventional information. (p. 6)

Unless it is inappropriate for your project, such prior preparation is only fair to your informants since you thereby do not waste their time and energy helping you rediscover what could have been easily learned beforehand.

Sample of Persons, Sites, and Situations

If yours is a case study of a few individuals, determining the boundaries of your study in terms of the persons, sites, and situations may be very easy. But use of appropriate sampling methods is key to many studies, and, depending on the purpose, a variety of forms of sampling are used in qualitative research. Further, since qualitative study samples are typically small, where representation of a unit is important, choice of persons and/or sites within that unit can be critical. *The key to qualitative sampling is choosing those cases from which one can learn the most!*[2] Miles and Huberman (1994) have an excellent list of sampling methods that includes:

- *theory-based sampling:* the theory determines who is included (e.g., a study of innovation and adoption: early adopters, influentials, followers, late deciders),
- *snowball or chain-referral sampling:* one determines the members of a group by asking each informant to name others in a particular group who in turn are asked that question (e.g., Who are the influentials in the state legislature?),
- *maximum variation:* persons are chosen for study across the spectrum of variation from one extreme to the other, and
- *extreme or deviant cases:* cases illustrative of some characteristic or set of them that helps us to see and understand the characteristic(s) in cases where they are less obvious.

Such sampling methods are commonly described in the proposal. They set the stage for entering a situation and determining what is of major significance. Once in the field, of course, an iterative process takes over as you choose new cases to test developing generalizations; to find contradictory cases, if any; to extend generality of conclusions by testing them in new settings; and the like. While you should typically describe this process in the proposal, it is difficult to anticipate its exact nature in advance. But a good basis for this section is what took place in a pilot study; it probably foreshadows what is to come.

If your study is intentionally designed to generalize to individuals like those studied (and not all studies are), then some discussion of the basis for that generality should be part of the description.

Qualitative Orientation

There are many points of view with respect to understanding people's behavior and to gathering and interpreting qualitative data. They go by many names such as ethnology, ethnography, symbolic interactionism (the one used by Warters), phenomenology, and literary criticism. To some persons, such orientations are extremely important since they determine how one views others, what the research process may be expected to produce, and how data should be

---

2. You might tend to think that those are the ones central to the study's focus. And certainly that is true for the bulk of the studies, but don't forget to sample the periphery. You can lose perspective if you sample too narrowly. Further, just as a different culture makes us newly aware of things in our own, so sampling the periphery, and/or contrasting persons or situations, even if seems like an empty exercise, sometimes pays off handsomely in insights that would have otherwise been missed.

gathered and interpreted. Others use qualitative data-gathering techniques such as interviews, open-ended questionnaires, and observation without consciously subscribing to any particular orientation.

In most institutions you are free to choose your orientation. However, because your chairperson and/or members of your committee may value particular ones over, or to the exclusion of, others, be sure to ascertain each one's willingness to support your orientation. Determine it before you extend an invitation to join your committee, and do not invite, or, if necessary, disinvite members who cannot be supportive. Otherwise, you tempt fate when you submit material for their approval.

How important is it that you declare your orientation in your proposal? For one thing, it ensures that your committee members are all committed to, or at least tolerant of, yours. From the outset, it gets any differences and difficulties out in the open. In addition, in selecting certain orientations, you consequently set boundaries around how the dissertation should be viewed and what they can expect you to do or not do.

Words can be slippery, and names like *ethnography* may mean something to you but something different for someone else. Therefore, both stating your orientation as a theoretical position and explaining what it will mean operationally for you as you conduct the study ensure that there is little room for misunderstanding and that you and your committee have common expectations about how the project will develop.

Researcher's Qualifications

Whether or not you lay out an orientation as just described, you need to assure your chairperson and committee that you have the competencies to carry the study to a satisfactory conclusion—or if you don't now, that you will attain them. Cite your relevant course work, prior research experience, if any, and any prior work you have done on this project to determine the problems and pitfalls you are likely to encounter. Warters's proposal is a particularly good example of assurances provided to a committee in terms of both prior work in the area (see paragraphs 31–32) and his pilot work (see paragraphs 25, 37–38, 45–48). Pilot studies are an especially good way of assuring your chairperson and committee that they are not letting you take on a project beyond your capabilities.

Pilot Studies

While it is possible to discuss the rationale and related literature sections of the proposal without having considered the role of pilot studies, the remaining sections of the proposal really almost require one for accurate formulation. Pilot studies help define the dimensions of the problem, the sample of persons and sites to be used, any instruments other than the observer(s), the behaviors to be targeted, the protections against reasonable alternative explanations, and the likely ethical problems to be encountered. Once one or more pilot studies are done, writing the proposal is markedly simplified.

Pilot studies often show that your preconception of a situation differs from what you find in the field.

> Bogdan (1971), for instance, began studying unemployment training programs as examples of adult socialization into the world of work. He found, however, that the program's difficulty in filling the classes was so great that the study became one of how people maintain programs that don't do the task they were created to do. Pilot studies would probably have uncovered this reconceptualization of topic before a proposal was submitted.

Pilot studies are especially useful for beginning researchers since they help them evaluate whether they are suited to doing a qualitative dissertation. Many students back into qualitative methods because the verbal aspects of qualitative methods are familiar, whereas they fear statistics. But not everyone is able both to empathize with their informants so as to understand what is behind the words they are hearing and at the same time to maintain enough distance that they can objectively observe, record, and interpret these events. Not everyone is able to bring order out of the mass of data that accumulates. And it takes analytic ability to sense the generalizations that are woven through those data. The pilot study helps you determine your readiness.

Since nearly every study benefits from doing pilot work, unless there is some reason not to enter the situation you plan to use until your study is fully cleared, do a pilot. If there is some reason not to, make that case in your proposal. Discuss your pilot with your chairperson and committee and keep at least your chairperson informed as it proceeds. You'll probably want to consult her as you go along anyway. Then, with the knowledge gained from your pilot study, prepare your proposal. You'll then be able to show it is solidly grounded and that you are competent in both content and method.

Data Collection

Describe the steps you will take to gather data in as much detail as you can anticipate at the outset of the study. Take a look at how nicely Warters does this, beginning with an overall description in paragraph 11 and then amplifying this with detail on the interviewing in 13 and 14, on the questionnaire in 15 and 16, and on the process of sampling in 17. Although some details may change, as a result of his prior experiences, he already has in mind much of what he will do—the value of pilot work.

Describe anticipated problems of data collection that may be in the minds of readers and how you will handle them. Entry problems and instrumentation are common areas of concern, and data quality is another. The latter is discussed in the next section, although protection against alternative explanations, an important part of it, is often included in this one.

Time schedules and work plans have already been discussed in chapter 6. Give at least rough estimates of data-collection completion dates. This sets goals for yourself that are important if you are to complete your work in a timely manner. Such goals also let you know when you are behind schedule, so you can make adjustments as appropriate. This is a deficiency in the Warters proposal.

Entry Problems

Entry to allow data collection needs to be described for nearly all field studies. It may have been accomplished if you have already negotiated entry with a pilot study or have entry by reason of your relation to the phenomena (e.g., you are a member of the group you are studying). However, nearly all institutions have protective measures against researchers collecting data within them without their permission. This usually means getting permission of some kind. Warters discusses entry problems in paragraph 20.

The proposal itself is a useful vehicle for negotiating administrative entry since it indicates in writing, and with more precision and detail than would typically be conveyed in a conversation, just what is involved. Use the proposal in preliminary form for that purpose. Assuming you want those studied to feel they are partners contributing to research (if it can be done, a good idea for most research, not just qualitative), discuss the study with them and make changes to accommodate their concerns. Then, when consent is gained, obtain a letter granting access to append to your proposal. Describe your entry process in the proposal, indicating what accommodations you made. The letter provides tangible evidence that entry has been negotiated and will help you when you request approval from your institution's Committee on the Protection of Human Subjects.

But as experienced researchers know, administrative approval is only the first step in entry; it must be negotiated at each level and with each new unit that is approached. It is well to indicate your awareness of this in your proposal. Having done a pilot study, describe what problems or lack of them you encountered and what you expect to find as you proceed past the administrative approval level.

Instrumentation

The use of instruments presupposes that, in choosing an instrument to measure a particular construct, you already know what constructs will be important. Few would argue that is appropriate for emergent studies. But researchers often use qualitative data analysis methods on verbal material gathered from open-ended questions. If such an instrument is to be constructed, indicate its nature with sample questions so your chairperson and committee have a more concrete idea of what you plan to do. Also indicate how you will pre-test it to ensure it is gathering the data desired. If already developed, place a copy in the appendix. Warters describes interview development in paragraphs 15–16.

Data Analysis

Describe the steps you plan to take to analyze your data. In some instances, you will follow a pattern ascribed to a particular qualitative approach or to leaders in the field. Warters, for instance, does this in his paragraph 18, indicating he is following Glaser and Strauss. But since even citing a particular orientation or reference usually allows for considerable latitude, he goes on to describe the steps that will be taken in the rest of paragraph 18 and into 19. This is typical of the kind of description to include.

As with data collection, setting at least a rough time schedule for data analysis has advantages in notifying you of a problem when you overrun an end date.

Because of the intense labor incurred, qualitative data analysis is increasingly being done using computer programs such as ATLASti (http://www.atlasti.de [accessed October 1, 2004]), N6 and NVivo (formerly NUD*IST) (http://www.qsr.com.au/products/productoverview/product_overview.htm [accessed October 1, 2004)]; for a comparison of N6 and NVivo, see http://www.qsr.com.au/products/productoverview/comparison.htm (accessed October 1, 2004) and winMAX (http://www.maxqda.de/maxqda-eng/start.htm [accessed October 1, 2004]). All the programs have downloadable demonstration software so you may try them out to see which one best fits what you are trying to accomplish. Once the data have been loaded into such programs, which in itself can be a laborious job, they make it so much easier to put similar data together, code them, manipulate the codes, recode, lay out diagrams of coding relationships, and the like. If your data mass is large, they are worth looking into, although they do require learning a new software program, hence a time investment. If your chairperson and committee are familiar with the program you decide to use, you may be able to shorten this section since you can assume some prior knowledge. But unless your committee is actively working with the program, don't assume they are up on the current version. Available programs, as well as new ones, are rapidly evolving as a search of "qualitative data analysis" by any Web browser will show. There are a number of helpful Web sites for qualitative research, a large number of which are listed at http://V.webring.com/hub?ring=qualres (accessed October 1, 2004).

Ensuring Research Quality

At least two kinds of research quality concerns need to be given consideration:

- that your readers may consider your observations, interviews, analysis of documents, or whatever to be less than "objective,"
- there are equally or more plausible alternative explanations than that which you advance.

In addition, you should provide an audit trail for those who have quality concerns about the study. Let us take these separately.

"Objectivity" Problems. The word *objectivity* is in quotation marks in the heading since it is a word with many different interpretations. Some argue that objectivity is a myth; there is no such thing—because of the freight of previous experience, everyone understands the same situation differently. Two persons looking at the same scene can have different interpretations of it, with both interpretations valid.

Whether the general research consumer would accept or reject that point of view, most of them would still expect researchers to be "objective" in one sense. Namely, if a second person, with the same focus of interest as you, were to observe the same phenomenon, that she would develop essentially the same record of what occurred, even though she might differ in her interpretation of it. In constructing an "objective" record, you try to prevent predilections, biases, attitudes, likes, and dislikes from affecting it. If they are likely to, you warn the reader of this fact. Miles and Huberman (1994) refer to it as "neutrality and reasonable freedom from unacknowledged researcher biases—at the minimum, explicitness about the inevitable biases that exist" (p. 278).

How do you handle such concerns in the proposal? If you are studying a phenomenon that has personal and/or emotional meaning for you, be up front with your chairperson and committee about this fact. Describe the possible conflict and indicate why you think you can adopt the role of a researcher and what you will do to ensure that role is maintained throughout the course of the study.

Studying one's own community, church, home, workplace, or the like is fraught with problems, but competent studies have been done under these circumstances. There may be ethical problems. And often there is a cost, especially if data gathering is done covertly and becomes known. Therefore, you and your chairperson and committee need to carefully consider the implications— another of the many instances where the proposal is the basis for shared decision making.

If you are using some of the more structured forms of instrumentation and have multiple observers or testers, be sure to indicate what training and/or other checks will be provided to ensure that the instruments are being used in the same way. Before using them in the field, for instance, you might indicate the provision for training until reliability checks reach a satisfactory level. Further, you might describe instituting such checks at random after field entry, or schedule two observers for the same situation and compare their records.

Eliminating Alternative Explanations. *If you are doing more than describing—for instance, trying to show how particular phenomena came about—you want the explanation you are advancing to be more plausible than any reasonable alternative explanations. Some alternative explanations, which both qualitative and quantitative researchers should be concerned about, were described in chapter 5, pp. 84–86—reactivity, researcher expectancy, selection, mortality, and instrument decay. If any of these is likely to be involved in your study, indicate how you will ensure that the case for the alternative is weaker than the explanation you advance. For example:*

- *Reactivity:* The individuals observed react differently during observation. Show how during the pilot study, they became accustomed to your presence and show what steps you will take to ensure that accommodation has occurred when the dissertation data are gathered.
- *Selection:* The findings depend on the particular persons or situations selected for study—the personality of certain individuals, the interaction of particular persons in a crew, the milieu created by the group, and the like. One alternative is to accept that the generality may be limited, and give a best guess of how limited, and where might comparable circumstances appear.

  A second alternative is to show generality by gathering data in a contrasting situation where the particular circumstances don't exist, yet one expects the phenomena to appear. Because the latter extends the scope of the study, it is a matter to be discussed with your chairperson and committee. Such problems are best caught in the pilot stage so that the data for the dissertation may be gathered in a contrasting situation.
- *Mortality:* The relationship appeared because certain persons dropped out of the study situation. Determine whether survivors are distinguished from nonsurvivors by reasons associated in some way with your explanation. If they are, like selection, this affects generality.

As can be seen from the examples, a pilot study can be very important in deciding what additional data to gather in order to defend against certain alternative explanations. There are many alternative explanations in addition to the ones discussed (see, for example, Krathwohl, 1998/2004, pp. 258, 317–320.)

Providing an Audit Trail. For your study's findings to become accepted into the realm of knowledge, ever widening circles of interested persons, each farther removed from the data, must accept your findings. This process begins with you in that you must be confident that you have honestly interpreted the data rather than forcing it in directions you would like it to lead. If you try out your interpretation of the data with your friends, they are the next circle. Your chairperson and committee are the next circle farther out to accept your dissertation findings, outside readers the next, and so on. Acceptance is facilitated if you help those in each of these circles to follow the path that led you to your conclusions. Such a path will also help researchers (possibly fellow doctoral students) who would like to either build on your findings or try to replicate them.

Miles and Huberman (1994) call such a path an "audit trail." It requires making the record of your methods and procedures detailed enough that another researcher could follow it (see their discussion, pp. 280 ff.). They note that many software programs automatically keep a record of decisions so the path is easy to reconstruct. While audit trails were rare in past research, they are increasing in frequency and seem highly desirable. If you plan to provide such a trail, mention that fact in your proposal and then make it part of your dissertation.

Ensuring Ethical Procedure

You will need to clear the ethical aspects of your study with the Committee on the Protection of Human Subjects at your institution. Note the detail with which Warters, paragraphs 45–47, 49, and 52, provides assurances of protection to his participants. But, fully aside from that, you will need to deal with the ethical problems that occur in the field. Such problems are quite likely when working with outlier populations or situations. At a minimum, a snap decision can spell success or failure of that data-gathering instance. Sometimes, the site as a whole becomes unusable. True, many of these situations cannot be anticipated, but many can.

> For instance, when one is observing a classroom, one can almost always expect the teacher to be curious about what you found; she expects some feedback. Since such feedback may compromise future observations, one needs to anticipate how this situation will be handled.

Foreseeing such situations, describe them in your proposal and try out your proposed solutions with your chairperson and committee. This is another example where shared decision making may enable you to strengthen your proposed response. Your chairperson and committee may suggest better alternatives or give a different evaluation of its effect. Again, a pilot study is good protection; the ethical problems you are likely to encounter are often suggested by events during the pilot stage even if they don't appear full-blown.

Finally, once you have produced a draft of your qualitative proposal, review Worksheet 7.1: Review of Proposals Using Emergent Qualitative Approaches to make sure you have paid sufficient attention to the special concerns of this type of proposal.

Review of Proposals Using Emergent Qualitative Approaches

How Well Does My Proposal Reflect the Special Concerns of This Particular Dissertation Approach?

How Well Have I Provided Strong, Detailed Descriptions of . . . ?	Strong	Acceptable	Weak– Improvements Needed	Not Applicable
Study focus or questions, boundary conditions, and study rationale?				
People, contexts, or sites to be studied?				
Qualitative orientation to be used in this study?				
My personal qualifications and experience with this research approach?				
Methods of data collection?				
Methods of data analysis, including quality control procedures?				
Ethical concerns and accommodations?				
Study timeline, resources, and management issues?				

SECTION 2: PHILOSOPHICAL AND HISTORICAL STUDY PROPOSALS

Philosophical and historical dissertations vary greatly in the extent to which they are structured in advance in contrast to being emergent. However, emergent philosophical dissertations tend to be rare in the social and behavioral sciences, historical ones less so, but they are still uncommon. The causes may be partly the unique kind of mind required to handle such material combined with a paucity of interested faculty. Add to this the risk of unsuccessful completion, and there needs to be a greater commitment to the problem by the student than is perhaps required by other kinds of dissertations.

The Nature of the Proposal

Emergent philosophical and historical dissertations are both similar to and different from qualitative ones. Like qualitative ones, they are emergent in the sense that you don't know for sure what you have until the study is finished. But unlike qualitative studies, in which a pilot trial is important to find the study's focus, philosophical and historical studies usually have some other prior basis for proceeding.

In the case of philosophical studies, usually you are expanding on previous ideas, trying them in a new context, or further developing them. In the case of historical studies, you are usually either pursuing the leads of a previous study, have found something not previously noticed that forms the basis for the study, or are transferring an approach pursued elsewhere to a new setting or time period. In all these instances, prior research forms the equivalent of a pilot study and provides the basis for a proposal that will guide the initial stages of the investigation. So most philosophical and historical studies have a basis at the outset for writing the proposal, which then provides the "contract" advantage of the proposal previously noted.

As noted earlier, the proposal will describe the germ of an undeveloped idea, and, except as it can be bolstered by what research has gone on before, may be fairly sparse in details. The checklist items for qualitative studies should be covered in philosophical and historical ones as well, but some topics require a bit of adaptation, and some additional topics should be added:

- the basis for the study, its conceptual roots,
- whatever conceptualization you contribute to the study,
- the assumptions on which the study proceeds,
- by what hallmarks of excellence the study should be judged if the criteria differ in some way from standard ones, and
- how you and your chairperson and committee will know when you are done with the study.

Let us examine these in more detail.

The Conceptual Roots of the Study

Since, as noted earlier, prior research forms the roots of the study for most emergent philosophical or historical proposals, especially competently describe those roots. Whereas the whole proposal is used to judge *general* scholarly competence, the analytic skills your chairperson and committee are evaluating in this section are the *ones that will be employed in the dissertation itself.* Demonstrate the kind of writing, logic, and analysis that the chairperson and committee can expect to see in the dissertation. Clarity of presentation is so essential that if those skills do not measure up, the committee may be hesitant about letting you proceed. So draft this section to your highest standards.

For historical studies, equally important is the availability and accessibility of the documents and/or artifacts that are critical to the success of the study. Suggest the basis for your confidence that the study is likely to be successful.

> For example, consider a study of the manuscripts of the Roman Curia to determine what mnemonic techniques helped monks remember manuscripts before the dawn of printing. Such a study may well have considerable present-day significance, if there is any reason to believe that those techniques were set down in useful form and are both retrievable and accessible. Give your reviewers what facts there are that lead you to be hopeful about the project.

Your Conceptual Contribution

This is your study, and in some way, you hope to make a unique contribution through it. Make the proposal show clearly what that contribution is. In conveying the conceptual roots of your study, it is easy to lose the thread of how your thinking has advanced the frontier. Perhaps it got buried in the presentation. How are you extending someone else's idea? For example, Fournier (1993) chose to extend Scriven's product evaluation logic to program evaluation. What original twist are you giving to the replication of someone's framework or process in developing a theory or in studying a new time or place? What ideas are you challenging? For example, Mauhs-Pugh (1992) in a historical study challenged the idea that school consolidation led to higher quality education. Your readers will be looking for your contribution, since it is the heart of a philosophical or historical dissertation.

If you don't make your contribution clear, your chairperson and/or committee, in their efforts to strengthen your dissertation, are likely to impose their ideas or framework on your problem. This is alright if you are comfortable with that—if you aren't like the adolescent who wants to exert his independence from past authority and will come to resent working on a problem he doesn't perceive as his own. The faculty mean well and are only trying to help you, but in doing so, they may change your problem to one you find difficult to live with. Preempt that possibility by stating your framework or contribution.

The Assumptions on Which Your Study Proceeds

Assumptions underlie all studies; why is it more important to make them explicit in a philosophical or historical dissertation than any other? Because there is always the possibility that your chairperson or a committee member may disagree with one or more of the assumptions of your study. In dissertations where the criteria of what constitutes an acceptable dissertation are clear, the direction for a solution or compromise can usually be found without undermining the whole dissertation. As noted below, that may be less true, however, of a philosophical or historical dissertation where the criteria are considerably more a matter for individual judgment and, except for errors in logic, less clearly agreed upon.

In those instances, disagreements about assumptions can have a fundamental effect on the acceptability of your dissertation. Better to uncover such problems at the outset than when the dissertation is further along. If you, your chairperson, and committee deal with them early, it is more likely that a satisfactory compromise can be found before you have invested much time and energy in the study and positions are more firmly entrenched.

The Criteria by Which Your Study Is to Be Judged

If yours is one of those dissertations where the criteria for judgment are not as standard as with many research methodologies, it follows that your proposal should do something about that problem. Quality is in the eye of the beholder; what one faculty member may consider a significant contribution, another may consider trivial. And it is here that the criteria for judging the study and the determination of when the study is considered complete become inextricably intertwined.

What makes it even more difficult is that there are usually so many configurations, each of which at least one committee member might endorse. You may think your research is finished, but your chairperson or a committee member may argue completion requires showing its applicability in other situations, fleshing out the steps in the logic more clearly and in greater detail, adding more examples, testing your point of view against another position, carrying it a bit further to greater generality, etc.

How Much Is Enough? As noted earlier, a dissertation is what your chairperson and committee decide it is! So that is a decision for them to make, and, if your institution requires outside readers or examiners at your oral examination, they may add their advice. What, if anything, can you do about this situation?

It isn't usually possible to specify the criteria and end point of the dissertation as definitively with a philosophical or historical dissertation as it is with other research studies. But you can set forth as clearly as possible your conception of what will be a complete dissertation. Attempting such statements avoids a problem later. First of all, it helps you and everyone else recognize when you are there. They may still not judge that to be enough, but at least it sets any additional requests in the context of having reached an end point that was initially agreed upon. That should moderate any supplementary requirements. Here are some examples from actual proposals of efforts to specify the scope of the study.

From a philosophical study:

> [I]n considering an aesthetic approach to evaluation, . . .I will analyze what it is that constitutes a *good* aesthetic argument . . . as discussed in the literature in aesthetics. . . . [O]ther types [of evaluation] to possibly examine are those which are primarily economic, political, causal arguments. This will result in the explication of the rules and standards that govern the justification of evaluative claims, or more specifically the clarification of the multiple *working logics*. . . . Once these logics are defined, the study will compare and contrast the various evaluation areas. Similarities will be extracted as a means of synthesizing an overall general logic of evaluation. (Fournier, 1993, p. 12)

Fournier provides fairly good specification of the idea by describing the steps in the process to be followed. This is comparable to describing the operational steps in an empirical study, and often works for philosophical studies. Note, however, that she left open the specification of the kinds of evaluation that were to be covered, something that would need to be resolved and could become a source of differences between herself and the committee—indeed, it did, though it was resolved after considerable discussion.

From a historical study:

> Although I have spoken about school consolidation thus far in generic terms, my research actually will be limited to a particular state: New York. And within New York, I will focus on a case study of two rural school districts. (Mauhs-Pugh, 1992, p. 5)

Could one generalize from two case studies about the value of school consolidation? Even though you and I might not agree, how much to require of a graduate student is for the chairperson and committee to decide; this committee said, "two cases are enough."

It is often easier to be specific about historical than philosophical studies since, as above, one can cite the operational instances that will be explored. But not always; consider this historical study of the presidency:

> By virtue of their high office and their access to the public through speeches, deeds, writings and images that are amplified by vigilant media attention, forty-two white men of Western heritage have presided from a "bully pulpit" with immense potential for educating the American public. (Cantor, 1994, p. 1)

> The researcher will make use of a wide range of presidential biographies and works of scholarship on the presidency to uncover evidence of presidential teaching, with an em-

phasis on "modern " presidents who have served since the First World War. Although this method introduces the biased influences of biographers and scholars, it has the distinct advantage over methods based, for example, on direct analyses of presidents' speeches. . . . This study will be concerned as much with the ways we choose to remember, or not remember, the past as it is concerned with the past itself; the words of professional rememberers—the biographers and scholars—are key. Collectively, their experienced insights and painstakingly-detailed toils far surpass any crude attempts this research might make. (Cantor, pp. 3–4)

The disclaiming modesty of the last sentence is a clever way of exempting himself from examining all the speeches and other documents. But this still leaves open all the biographies of presidents. Even with an emphasis on "modern" presidents from 1918 on, how are he and his advisors to know whether he has omitted a key biography? At the oral examination an outside reader may ask, "Why was so and so omitted?" Further fencing in the relevant territory would be wise, perhaps by including all autobiographies and one biography on each president. The latter could be chosen by asking one or more experts on the presidency to recommend the biography most likely to include aspects relevant to the topic.

It isn't always possible to make such concrete statements at the outset of the dissertation process. Coming as close as one can provides some measure of security as to what is a viable dissertation.

In Any Kind of Study, How Much Is Enough?

It is perhaps worth noting that, although described in the context of philosophical and historical dissertations, including the criteria by which the dissertation is to be judged may be useful in other contexts as well. Indeed, *it is worth considering whenever students have any reason to be concerned that their conception of "how much is enough" may not be congruent with the faculty's.* This can especially be a problem for historical and philosophical studies; there is always one more angle to explore, another point of view to take into account, a potential treasure trove of information not tapped.

When does one say "enough!"? If there is likely to be any doubt as to the answer, this is a topic to discuss with your chair and committee BEFORE the question must be faced. It may be difficult to set firm boundaries, particularly in an emergent study. But starting everyone thinking about the issue early means that termination criteria likely become included in the decisions as one makes important design or directional changes to accommodate emerging findings.

Finally, as with emergent qualitative studies, proposals for philosophical and historical dissertations include special considerations. Review Worksheet 7.2: Review of Proposals Using Philosophical and Historical Approaches to ensure you have well attended to these aspects.

Review of Proposals Using Philosophical and Historical Approaches

How Well Does My Proposal Reflect the Special Concerns of This Particular Dissertation Approach?

How Well Have I Provided Strong, Detailed Descriptions of . . . ?	Strong	Acceptable	Weak–Improvements Needed	Not Applicable
Study focus or questions, boundary conditions, and study rationales?				
Conceptual roots of the study, including the assumptions from which it proceeds?				
The conceptual framework to be used in the study?				
My personal qualifications and experience using this conceptual framework?				
The people, events, situations, and concepts to be studied?				
Methods of data collection?				
Methods of data analysis including quality control procedures?				
Ethical concerns and accommodations?				
Study timeline, resources, and management issues?				
Criteria for judging study completion and quality?				

CHAPTER 8

The Special Requirements of Proposals Using Quantitative Approaches

Experiment, Causal Modeling, Meta-Analysis

CHAPTER CONTENTS

This chapter discusses three kinds of studies, all of which use quantitative approaches in quite different contexts: Section 1: Experiments, Section 2: Causal Modeling, and Section 3: Meta-Analysis. While experimentation clearly builds on the generic proposal structure described in chapters 4–6, to some extent causal modeling and even more so meta-analysis call for its modification with special attention to certain parts. If you have not yet read the annotated Beissner or Phelan proposals (chapters 12 and 13), do so either now or as you study this chapter, which uses them as examples.

SECTION 1: EXPERIMENTS

The rationale, hypotheses, design, and analysis of data are four major aspects that need extra attention in a proposal to do an experiment. You'll be helped if you also do a careful time schedule as discussed in chapter 6.

Rationale

The rationale for the study is important, since the value of an experimental study lies in its contribution to knowledge (or in showing that what has been accepted as knowledge was wrong, thus warning others about it). Your rationale will explain how the study relates to previous findings and what is to be added to them. Place the rationale in the problem statement, in the review of related research, or even in the objectives section, but be sure it is there.

Beissner's proposal does a nice job of explaining the rationale up front. Her first paragraph summarizes it very briefly. Then, in spiral fashion, giving greater detail each time around, she starts with medical problem solving in general (paragraphs 2–5), then focuses on the clinical reasoning process (paragraph 6), and then gets down to the rationale (paragraph 7) for the specific intervention she plans to use (paragraph 8).

Studies that have no rationales seem to be plans to try something to see what would happen. They are less likely to gain approval than studies that build on what is known. But consider for a moment. Your study isn't a random collection of activities. You intentionally decided to look in certain places and not others and chose to perform certain actions; give your rationale for these choices.

Hypotheses

Experimental studies are nearly always intended to demonstrate a relationship or the effectiveness of a treatment or to confirm a prediction. In all of these, since the study builds on what is known (or challenges it), the outcome can be anticipated. As suggested in chapter 4, translate those expectations into directional hypotheses, hypotheses that predict what will occur—the most specific hypotheses that are reasonable, based on what is previously known. If you can, not only state that something will become larger than something else, but better still, state how much larger, how it relates to the strength and/or timing of treatment, how the change behaves over time in terms of increasing, decreasing, or staying the same, and so on. Then show through your study that what you have predicted is true. If your hypotheses are stronger predictions than those that have gone before and are supported by the data, you have contributed new knowledge about the phenomenon.

> Beissner first describes her independent and dependent variables (paragraphs 9–14). Having established what these are, she then states her objectives in directional form in paragraph 15. They are stated in both verbal form and then in symbolic form.

Design or Procedure

In experimentation, the design or procedure covers all six of the rings joining the procedure to the data level in the chain of reasoning. The proposal must discuss each of them.

Participants—Population or Sample

Nearly all experimental studies are concerned with showing an effect that has generality beyond the study's sample. While some results may be specific to a particular kind of individual or situation, most are concerned with generalities that apply to anyone—that is, at least anyone in the same culture. (We don't really know how many of our social science generalizations are culture bound; that kind of research has been done in very few areas and needs to be done more often.)

Where the results of a study ought to apply to anyone, anyone can be the subject of the study. But only as we can show that no matter which sample we draw the proposition holds is it eventually accepted as having universality. Even then, there is always the concern that there might be a new sample in which it does not hold. Ideally, each test of the proposition would be on a sample that was representative of the population to which we wish to generalize— for example, a random sample of U.S. citizens or of humanity. Obviously, that is impractical. But is such a sample necessary? Only if there is some reason to believe that the sample used is atypical in some way that would affect the results.

Because college students are conveniently available and, in many characteristics, like the general public, they are often used. And to the extent the characteristics in which they resemble the public are the subject of the study, there is no reason not to use them. Yet, beware, this point of view has led to many studies based on samples of Caucasian males—with results being generalized, sometimes wrongly, to any female.

Of course, such convenience samples leave the study open to criticism if anyone thinks that some particular characteristic of the sample did affect the results and can present a plausible argument as to why this should be so. Without a study that controls for that sample characteristic, one can't be sure. The problem with convenience samples is that usually they are assembled for some purpose (e.g., a college freshman class in art appreciation), and you must rule out the implications of that purpose from your study.

But while the choice of individuals for many studies may be a convenience sample, that does not mean that they may equally comfortably be formed into groups for study purposes. Indeed, assignment to treatments within the study should, if possible, be random or involve control of one or more relevant characteristics. Control could be by random assignment after blocking (which is basically stratification) or pairing (the extreme of blocking, where the block is two individuals). Random assignment to groups is the definitive characteristic of those designs designated as "true experimental designs" by Campbell and Stanley (1963) in contrast to those designated as "quasi-experimental designs." But remember, even "true experimental designs" do not control for all alternative plausible explanations, just more of them than quasi-experimental ones.

Where random assignment is impossible, a variety of quasi-experimental designs have been studied that may be substituted. (See Campbell and Stanley, 1963; Cook and Campbell, 1979; or Shadish, Cook, and Campbell, 2002). However, random assignment is possible in many more situations that would have been thought possible, as Boruch and Wothke (1985) have shown (see also a good discussion of this problem in chapter 14 of Shadish, Cook, and Campbell, 2002).

We typically assume that the sample size is simply the number of individuals involved in the study. That is not always the case. A common problem is lack of congruence between the unit of analysis and the sampling procedure. The unit of analysis should be the smallest group that is uniformly exposed to the treatment. If conclusions are to be drawn about teaching methods, assuming the class as a whole will be exposed to the treatment, then the classroom rather than the individual student is the sampling and analysis unit. Even though it is tempting to use students as the unit because this makes the sample size much larger, make the unit of sampling match the unit of analysis.

Where the sample is split into many smaller groups as a result of using a complex design such as factorial, Latin square, or nesting, readers will be interested in the available cases for each of the variables to be analyzed. Include this information in the design description part of the proposal as well as the minimum cell size for a given set of conditions of treatment.

Treatment

Experimental studies involve a treatment that is directly under the control of the experimenter. There are four aspects that should be covered in the treatment section of the proposal:

1. the conceptual definition of the treatment,
2. the translation of the conceptual definition into an operational one that is representative of the conceptual definition,
3. ensuring that the treatment was administered as intended (fidelity of treatment), and
4. ensuring that the characteristics essential to the conceptualization of treatment are the ones, and the only ones, causing the effect.

Except the third one, these apply to any independent variable as well. The fourth is discussed more fully when we take up the ring "Comparison and Contrast—The Basis for Sensing Attributes or Changes." Let us examine the others here.

Conceptual Definitions of Treatments. All treatments need to be placed in some kind of conceptual context, even those that are defined by materials and/or equipment such as, for instance, a rapid presentation of specified reading material to improve reading speed. Even here, it helps to understand that the treatment consists of forcing the student to expand the number of words encompassed in each fixation on a line of print. The point of the conceptual definition of the treatment is to delineate its "active ingredient(s)" in a way that has generality beyond any particular operationalization.

A treatment such as "outlining a theme before writing" needs to be conceptually defined to determine what is meant by "outlining." Is it the written framework of the theme with major and subordinated headings? Is it forethought about the topic even though a written framework is not produced? Is it the determination of a place to start and the end goal, without all the intermediate steps identified? Is it a determination of how a given individual best is able to assemble a theme, regardless of which of the above is determined to be the mode? Which of these are we seeking? What is our ultimate goal, and how are we seeking to attain it? This is the material that makes up the conceptual definition of a treatment.

The conceptual definition can be derived from the theory on which the study is based (e.g., reading speed increases without loss of comprehension as one takes in larger and larger groups of words). In that sense, the research is a test of the theory that readers extract meaning from whole blocks of text at a time, and the larger the block, the faster the reading speed. This may extend the theory in a way that may not have been studied before, allow new operational definitions and implementations, and help one see the implications of the theory in a new way. Such a theory-linked definition provides generality beyond this particular study. Thus, the conceptual definition of the treatment is very important and should be included in the proposal.

It is interesting that both of the sample quantitative proposals, Beissner and Phelan, come up short in describing their treatment. The closest that Beissner comes to a conceptual definition of treatment is in paragraph 7, which talks about the spatial representation of ideas in a general way. Nowhere in Phelan is there a conceptual discussion of treatment, though there is considerable material on self-directed learning in general. Self-directed learning is the topic of the workshop that is his treatment, and a description of the workshop (its operational definition) is in the appendix. But some kind of conceptual definition, and an indication of why self-directed learning is amenable to change with a single workshop, is what the reader expects to find and doesn't.

Translation of the Conceptual Definition into an Operational One that Is Representative of the Conceptual Definition. Sometimes one starts with a concrete definition of treatment and must work backward to the conceptual definition and an understanding of what is taking place. The reading treatment above started with the rapid presentation of specified reading material and worked back to what was happening. But this is rarer than the other way around. One usually starts with a conceptual problem, increasing reading speed, examines the literature for ways of doing this (increasing the eye's grasp at each fixation), and then seeks a way to translate this into a treatment. This latter is the operational definition—the actions, materials, and/or equipment that are the actual representation of the treatment in the study. Further, whatever operational definition is chosen is a sample of the possible ways of operationalizing the conceptual definition of the treatment.

Searching alternative operationalizations sometimes leads to a better one. For instance, instead of simply presenting whole sections of text for shorter periods of time, suppose one started flashing just one word and then increased the words on a line. One would check comprehension after each presentation and not increase the number of words at a given level until comprehension was consistently established. Such a treatment is much more congruent with the conception of the treatment than the initial operationalization.

The list of characteristics that are involved in determining whether a treatment is representative and authentic can be quite large if there is much freedom in administration. Consider this sample of questions that might be applied to treatments as varied as a school curriculum and a counseling intervention:

> How long must it be applied?
> Must all aspects be covered?
> If not, how much can be omitted?
> Can it be spread over a time period, or can it be concentrated?
> What level of absenteeism from sessions will be permitted?
> What is the minimum level of cooperation on the part of the subjects?

Appraise your treatment for comparable questions and preempt concern by providing treatment specifications in the proposal.

Things like training in the treatment's administration can affect representativeness. If such training would be atypical of situations to which the findings are intended to apply, generality is limited. Similarly, the freedom to adapt the treatment may be greater in the situations to which you hope to generalize than in the instance in which you plan to study it. Initially studying the treatment in a highly standardized format may be justified by the need to ensure that the treatment has the intended effect. Since you can't be expected to do everything in one study, be sure to indicate the limited generality and its reasonableness. Generality is greatest when freedom to adapt is comparable in the study to that to which it is intended to generalize.

If different levels of treatment effect will be used, be sure to describe the levels and explain: (1) why these levels were chosen, (2) of what the levels are representative, and (3) how you will ensure that these levels of treatment are obtained (see "Treatment Fidelity," below). For example, in the reading improvement study, how was it decided that text at specified levels of difficulty would be used? Are they representative of the levels usually used in these grades, and how will one determine that the text is at the intended level of difficulty?

In many instances, it may be well to indicate other operationalizations that were possible and suggest why this particular one was chosen. If others are equally suitable, indicate how your choice is representative of those possibilities. In choosing a particular operationalization (e.g., presenting phrases to be read via a computer), one may be limiting generality. Mention this while noting the boundaries of what is practical in a dissertation and show how despite such limitations, the dissertation will make an important contribution.

We are much closer to operational definitions of treatment in the Beissner proposal than to conceptual ones. It is as though giving the details of the experimental design is what is important and the treatment is just a detail in it. Okay, but it is a critical detail. As noted in paragraph 26, the appendix where the description of the workshop appears is not included in Phelan's proposal for reasons of space. But it was longer on operational details than conceptual definition.

Beissner provides some operational details of concept mapping in paragraph 8, but further description of concept mapping is in terms of scoring (paragraphs 14 and 46). The closest she comes to describing the training is in paragraph 46: "The training will follow the suggested outline provided by Novak and Gowin (1984)." But nowhere is that "suggested outline" described, and there is no reason to assume all the members of the committee would be familiar with it. It should have been reproduced in the appendix and/or its essentials described in the proposal. The latter would describe the "active ingredient." Neither Beissner nor Phelan is a good example of what should be covered in a treatment description.

Placebo Treatments. If you have a control group, be sure that it is given a treatment that is in all ways identical to that of the experimental group except for the "active ingredient"—a so-called placebo treatment. Such a treatment controls for reactivity (see pp. 85, 134), as well as for other plausible alternative explanations. Describe how the treatments will be made similar except for the variable of interest. Creating an equivalent control treatment is sometimes a serious problem. For example, considerable ingenuity may be required where the amount of time required for instruction is greater in the experimental treatment than can be profitably used by a control or placebo treatment.

Treatment Fidelity. Was the treatment given as intended? The latitude accorded to the individual responsible for giving the treatment may be such that his attempts to "improve" it result in its no longer being what was originally envisaged. Training may help ensure treatment fidelity. Often observers are used to determine fidelity. Either covert observation or unannounced visits help ensure that fidelity is practiced regularly, not just when a researcher is present. Observer checklists of all those aspects deemed essential to treatment success (the active ingredients) help ensure that the necessary data for determining fidelity are gathered. Fidelity of administration may be important in your study; if it is, be sure to indicate what steps you will take to ensure it.

Records—Observations and Measures

Observations and measures serve several purposes in a research design: (1) assessing prior characteristics that might affect the result, (2) determining whether the treatment did cause the change that was anticipated, and (3) ensuring treatment fidelity as noted in the paragraph above. Regardless of which of these purposes is involved, the usual questions regarding observations and measures need to be answered in the proposal. This means assuring the reader that the record obtained is a valid one that appropriately represents whatever was to be observed or measured without bias or substantial error. To adequately meet such standards may require changing from unstructured observation to more structured checklists or interview schedules—for measures, this may involve obtaining statistical evidence of reliability, validity, and objectivity.

What standards will be held for specific observations or measures will depend on how critical they are to the study, and the precision with which they will be expected to delineate between individuals and/or groups. Clearly, using instruments with a history of prior satisfactory development and application simplifies presenting your case for their choice. Your decision about what data to include gives some indication of your capability, just as does the literature review. Carefully consider what is needed and supply it.

Both the Beissner and Phelan proposals are much better in regard to this link in the chain than the previous one! Beissner, in fact, devotes a separate section to it, "Instruments" (paragraphs 28–47), a large chunk of her proposal. Further, she gives extended discussions of the quality of the instruments she intends to use, as well as in one case an alternative measure. This is appropriate since the concept that is the focus of her study, problem solving, is difficult to measure.

Phelan is faced with a similarly difficult concept to measure, self-directed learning. Instead of making it a separate section, he embedded the discussion of his measure of effect in the literature review paragraphs that were omitted (end of paragraph 8), examining its use in other studies. Then in paragraph 18 of the "Research Method" section he simply indicates he will use the Self-Directed Learning Readiness Scale (SDLRS).

Either way of handling the operationalization of concepts is fine, so long as the information is there. Readers are more likely to look for it in a design, procedure, or methods section. In this instance, however, having read the literature review section, they have the necessary information, and that is what is important.

Comparison and Contrast—The Basis for Sensing Attributes or Changes

For experimental studies designed to show the effect of some variable or treatment, the design structure is the main protection against plausible alternative explanations—proper design makes them implausible. If the design structure is not adequate to ensure the integrity of the study's chain of reasoning against alternative explanations, the study is largely wasted effort! The importance of this section justifies some repetition and expansion of the previous discussion of these matters.

For the study corroborating a hypothesis, the design shows how the study will be structured so that data can be gathered with the least contamination by factors providing alternative explanations. If such factors have an effect, they are built into the comparison—as when control and experimental groups are equally affected. This means the proposal must include a *discussion of which variables to control and how to control them.*

For example, in a study of the effect of two different curricula, you would want to control for any initial differences in the groups that might be reflected in their after-treatment performance. In this situation, you might be expected to control such potentially alternative causal factors as the beginning level of competence or achievement, general academic ability, and motivation. Be especially careful to explain what is and what is not controlled and the reasoning behind the choice of variables to control and the choice of methods for controlling them.

Random Assignment. Certain design configurations provide a lot of protection, others less. For example, the learning resulting from an experimental curriculum in a single experimental group might be explained by the nature of the persons initially selected, those who stayed through the length of the study, normal growth patterns, or a variety of other factors. However, when you randomly assign a pool of subjects to control and experimental groups, many alternative possible causal factors are eliminated because they would be expected to affect both groups equally—differences between the groups are not likely to be due to these factors. *When comparing groups, you buy a lot of protection by randomly assigning individuals to them.* On the average, random assignment to groups equalizes everything from intelligence to size of belly button.

Preferred Methods of Controlling for Alternative Explanations. The sensitivity of a study to statistically significant differences is greater if one can eliminate a factor rather than spread its effect equally to both treatment and experimental groups. For example, suppose that a test of letter recognition was part of the evaluation of an experimental kindergarten program. If the university researcher conducted that test, some children might be uncomfortable and not do as well as if their regular kindergarten teacher had given it. By having the university researcher test both experimental and control groups, such an effect should be as much represented in the control group as in the experimental.

But this introduces another factor, the child's reaction to the test administrator, some of whom will react badly, some of whom won't. This added variability to the test scores might be enough to mask the experimental effect of the curriculum, thus causing it to be judged ineffective when it actually was effective. Eliminating that variability by having the classroom teacher give the test would make for a more sensitive test of the experimental effect. *If possible, elim-*

inate a factor to control it; if you can't, then be sure that it equally affects the control and experimental groups.

Consider another example and a slightly different solution. Suppose that in order to measure gains, you plan to give both a pretest and a posttest to an experimental group. Taking the pretest may result in higher posttest scores; the subjects may be more at ease knowing what to expect on the posttest or may have reconsidered their answers and be ready with correct ones. One way of eliminating this alternative explanation of the effect might be to create a control group and give a pretest to both groups. But students will react differently to the pretest, some benefiting greatly, others less so, and this variability overlays that of the treatment effect. Again, this reduces the sensitivity of the study, making it more difficult to discern the treatment effect.

A better solution is to eliminate the pretest and use experimental and control groups that are given a posttest only. But this presupposes that random assignment created two groups that were equivalent at the beginning, and you may be uncomfortable with this assumption. In that case, create four comparable groups by random assignment of subjects, a control and experimental group that undergo both pre—and posttesting and a control and experimental group that take a posttest only. (For additional assurance, you might also stratify or block on a relevant variable. For example, divide the sample into thirds on the basis of a test of learning ability and randomly assign to experimental and control groups within the thirds. Since this will create twelve groups, you will have to have a large sample to begin with; nearly everything comes at a price.) The pretest groups provide an indication of the comparability of groups created by random assignment as well as the change from their initial level; the posttest-only groups show the effect of the treatment, unaffected by pretesting. This design, called the Solomon Four-Group Design, is just an indication of the possible design choices; there are many more.

For an example of a modified Solomon four-group design, see paragraph 12 of Phelan. He uses random assignment to determine who is assigned to which measurement pattern of pretests and posttests, providing protection as indicated above. Group 5 is a second control group, Group 4 being the first. Presumably, it would show any difference over the time period in which the treatment is administered to the experimental groups that was due to some external influence other than treatment. Without some indication from the writer, however, it is unclear why this protection is necessary. Apparently, the reference to Durr is supposed to tell us, but we shouldn't have to trot to the library to find out.

A number of such arrangements of groups and measures into designs have been analyzed for their strengths and weaknesses with respect to the alternative explanations commonly found in behavioral science studies. (See, for instance, Campbell and Stanley, 1963; Cook and Campbell, 1979; and Shadish, Cook, and Campbell, 2002.) Such references are extremely valuable aids in picking a configuration that eliminates plausible explanations for your particular study.

Additional Alternative Explanations in Experimentation. Four plausible alternative explanations were described in chapter 5. When present, these need to be controlled. But they are by no means the totality of common plausible alternative explanations. Not only are there others, but many studies involve alternative explanations that are unique to either that study or that type of study. Look for others in your study (see Krathwohl, 1998/2004, pp. 527–530; or Shadish, Cook, and Campbell, 2002, for other common ones). Then point them out in your proposal and show how you have made them implausible or minimized their effect.

Additional Procedural Details

For many studies, the description of the study's design contains all the information needed on procedure. However, there may be certain aspects not central to the design, but important to the integrity of the study. For instance, it is common to interview a sample of the experimental and control subjects after the completion of the study (and sometimes during it) to determine such things as: Was the situation perceived as an experimental one? What did they think was the treatment? Did this change how they reacted? Tried harder? Or less hard? Were there side effects? Were there unexpected interruptions? Etc. Either include these as part of the design description or in a section perhaps called "Additional Procedural Details."

Analysis of the Data

Describe how you intend to analyze your data. For new statistical procedures that are unlikely to be familiar to your chairperson and/or committee, provide references (they may appreciate a description in the appendix or a photocopy from the journal where it was described).

Thinking through your plan of analysis will ensure that you gather the information you need while it is still possible to do so. According to Murphy's law: "If anything can go wrong, it will!" Nothing is more discouraging than to have gathered all the data only to find that some essential piece is missing. To avoid this, many advisors ask their students to include dummy tables in the proposal that are complete in all details except for numerical entries. Clearly, this makes it easier to write the results section of the dissertation—just plug in the numbers. (This assumes all will go as planned!)

Laying out the tables in advance has an additional advantage, however, if one considers alternative outcomes. It forces you to consider what additional information might be needed to explain your results if they don't turn out as expected. That way, you can plan to collect that additional information, instead of either having to go back and obtain it or, perhaps, find that it is no longer available. For instance, suppose the sample included persons for whom the treatment turned out to be ineffective. Did they complete the treatment, or was it ineffective because they were absent for part of it? Unless you have appropriate records, you won't know. Anticipate what extra data are essential and explore with your chairperson and committee what supplementary data might reasonably be collected. Then provide for these data either in the "Design" or "Additional Procedural Details" section.

Experimental studies typically use inferential statistics to show the treatment had an effect. Typically these involve t tests, analysis of variance, chi-square, or some variant thereof. It is worth noting that because hypotheses tend to be worded in terms of differences, one therefore tends to translate them into studies examining differences between groups.

Ultimately, however, we are interested in the strength of the treatment and how to modify the treatment to do its job better. This requires studies designed with different levels of treatment and with groups with various characteristics interacting with treatment effectiveness. This typically leads us to use analysis of variance. But it is correlations that give us information on the strength of relations between, for instance, length or strength of treatment and their effects, or of ability grouping on treatment.

Multiple regression or structural equation modeling will work with any problem that can be handled by analysis of variance and, in addition, give estimates of strength of the relation between variables. This provides better information for increasing a treatment's effectiveness. Consider these possibilities when designing your study. Computer programs such as SAS, SPSS, MINITAB, and others are comprehensive enough to provide computations for most procedures you might consider using.

To be sure your proposal contains the appropriate information, check it against Worksheet 8.1: Review of Proposals Using Experimental and Causal Modeling Approaches.

SECTION 2: CAUSAL MODELING

As we learn more about the interrelations of variables, we are able to construct chains of variables—causal models—that lead to some behavioral outcome. An increasing proportion of published research is devoted to causal modeling studies. These studies can be thought of as synthesizing prior research since they derive the basis for their model from simpler studies, perhaps of a couple of variables. Their contribution is to assemble simpler ones into a larger whole—a model—and test it to see whether it is supported by new data.

What does this call for in a proposal? Clearly the background research is crucial to convincing readers that a basis for the model exists. Assemble the prior research that undergirds each of the parts of the model and supply the rationale to piece together the literature.

The basic literature review will quite naturally lead into a description of

Review of Proposals Using Experimental and Causal Modeling Approaches

How Well Does My Proposal Reflect the Special Concerns of This Particular Dissertation Approach?

How Well Have I Provided Strong, Detailed Descriptions of . . . ?	Strong	Acceptable	Weak– Improvements Needed	Not Applicable
Research problem and study rationale?				
Relationship to be examined, treatment effectiveness to be assessed, or prediction to be confirmed?				
Population(s) and sample(s) to be studied?				
Treatment conceptual definition, operational definition, and fidelity of implementation?				
Methods of data collection including development and quality of instrumentation?				
Procedures for assessing change and eliminating or controlling alternative explanations?				
Methods of data analysis including quality control procedures?				
Ethical concerns and accommodations?				
Study timeline, resources, and management issues?				

your proposed model in conceptual terms. Because the conceptual definition of a variable is often at variance with its operationalization, describe the operationalization in the original research as well as that in your planned study. Then readers can judge your operationalization in relation to the original. For those variables for which you use different instruments, or where multiple research studies used different operationalizations, provide a justification of your choice of operationalization. In order more fully to portray a variable in all its conceptualized aspects, it is common to represent it with more than one operationalization. Indicate in the proposal where you do this and describe the advantage, if any, this gives your study over previous research.

Most structural equation modeling approaches provide neither for interacting variables nor where feedback moderates certain variables. Further, they assume only linear relationships. Note this limitation if it confines the findings you expect. It may be that your model flows only in one direction, and that all the variables can be represented well enough by linear equations so that this will be no problem; then so indicate in the proposal. However, if there are recursions or feedback you will want to use LISREL or some other modeling program that handles such problems. If you don't, you'll need to indicate why you are using a less than adequate modeling technique.

Some phenomena involve step functions. These are variables that react to the strength of a stimulus only on reaching a certain threshold; sometimes in an all or nothing fashion. Because such variables are not well handled by conventional statistics, where you suspect their presence, speculate on the adequacy of your model and indicate how seriously you think your conclusions will be limited.

Finally, you will want to describe the structural modeling technique that you plan to use in this study. Since this field is continuously evolving, unless you have training in this field, you may want to consult a statistician to insure that what you plan is currently sound. Then describe it in sufficient detail that your chairperson and committee will have little trouble in following your plan. Although some members of your committee may have a general idea of what structural modeling is, they may need some explanation in order to follow and discuss what you plan to do. Provide them with enough that they can intelligently contribute to your discussion.

To be sure your proposal contains the appropriate information, check it against Worksheet 8.1: Review of Proposals Using Experimental and Causal Modeling Approaches.

SECTION 3: META-ANALYSIS

Meta-analysis began as a descriptive tool to portray the combined results of quantitative studies, converting them into a summary of the results. Sometimes this summary is a simple vote count. More often it is a kind of standard score called an effect size. But the method has evolved beyond this. Where there are enough studies under each of several different conditions, it has become an investigative tool to determine the effect under these conditions taken singly and/or in combinations.

Investigative meta-analysis requires assembling past data into subsets contrasting certain conditions—for example, differing levels of socioeconomic status (SES). This allows one to find how circumstances change a relationship—for example, high classroom structure facilitates learning for low SES students. But one may also find that too high and inflexible a structure reduces learning for high SES students. The shape of the relationship of a measure of classroom structure to SES may be plotted to determine where it is maximized or minimized and for whom.

For instance, Glass and Smith (1979) and Glass, McGaw, and Smith (1981) plotted class size against achievement. They found that achievement increases only very slightly from huge class sizes into the low teens and then accelerates rapidly, especially with class sizes below ten. It reaches a maximum with a class size of one—tutoring. By plotting the effect sizes against class size, a much clearer idea of the nature of the relationship was gained. Incidentally, stronger designs yielded larger effect sizes than did weaker ones.

Light (1984) notes that research syntheses can answer several important questions. They can explain which features of a treatment are critical.

For example, Raudenbusch (1984) examined eighteen studies of expectancy effect. He found only a small effect overall (an effect size of 0.11). But by comparing the studies with a strong expectancy effect with those with a weak one, he discovered an important finding. Teachers, who met their children *after* they were given the information intended to create the expectancy, showed a strong effect. Those who met the children first showed almost none. Unless this were hypothesized, it is unlikely that it would be determined from a single study.

Meta-analysis has become increasingly sophisticated to answer the concerns of critics. As Russell Sage's series of volumes on meta-analysis indicates (Cook et al., 1992; Cooper and Hedges, 1994; Wachter and Straf, 1990), it has become a method of research in its own right. Other books reinforce this (e.g., Hedges and Olkin, 1985; Hunter and Schmidt, 1990; Lipsey and Wilson, 2000; and Rosenthal, 1991).

Special Requirements of a Meta-Analysis Proposal

A proposal to do a meta-analysis for a dissertation needs to give special attention to four questions:

1. What question are you seeking to answer, and what areas and variables does this entail?
2. Is the pool of studies sufficient that a meta-analysis is feasible? What lit-

erature will be searched? What criteria must studies meet to be included?

3. Is this a descriptive or investigative meta-analysis?
4. How will the results of individual studies be combined and analyzed?

The Research Question and Literature

The first three questions are so intertwined that the answer to one implies certain answers to the others. For instance, what variables are involved in defining the question one seeks to answer determines the literature to be searched. The size of that body of literature, in turn, determines whether an investigative study is feasible.

While the first task of a meta-analyst is to define the area of study, that area is often enlarged by the nature of the available studies. Pilot work is necessary to determine their nature, what independent variables will need to be included, and whether enough studies involve the latter that an investigative study is feasible.

> For example, consider a study of the effectiveness of different patterns of part-whole practice (the independent variables—the causes) on learning of psychomotor skills (the dependent variable—the effect). Using the symbol W to designate learning a psychomotor act as a whole, and P to designate learning a part of the action with numbers to designate the order of their assembly (e.g., P1 for part 1, etc.), we can designate the patterns. These patterns were found in the literature:
>
> W, P, W
>
> (P1), (P1 + P2), (P1 + P2 + P3), and so on;
>
> P1, W, P2, W, P3, W, and so on.
>
> These variations of treatment were found to be administered under conditions of massed practice (all at one learning session) or distributed practice (distributed over several sessions), or both. So this second variable had to be added to the study, and studies had to be sorted into the different possible combinations of variations of whole versus part learning with massed versus distributed practice as shown in the cells of Table 8.1.
>
> By classifying studies into the cells of such a matrix, one can determine which rows, columns, and cells have sufficient data and which distinctions need to be collapsed.

Developing such a structure from an analysis of the literature is one of the most important tasks of the quantitative literature reviewer. The structure facilitates understanding the field and both determines how well a meta-analysis illuminates the interrelations of independent to dependent variables and shows where new research is most needed. Light and Pillemer (1984) emphasize that

TABLE 8.1

Matrix Showing the Combinations of Variations in Whole-Part Learning with Variations in Massed vs. Distributed Practice. Studies to be Included in the Meta-Analysis Would Be Sorted into the Blank Cells.

	Massed Practice	Distributed Practice	Both Massed and Distributed Practice
W, P, W			
(P1), (P1 + P2), (P1 + P2 + P3), and so on;			
P1, W, P2, W, P3, W, and so on			

the decision of what studies to combine and how to combine them is a critical feature of meta-analyses.

You need not have completed the literature review before doing your proposal, but you should have done enough of it to be able to present the kind of structure you plan to use in classifying the studies. On completing the review, you may need to combine rows and/or columns for the meta-analysis itself where there are insufficient studies. If you anticipate this happening, foreshadow this possibility in your proposal and indicate its consequences for your study.

Your proposal should also indicate the search plan you will use to find studies. For instance, will you be seeking only published studies or include fugitive ones as well—other dissertations, unpublished papers from conferences, government reports, etc.?

If you have enough studies you can afford to be fussy; indicate the criteria you will use to include and exclude studies—for example, including only those using random assignment. More often, however, all studies are included, and judgments of a study's research quality become part of the coding scheme. Then meta-analyses for well and poorly controlled studies can be compared. Sometimes, the better studies have shown a larger effect, suggesting that the true effect size is closer to that of the better studies.

Investigative vs. Descriptive Meta-Analyses

All meta-analyses are descriptive, but whether one can also make a particular meta-analysis investigative depends on the classification structure used and whether sufficient numbers of studies can be found to fill the cells where the rows and columns indicate combinations of different sets of conditions. Your proposal should indicate whether you anticipate being able to do an investigative study and which variables you expect to examine. There is no minimum number of studies for a meta-analysis; after all, two studies of good quality provide a better estimate than one.

Combining the Studies and Analyzing the Results

Meta-analyses usually report strength of association either as a correlation or as an effect size. The latter is comparable to a standard score and is expressed in standard deviation units. Thus, an effect size of 1 indicates that a member of a treated group would, on average, have a treatment effect one standard deviation larger than the untreated group. To get an effect size, the effect (for instance, the difference between treated and untreated groups) is divided by a standard deviation uncontaminated by treatment. Usually, this is the standard deviation of the control group, but if analysis of variance is used, it may be a residual after other influences have been removed. Indicate in your proposal's discussion of the data analysis what effect size will be used and how it will be determined.

Translation of Study Data into Effect Sizes. Although some current studies report effect sizes in addition to the usual statistics, few past ones do. Turning the data in old reports into effect sizes requires some backward reasoning and often some assumptions when the required data were not reported. Glass, McGaw, and Smith (1981), Hedges and Olkin (1985), R. Rosenthal (1994), and Cooper and Hedges (1994) provide instructions for translating most statistics into effect sizes or, alternatively, into a combined significance test, if that is preferred. Indicate what assumptions you must make to obtain the effect sizes.

In studies that used more than one measure to determine effects, each yields an effect size. Combining such multiple estimates with data from other studies gives the studies with multiple estimates extra weight and overrepresents their strengths and flaws in any overall effect size. Choosing one effect size from each study to enter a combined effect size takes the study as the unit of analysis instead of all the individual findings within a study (Mansfield and Busse, 1977; Bangert-Drowns, 1986).

But choosing one effect size to represent each study may throw away valuable information. For example, a study might show that a curriculum had three positive effects: achievement, attitudinal, and study skills. (If other studies also gathered attitudinal and study skills effect data, however, you could do two additional meta-analyses, one on attitudinal and one on study skills effects.) You may also weight the studies in the overall average in relation to sample size, thus giving more weight to the better estimates from larger samples. Indicate in your proposal how you will decide to represent each study (allow multiple effect sizes, weight by sample size, weight by quality of study, etc.) and your basis for this choice.

Variance-Partitioning for Investigative Meta-Analyses. Ideally, if studies were replications of one another, instead of using the study as the unit, perhaps we could pool the individual subjects into one huge study. Since the studies are not replications, we can only approximate data pooling. Further, where the variability in the results across studies is great, the results are usually the consequence not only of the treatment variable but also of variations in method, instruments, and so on. Using an analysis of variance analogy, researchers developed variance-partitioning meta-analysis to determine the effects of the various sources of undesired variability and correct for them to determine the effective size of the independent variables of interest.

Researchers are attempting to find the potential inaccuracies in the estimates provided by simple meta-analytic methods and to find ways of making allowances for them. Hedges (1982), Rosenthal and Rubin (1982), and Hunter, Schmidt, and Jackson (1982) worked out the required statistical tests to partition the variance into subgroups such as outcome measure, treatment variation, gender of subjects, research study quality, etc. Hunter and Schmidt (1990) also make corrections for the unreliability of the instruments. Clearly, many assumptions are involved in these procedures.

Meta-Analyses and Research Judgement. With so many analytic and interpretive possibilities, clearly the proposal should indicate your judgement of which to select so your committee will know what to expect. Not all the various corrections that have been proposed will make sense in every study. Indicate those that you have chosen for yours, and give your rationale for the choice. After enough pilot work to be able to judge the size and nature of the available literature, you should be able to lay out the structure of the analysis in some detail, thus providing a rather complete work plan for the study.

Although meta-analysis substitutes statistics for some judgments, many remain to be made. If one of the studies has flaws, does combining them provide an improved estimate? Judgment regarding the effect of the flaws is required. Many believe that the best research syntheses are combinations of the old-style judgmental literature analyses and meta-analyses. Indicate where you stand with respect to this issue, and what kind of analysis you expect to provide.

To be sure your proposal contains the appropriate information, check it against Worksheet 8.2: Review of Proposals Using Meta-Analysis Approaches.

Review of Proposals Using Meta-Analysis Approaches

How Well Does My Proposal Reflect the Special Concerns of This Particular Dissertation Approach?

How Well Have I Provided Strong, Detailed Descriptions of . . . ?	Strong	Acceptable	Weak– Improvements Needed	Not Applicable
Topic and structure of study based on literature reviewed?				
Criteria for inclusion of studies and search procedures?				
Methods for combining studies and analyzing results?				
Results of preliminary analysis and pilot work?				

CHAPTER 9

The Special Requirements of Proposals Using Qualitative and/or Quantitative Approaches

Survey, Evaluation, Development, Demonstration

CHAPTER CONTENTS

Many studies do not hew to either quantitative or qualitative traditions, but, instead, borrow whatever methods might prove useful in reaching their goal. For example, sample surveys may use interviews that are analyzed qualitatively, or structured questionnaires that are analyzed quantitatively.

Depending on the goal and the approach, there is a wide variety of such proposals, and they can differ too much from one another to cover all the possibilities here. Instead, we will focus on several commonly traveled paths that we hope will provide adequate guidance for writing proposals not otherwise covered. The chapter is divided into four study types: Section 1: Sample Surveys, Section 2: Evaluation Studies, Section 3: Development Studies (e.g., Curriculum, Equipment, Instruments, Software, and Methodology), and Section 4: Demonstration and Action Research Studies.

SECTION 1: SAMPLE SURVEYS

Survey studies, by describing existing conditions, contribute to a better understanding of our world. Their social bookkeeping provides data that describe conditions, opinions, attitudes, and relationships; they can add precision to qualitative descriptions of phenomena. In addition, such studies may confirm hypotheses and contribute to theories and models. The proposal requirements for social bookkeeping studies differ slightly from those providing support for hypotheses, theories, points of view, and models.

Social bookkeeping is mainly descriptive. The proposal consists of a justification for gathering the data including previous literature, a description of how the data will be gathered, and how they will be displayed so as to facilitate understanding by those audiences the researcher intends to reach.

Surveys supporting hypotheses, theories, points of view, or models are written as chains of reasoning that show how they build on the previous literature, advance it in some way, and can be operationalized into a study. Both bookkeeping and generalizing studies are discussed under each heading below.

Problem

In this section you will describe the facts you wish to gather and/or the hypothesis, theory, point of view, or model you wish to test. If you are gathering facts about society, the justification usually rests on the survey's having some important consequences, often for public policy or that of an organization. Indicate the need for the information and what group (if any) will be in a position to use and follow up on it. If it is a public policy study and you can tie into a contemporary interest such as social indicators, the importance of the study may be enhanced.

If you are gathering information in support of a hypothesis, theory, point of view, or model, it is the use of the information in their support and development that provides the justification. Indicate where the hypothesis leads; the implications that supporting a particular theory, point of view, or model might have; and how any of these might lead to further developments and/or greater understanding.

For example, consider understanding how attempts to empower teachers are perceived by the teachers themselves. One could discover whether they perceive these efforts as another top-down imposition on their time and energy, a temporary sharing of power until this fad blows over, a sharing of power only on issues where it has little significance, etc. Such insights might help predict the success of power-sharing administrators in achieving real school reform; it could provide guidance about how to bring about real empowerment and could contribute to the organizational theory of school administration.

Review of Previous Research

Building on the past is good practice even for surveys that are concerned with the present. Past surveys may suggest questions to ask and appropriate formats to ask them. They may provide ideas for question types. They may suggest new formats for your data collection instruments. Their data may provide the basis for establishing trends. Differences in past results may show areas particularly sensitive to question wording. Energy spent finding past similar work may pay dividends in time saved on current efforts.

Past data are available on a variety of topics and are increasingly available for secondary analysis as computer-based data sets, especially from the U.S. government—e.g., the Census Bureau and the National Center for Educational Statistics. There are useful printed collections of instruments and polls, many in libraries. Search library and Internet headings like Gallup Organization (http://www.gallup.com [accessed October 1, 2004]), Harris Organization (http://www.harrispollonline.com [accessed October 1, 2004]), National Opinion Research Center (http://www.norc.uchicago.edu [accessed October 1, 2004]), Roper Organization (http://www.ropercenter.uconn.edu [accessed October 1, 2004]), and the Survey Research Center, Institute for Social Research (http://www.isr.umich.edu/src/ [accessed October 1, 2004]). The Survey Research Center site also lists their research working paper series [www.isv.umich. EDU/SRC/SMP (accessed October 5, 2004)]; many can be downloaded.

Because experts in the field have done these studies, their analyses frequently not only warn of potential problems in specific research areas, but also increase your sensitivity to these problems in a general way. For example, they may point to the significant effect of the order of questions on data interpretation and subtle shifts in respondent perception caused by minor changes in wording.

Further, past data add perspective over time to the understanding of phenomena. This is frequently important since the interpretation of what may seem like a sudden surge and change in speed and/or direction, when viewed in a historical perspective, becomes part of a periodic variation that has occurred before. This likely changes interpretation significantly. Two collections of questions that were administered at different times are Hastings and Southwick (1974) and Martin, McDuffee and Presser (1981). Use these in the *Social Science Citation Index* to find others.

So, given the wealth of archival material, and its possible timesaving and interpretive significance, whether social bookkeeping or supporting hypotheses, theories, or models, a search for previous research may be in order both for the findings and for the instruments.

For studies supporting hypotheses, theories, points of view, or models, see the suggestions given in chapter 4 and show how the hypotheses, theories, or models grow out of past research.

Design

Social bookkeeping studies require primarily a description of the operational details of the study. Studies supporting a hypothesis, theory, and/or model, having shown their derivation from previous research and literature, need to show how operationalization will contribute supportive data. In both instances, indicate why it is reasonable to assume the survey instrument taps the conceptual variables of concern in the study.

A Representative Sample

The representativeness of the sample is most critical with social bookkeeping because the whole point of the study is to be able to generalize from the sample to the larger society. Perhaps more than in any other kind of study the nature of the sample and sampling procedures should therefore be described in detail and some indication as to why generalization to the target population is justified.

The sampling plan should be worked through carefully. This is often a good place to seek expert help if sampling theory is not your strength. Provide information about details of the plan. If stratified, or cluster sampling is used, describe the nature of the strata, or clusters, along with the rationale for your choice. Surveys can be large or small, and their size depends on many factors, prime among them the size sample needed to provide desired precision. Some explanation of the basis for the sample size selected should be given. Data from pilot studies provide the most accurate size estimates. In addition, they also provide an opportunity to pretest one's instrument—an essential.

Surveys intended to provide evidence supporting a hypothesis, theory, or model need to be representative in the sense that the sample is drawn from an appropriate population. However, assuming that the hypothesis, theory, or model is intended to be generally applicable, then you may use any unit that is typical.

Be sure the sampling unit used is consistent with the hypotheses. For example, often the hypothesis deals with the effect of some intervention on a classroom and the sampling unit is thought to be the student. In such a study, the classroom is the unit; the sampling unit is the smallest unit uniformly receiving the intervention.

Longitudinal, cross-sectional, cohort, and panel studies all require detailed discussions of how the sample will be chosen to be representative. In addition, describe planned replacement strategies for losses of sample members. Where a cross-sectional study is used in place of a more preferable longitudinal one, indicate why the cross-sectional is a satisfactory substitute—other than its obviously greater convenience and comparatively lower cost.

Instrumentation

As previously indicated, already developed instruments are often available and are a source of both ideas and actual items. Although it is tempting to use previously developed questions without a tryout, pretesting is advisable because intervening events may have changed both the meaning and the effect attached to certain words.

> Converse and Presser (1986), for example, note that responses to a question previously used to measure confidence in government ("Do you think the people in Washington are smart people who know what they are doing?") acquired new meaning after the Watergate scandal. Respondents gave it a wry twist: "Oh yeah, those guys know what they're doing, all right—they're plenty smart." (p. 51)

Using an item in a new context may change responses significantly.

> They also note questions acquire meaning from the context of neighboring questions: "[F]ew people say their taxes are too high after being asked a series of items about whether government spending should be increased in various areas (Turner and Krauss, 1978)." (p. 40)

If you are recycling a previously used instrument, indicate your protections against changed meaning and/or context. Also be sure to give credit in your proposal to the original source, indicating how you have secured permission to use the instrument and have abided by copyright restrictions.

If you are interviewing, indicate the kind of interview you plan to conduct. Will it be:

- open-ended?
- unstructured, with just the general area prescribed?
- partially structured, with freedom to modify questions and order?
- answers coded as they are received?
- a focused or funnel-shaped set of questions starting broadly and narrowing to a focus?
- a nondirective approach?
- a panorama of questions from which you will pick as you go?
- tandem interviewing with a coworker?
- focus groups?

As with any study using qualitative methods, some pilot work that helps one anticipate what to expect provides the basis for constructing the proposal. Where you are working with an emergent focus to your problem, pilot work indicates what is likely to emerge.

If you are planning to use computer-assisted telephone interviewing (CATI), there are now a number of "shell" software programs into which you can place your questions. Describe what software you plan to use. How will you determine whom to call? What will be your callback procedure if a person is not reached? How does the software provide links between questions? Does the software link responses to a statistical procedure for determining when sufficient responses in a given category have been received? If it does, how?

There is increasing interest in using the Internet for surveys. It has the advantages of minimal or no cost and great ease to send the instrument, receive returns, and send follow-ups with little time lost in transit. It has the disadvantages of limiting the respondents to those with access to computers and the Web or e-mail. It is difficult to make returns anonymous (although one could have all returns sent through an anonymizer). Reasonably priced software is available, including some that will provide shell questionnaires, host receipt of your returns, and provide an analysis of the responses. You locate your sample and provide them with the access password and URL. Some software can be downloaded to run your own site. To find this software, put something like "sample+survey+software," "survey+analysis+software," or "survey+web+software" (without the quotation marks; use them when you want to search for an exact phrase) in a search engine; the plus signs ensure all three words will be in the sites the search engine returns. Anyone planning surveys on the Web may find Shannon, Johnson, Searcy, and Lott (2002) of help (abstract available at: http://edresearch.org/scripts/seget2.asp?want=http://edresearch.org/ericdc/ED470202.htm [accessed October 1, 2004]). They compiled the suggestions of sixty-two experienced survey researchers regarding electronic surveys.

Place a copy of your interview schedule or questionnaire in the appendix if you have already developed it or have borrowed one. For a mailed questionnaire, include the letter of transmittal, and indicate how its appeal has been tested and the basis for expecting a good return. For a Web—or e-mail-based survey, include the letter of invitation and the basis of its appeal. If the instrument is yet to be developed, give examples of the kind of instrument that will be used—e.g., sample questions or examples of existing similar instruments. Describe your plans to check the instrument's effectiveness—pretests for new instruments are essential and for previously developed instruments used in a different time and context equally so.

Comparison and Contrast: The Basis for Sensing Attributes or Changes

In a cause and effect study, indicate clearly the basis on which the effect will be sensed, whether this is by contrasting groups, using the sample as its own control, or using some standard, such as test norms, to judge change. Usually, this is discussed in the design section of the proposal and is one of the most carefully scrutinized.

All research methods are vulnerable to alternative explanations; survey studies are no exception. Catching changes by comparing groups, time periods, etc., enables you to spot and often to correct for them. Make clear the basis on which you are able to rule out alternative explanations that may seem reasonable to your audience. Usually, this requires certain procedural steps. For example:

- *instrument decay*—Interview procedures may change with experience or from individual to individual, requiring training and retraining to ensure standardization of procedure.
- *mortality*—Dropouts from the originally chosen sample can markedly affect data patterns if the lost responses differ significantly from those collected. What procedure you will use to follow up nonrespondents is especially important: callbacks, interviewing a sample of nonrespondents, tracking questionnaire responses by date of receipt for trends, etc. Give details.
- *acquiescence response set*—The most prevalent of the response sets, acquiescence, often results whenever the question calls for a "yes," "true," or "agree" response. Particularly where there is uncertainty on the part of the respondent on how to respond or ambiguity in understanding the question, the respondent tends to say to herself, "Yes, I guess so," and responds affirmatively. This can mask the true response. Questions likely to elicit response sets can be caught at pretest if one interviews respondents to determine the basis for their answers.

Time Schedule: The Procedure

The steps involved in the study from beginning to end will probably have been covered in the instrumentation or preceding sections, but if not, describe the procedure of the study in a separate section. The work plan section may provide much of this detail.

Data Analysis

The basis for coding interview responses should be described. Again, if this is an emergent study, the final codes will not be known until the study is done. But the pilot study can provide the basis for anticipating their nature, what themes are likely to be most prominent, and how these relate to the hypotheses, theory, point of view, or model being studied. Make the relation clear. If you have begun a coding manual, and it is not too extensive, you might want to include it in the appendix.

Indicate what controls you will institute to ensure that coding is consistent as well as checks you will make to maintain consistency across multiple coders and over time. Establish rules for handling and coding the causes for missing data: doesn't know, refused to respond, indecipherable, inappropriate response, etc. To achieve consistency, establish rules for handling multiple responses and for distinguishing multiple responses in data presentation and analysis.

The nature of data analysis varies considerably in sample survey studies depending on the kind of data gathered and the method used in gathering it. With computer-aided telephone interviewing, the computer can often be programmed to analyze the data as the interview progresses. The interview is pruned as sufficient data are obtained in certain areas; interviews are terminated early when the responses to the opening demographic questions show sufficient similar cases have already been contacted.

On a less rapid interactive basis, continued analysis of responses with traditional interviewing techniques may also result in interview schedule modifications as new leads appear or as certain points are covered with enough data while others need more.

Questionnaire responses are usually treated graphically or statistically, sometimes being combined into indexes. Claiming to be solely descriptive, many surveys state no hypotheses about what they expect to find. Nevertheless, the researcher who has thought through what to expect will be in a much better position to delineate fortuitous and chance findings that would not stand up under repeated research from generalizable ones that would. State your expectations if at all feasible, but then take steps to protect against researcher expectancy so they do not become self-fulfilling prophecies.

Because of the wide variety of analysis patterns for surveys and the fact that the analysis plan is so important to interpretation, readers will expect it to be described in some detail in your proposal. Don't disappoint them.

Querying Sensitive Topics

If you are querying respondents about topics that may cause considerable affective response, or that the general public considers taboo, you will need to take special steps to protect both your respondents and yourself. First of all, be sure that you go through whatever protection of human subjects procedures are in place at your institution, and, if you are gathering data in other institutions with such protections, in those as well. You may need parental permission if you are working with children. Describe these steps in your proposal.

In addition, consider various techniques that make it obvious that the interviewer cannot tell whether the respondent's answer falls in the sensitive class or in a neutral one. For example, phrase the question so the sensitive response is a "yes." Then, ask respondents to flip a coin but *not* show it to you. Tell them: "I'm going to use a procedure that hides your response so I can't tell which question you answered. Don't tell me yet, but if it came up heads, answer this question (insert the sensitive question here) with an honest 'yes' or 'no.' But if it came up tails, answer the question: 'Is your birthday in December?' Now, is your answer 'yes' or 'no'?"

Since birthdays are spread about equally throughout the year, 8.33 percent per month, then 8.33 percent of half the group, or 4.17 percent of the whole group, will answer the second question "yes." To estimate of the percentage of "yes" responses to the sensitive question in the total group, subtract 4.17 percent from the percentage of "yes" responses in the total group and then double what is left. This yields a good estimate, though one can never identify a single one of the persons who answered "yes."

If sensitive responses need to be linked to other responses for the individual, putting all the questions in a single instrument without any personal identification may handle the situation. But make clear how you will convince respondents that their group's answers will be kept anonymous.

If the responses need to be linked to another instrument, have them make up a code that they reconstruct on each instrument as you ask them certain questions. Then ask the same successive questions prior to each testing: "On the top line, write the first letter of the month in which you were born, next the last letter of your mother's first name, then the second letter of your street, etc." (Carifio and Baron, 1977).

Use items that would be difficult or impossible for the interviewer to ascertain. In most states, certain school information is considered privileged as a matter of law, so could not be revealed to you. Whether you use these techniques or others to gain information on sensitive issues, make clear how you will handle the matter of privacy of responses in your proposal.

Finally, use Worksheet 9.1: Review of Proposals Using Sample Survey Methods to ensure your statement includes the key elements of a sample survey study proposal.

Review of Proposals Using Sample Survey Methods

How Well Does My Proposal Reflect the Special Concerns of This Particular Dissertation Approach?

How Well Have I Provided Strong, Detailed Descriptions of . . . ?	Strong	Acceptable	Weak– Improvements Needed	Not Applicable
Research problem and study rationale?				
Facts to be gathered and any hypothesis, theory, point of view, or model to be tested?				
Review of past research findings and methods?				
Study design, definition of population, sampling strategy, sampling units, and units of observation and analysis?				
Data collection procedures?				
Instrument development process including draft questionnaire and transmittal notices?				
Procedures and results of pretesting and pilot testing?				
Procedures for assessing change and eliminating or controlling alternative explanations including assessments of non-respondent bias?				
Methods of data analysis including coding, data cleaning, and other quality control procedures?				
Ethical concerns including confidentiality/ anonymity and human subjects review procedures?				
Study timeline, resources, and management issues?				

SECTION 2: EVALUATION STUDIES

One can evaluate persons, programs, or products. Since few dissertations evaluate persons, and evaluation of products is covered in the next section of the chapter, this section deals with evaluation of programs. Program evaluation studies use any of the methods previously discussed (as well as others), so advice given elsewhere in this book is also relevant.

What is unique about program evaluation study proposals? Consider these concerns for starters. The proposal should define:

- Who, if anyone aside from your chairperson and committee, are its audiences?
- Who will define those audiences (e.g., you, your chairperson, your committee, a sponsor, the program's administrator)?
- Are all possible stakeholders (persons with a stake in the study's outcome and its implications) to be included as audiences?
- Are any audiences expected to play a role in the evaluation and if so what?
- Who defines the criteria or standards against which whatever is being evaluated is to be judged (e.g., the program's goals)?
- What evaluation orientation will be used (e.g., goal-free evaluation)?
- Is it to be summative or formative (in a sense, all evaluations are formative, but some more so in a short time sense than others)?

Clearly, a number of questions are pertinent to an evaluation study proposal that are less relevant, or do not even arise, in other studies.

Guidance for some of these questions, as well as others, is provided in the set of standards for evaluations prepared by a committee of professional association representatives (Joint Committee on Standards for Educational Evaluation, 1994; to see a summary of them, click on "Program Evaluation Stds" at http://www.wmich.edu/evalctr/jc [accessed October 1, 2004]). Although addressed to educational evaluation, their applicability is much broader. Where they address problems relevant to your situation, following their recommendations will help you build appropriate comments into your proposal. Indeed, your committee may expect it.

Let us examine in more detail the questions posed above with respect to evaluation proposals.

Audiences

The first four questions above all deal with the evaluation's audiences because their determination is a key judgment from which many of the later aspects of the study flow. Such evaluations may be developed as either applied or basic research.

Applied or Basic Research?

Most evaluations are applied research, undertaken to facilitate a decision about the worth or merit of whatever is being evaluated. We say such evaluations are decision-driven because determinations about what evaluation steps to take are based on how they contribute to the decision-making apparatus and the decision itself. Some evaluation dissertations, like applied research, are decision driven; they are application studies whose local findings (see chapter 2) are intended to be useful to an organization or program as well as to contribute to the doctoral student's education.

In these cases, the audience for your study is broadened considerably over the typical dissertation. Besides your chairperson and committee, it can include whomever you decide: the administrators and/or the staff of a program, its clientele, and/or other stakeholders. Your choice of audience basically comes down to your intent.

Applied evaluation studies take place within specific political arenas in which many participants may gain or lose resources, reputations, professional positions, etc., as a result of the evaluation. Therefore, the sociopolitical context of the study is often an important factor in the success of your research. Further, if the purpose of the evaluation is to influence local decisions, shape current practice, or change operating policy, dealing with political issues can add a significant new dimension to your dissertation work.

The findings of evaluations done as basic research studies may or may not have action consequences; their intent is more to make generalizable statements of program worth. If your study's sole purpose is to complete your education, your prime audience, like a basic research study, is your chairperson, your committee, yourself, and ancillary readers. The study can be much simpler if you and your committee can be satisfied solely with whatever you learn from doing the study without action consequences in a specific local context.

Applied Research: Getting the Evaluation Used

What if you are in the program's decision-making loop? Perhaps doing the dissertation while on the job? Perhaps even getting support to do the evaluation in the hope the organization will benefit from its results? Now your dissertation audience is expanded to the decision makers you want to help use the results and whoever you and they recognize as significant stakeholders—persons whose acceptance of the results is critical to the success of the evaluation. Further, their concerns may differ, sometimes considerably, from those of your chairperson and committee. Yet the latter must still be considered your prime audiences. That doesn't always present a problem; indeed, your chairperson and committee, if they are at all savvy about evaluation, are likely to be most helpful in suggesting ways of avoiding conflict among audiences. But be aware of such possibilities—the divergences could stretch you thin.

Audience Involvement in the Evaluation

If the evaluation study is to have stakeholders as audiences (using the term broadly to include administrators and staff as well as clients and others), you must make some decision about whether and how to involve them at the proposal stage. The demands for accountability, which bring evaluation to the fore, often make it the center of political action with stakeholders. Depending on the situation, it may be too late to bring them into the evaluation process once the evaluation plan is formulated. If not involved early, they may perceive the evaluation as threatening their interests and be unwilling to accept its results. Therefore, before formulating the proposal, it is essential to obtain the best understanding possible of which stakeholders are involved, their relation to the decision maker(s), and to each other. Are they opponents? Advocates? Informed? Acting from stereotypes? Need they be involved in the development of the evaluation proposal? How?

That is a lot about audiences, but clearly, it is enough to indicate that

- the proposal must contain statements about your purpose for undertaking the study, and therefore
- which audiences you accept as the guiding ones for what the study must include if the results are to be accepted as:
    satisfying the requirements for the degree and, if relevant,
    satisfying other audiences so that the results of the study are used as a basis for their decision making.

Remember, it is your study; this is a decision you must make. If you conclude others beside your chairperson and committee are to be audiences of the dissertation, you must get your chairperson and committee to concur.

Clearly, the definition of who the audiences are is an important part of the proposal together with your rationale for the choice. If you include multiple audiences, discuss their respective roles and how differences, if any, will be reconciled.

Who Defines Program Goals or Standards?

Evaluation involves the determination of the value of something usually by comparison with standards, with something else such as another program, or with the achievement of its own program goals. These may be the goals around which the program was originally designed or modifications of those goals as the project progressed. Some programs turn out to achieve outcomes for which they were not designed.

A toy lending library was developed to help inner-city children overcome the effect of the "hidden curriculum" in the middle-class home by providing toys equivalent to those played with by the latter group. But the program's greatest value turned out to be the parenting education provided by the "librarian" when mothers asked what toys to select for their children.

If the evaluation is to determine whether certain goals were achieved, your proposal must answer such questions as:

- Where did these goals come from?
- Were they the original goals of the project?
- Has the project changed goals as it developed?
- Are they the goals of the agency that granted funding for the project? For the evaluation?
- Were those goals accepted by those involved in the project?
- Do the goals reflect those of the personnel who now control and administer the project?
- Were those goals based on a needs assessment that determined the discrepancy between what currently is and what is needed or wanted?
- Do clients and other stakeholders perceive the goals of the project in the same way as those running the project (e.g., mothers who were more attracted to employment training centers because they provided child care than because they provided training)?

If only certain goals are included in the evaluation, who determines which they are? You, with the approval of your chairperson and committee? If the evaluation is done as basic research, yes. If done with additional audiences, the answer can be considerably more complicated, especially if stakeholder audiences do not agree with you and/or each other. If the evaluation is funded, should the funder's or client's goals be those against which the project is evaluated? Provide a justification for whatever goals will be used in the evaluation, and indicate congruence, neutrality, or opposition of various stakeholder audiences and the likely consequences.

What Evaluation Orientation Do You Bring to the Study?

Program evaluators used to automatically compare a program with the goals its originators designed it to achieve. Today's evaluators choose among an array of evaluation approaches. For example, Scriven's (1972) "goal-free" evaluation contrasts with past approaches. He suggests entering the scene without knowing the program's goals. Evaluate the program on the basis of whatever changes it seems to have brought about, then compare these with the significant needs of program participants. This permits greater sensitivity to important but sometimes unintended side effects, such as that of the "librarian" above. Another example of an evaluation uncovering a significant unintended side effect is the family breakup that resulted from the guaranteed-income experiment (Rossi and Lyall, 1976). Whether or not goal-free evaluation is used, provisions in the proposal for observing and recording unintended consequences and side effects may be very important.

Management-oriented approaches are typified by Stufflebeam's CIPP approach (Stufflebeam and Shinkfield, 1985). The initials stand for the four kinds of management decisions involved and their equivalent evaluations:

C. *context evaluations* that determine the target audience and the needs to be met,
I. *input evaluations* that determine the resources that can be used to meet the needs,
P. *process evaluations* to determine how well a plan was implemented, where there are problems, and what can be done about them, and
P. *product evaluations* to examine the results obtained, whether needs were met, and what plans to lay for the future.

Cost-benefit analyses to determine the value of the program's outcomes in relation to costs are a frequent part of such evaluations. Cost-effectiveness analyses compare the efficiency of two or more programs in the use of resources to meet needs.

Expertise-oriented approaches, as represented by Eisner (1976, 1981) who calls this a connoisseurial approach, involve the use of experts to make evaluation judgments. This approach is often used where there are so many ways of meeting needs, and/or programs are so complex, that measurement or other evaluation techniques fail.

In contrast to the expertise orientation, transactional or participant-oriented approaches provide greater equality of power in determining the course of the evaluation among the evaluator and sponsor, staff, and other stakeholders. Such an orientation involves discussion among these parties to determine the purpose of the evaluation, the standards for evaluation, and the course of the evaluation itself. The evaluator acts more as a consultant than as a prime mover (Guba and Lincoln, 1987; Patton, 1997; Fetterman, Kaftarian, and Wandersman, 1996).

With these choices and more, it is clear that an evaluation proposal should contain a statement about the orientation chosen. (See Shadish, Cook, and Leviton, 1991, for an in-depth comparison of seven major evaluation approaches.) Depending on which it is, that orientation will determine what is appropriate at a number of places in the proposal and how definitively the process can be anticipated. Much less process detail can be concretely predicted if a participant-oriented approach is used than with others. Evaluation studies following collaborative, participative, or empowerment approaches often employ more emergent than prespecified design strategies. This will be reflected in your proposal.

It is usually preferable to describe the evaluation orientation early in the presentation; describe whether you are following it in "pure" or modified form and how it will manifest itself in the study. Include your rationale for the choice of this orientation in contrast to some other approach. Be sensitive to the fact that you should consider compatibility with your preferred evaluation orientation in your selection of chairperson and committee members.

Formative or Summative?

Is your evaluation intended primarily as a formative evaluation? Will it be used to find better ways of carrying on the project or to plan or improve new programs? Alternatively, is it intended to help make a summative decision such as whether to increase, continue, decrease, or terminate the program? If yours is a basic research study, it is most reasonable to assume a summative stance. Without the decision makers being part of the intended audience, you can't ensure they will use the results formatively.

If formative use is intended, there are a lot of questions to consider answering in your proposal:

- How will the information be made available to those who will use it?
- How will they be helped to understand it?
- What steps will be taken to ensure acceptance and utilization?
- What is the expected effect of the evaluation on the staff of the project?
  On the sponsoring agency?
  On similar projects in the future?
- How are positive effects being enhanced?
- How will the evaluation's conclusions be communicated and disseminated to the participants, the agency, future project participants and directors, and relevant policy makers?

Just how far you and your chairperson and committee will want you to go in answering the above questions is something you should determine in the evaluation's planning stages and include in the proposal. Otherwise, the decision about when to terminate dissertation work is fuzzy, subject to different interpretations, and therefore has potential for conflict.

Decide, first of all, how far you personally want to carry the evaluation. Is it important to you that the results of the dissertation be used in some way? Is it enough that the study was done well and can now take its place with other research on the shelves? Considering that one purpose is as a learning experience for your degree, that is not an inconsequential result, and if you want to stop there, you shouldn't feel guilty about it.

On the other hand, your motivation for undertaking the evaluation study may compel you to consider the project complete only if it has some consequences in the context evaluated. Your committee may feel that is not part of your responsibility, nor theirs, and beyond their interests. Discuss this with them before completing the proposal so that it can appropriately reflect your understanding of what you and your committee agreed to.

Describe the Research Method

Evaluation studies can be conducted using experimental methods, either studying a single group or comparing different programs, perhaps even with control groups. They can use quantitative, qualitative, survey, and historical methods. In addition, certain research designs have typically been found to be more compatible with selected evaluation approaches. Describe the research method used much as you would in any other study, but ensure that congruence with your evaluation orientation is also made clear.

Worksheet 9.2: Review of Proposals for Evaluation Studies will help you ensure you have discussed the important aspects of an evaluation proposal.

SECTION 3: DEVELOPMENT STUDIES (E.G., CURRICULUM, EQUIPMENT, INSTRUMENT, SOFTWARE, AND METHODOLOGY)

Construction of a new curriculum, invention of a new piece of instructional or research equipment, creation of a new measuring instrument, generation of new software, and conception of some new wrinkle in research methods share the characteristic of being development dissertations. Like the emergent philosophical and historical studies discussed in chapter 6, you venture into new ground in such studies, and so incur some risk. If the project doesn't work out, there may not be much to make into a dissertation.

In this part of the chapter, we discuss aspects requiring special attention in such proposals, specifically:

- the problem statement—the need for what is being developed, where it fits in the current context, how this effort differs from past ones, and what path it follows;
- who will be involved besides yourself and what approval or evidence of concurrence of interest you have in hand;
- what is involved in the actual development process and how much of that can now be anticipated and described;
- whether, how, and how thoroughly whatever is developed should be evaluated;
- the work-plan section; and
- protection of the end product—copyright and patent issues.

As previously, these topics constitute the organization of this section.

Review of Proposals for Evaluation Studies

How Well Does My Proposal Reflect the Special Concerns of This Particular Dissertation Approach?

How Well Have I Provided Strong, Detailed Descriptions of . . . ?	Strong	Acceptable	Weak– Improvements Needed	Not Applicable
Purpose of the study (formative, summative . . .) and the program to be evaluated including its political context?				
Primary client and audiences and their role in the proposal development and study?				
Evaluative criteria or goals to be used in judging the program, their source and justification?				
Evaluation orientation to be used and how it will be operationalized procedurally?				
Research methods to be used in the study (qualitative, survey, historical, . . . see relevant Worksheets)?				
Unique reporting requirements (e.g., separate reports to clients, stakeholders, etc.)?				
Ethical concerns and accommodations?				
Study timeline, resources, and management issues?				

Special Emphases in the Problem Statement

Many social science development projects will be following development procedures used in previous projects. It helps to place your contribution in that context. To what extent are you following the same path that others have trod, and where do you diverge?

You are building a new scale for measuring anxiety. How does your conceptual definition of anxiety relate to the previous ones? How are you operationalizing yours differently? Developing more relevant and useful norms? What are the implications of doing so for improving measurement in the field?

You are building a new American history curriculum. How does it relate to the national standards that have recently been established? Some previous curriculum efforts have been backed by substantial foundation grants; what makes you think you can improve on them?

Clearly, one of the major points to stress in a development project is the newness of the approach to be studied and its potential advantages over past efforts. If your different way of measuring, new computer program, or unique method of observing has important consequences, point them out.

Needs Analyses

Along these same lines, indicate the need for whatever you are developing. If you are trying to help a group and a needs survey has been done, cite it. If it hasn't, to ensure that what you have in mind is the answer to expressed needs, consider one. It could be a pilot project or a preliminary phase of the study. The needs survey may seem unnecessary with projects that are a logical extension of the direction the field has been moving. However, such a survey can also turn up previous efforts of which you are unaware that make your study unnecessary or of lesser incremental value. You need to know this before starting.

Sometimes, too, we think that we know the prime need of a group, but a needs survey turns up a different pattern of lacks.

> Lack of a computer program to easily display instructional material may appear to be holding up the field. But needs surveys show most individuals, at least initially, are afraid to install new software. Each new program adds potential conflicts that are likely to crash the computer. As a result of the needs survey, the developer adds code that senses such conflicts in advance and either defuses them or alerts the operator to potential troubles so they can be avoided.

Bauer (1984) has a useful section on needs analysis, and Kaufman (1979) has a book on the subject. Witkin (1994) described the current use of needs assessments in federal programs. See also Romiszowski's (1981) discussion of front-end analysis of instructional problems.

Significance

Development is the means for achieving an end. Stress the consequences of a successful project for achieving its goal. "A new measure of anxiety will lead to better estimates of psychotherapy success and to better diagnoses of mental health problems." How important is it to achieve these goals? Tell them! If it is unlikely that this development will take place if you don't do it, indicate why you think this is true. Include ancillary benefits not central to the major thrust of what is being developed.

You are developing a body-image self-report test. Although your instrument may not be designed as directly applicable to the handicapped, recognizing this is a special problem for them, note how it may hasten the day when they have a useful instrument available. If it is an easy outgrowth of your development, note that as well.

Who Will Be Involved?

Most development projects will involve others—for example, consultants (e.g., subject matter experts for a curriculum project or technical specialists for a new statistical method). Some may be gatekeepers involved in tryout sites for formative and/or summative evaluation. Still others may involve permissions—for example, to use equipment or to build on earlier versions, thus avoiding possible copyright or patent infringement. In all such instances, it is wise to get the approval of the persons involved before completing the proposal. This gives your chairperson and committee greater assurance of the feasibility of the project.

Equally important, however, when you consult these individuals for their approval, you will need to explain the project to them and their role in it. This gives them a chance to have some input into the project before it is "set in cement." It makes them feel as though they are an integral part of the process and gives them some "psychic income" from participating in it. After all, that is likely their only pay. It also indicates that you valued them highly enough to let them in at the beginning rather than as an afterthought.

Where you plan to use institutions as tryout sites, you may need permission from their review board. Having such permission in hand will also help you clear your own institution's review board. Append those permission letters.

Describe the Development Process

Assuming that your project is not breaking new ground in the development process itself, the set of activities involved will likely have been previously established. Write a description of the procedure in a straightforward, logical manner; a set of sequential steps is usually easiest to follow and to explain.

In many projects of this type, if a particular development path is followed, success is ensured. All that has been lacking is the time and energy and/or someone with the skills and motivation to do the job. In others, the chances of success may be less certain. Indicate the likelihood of success that you can follow the development process that has been laid out and that it will arrive at the expected product. Be sure to provide the basis for your estimate.

Work Plan

Where the steps follow the paths of previous development studies, work plans can be charted in detail and are often turned to first as a quick way of understanding the study. Hence their special importance in development studies. Inclusion of a well-laid-out work plan that gives every indication it will do the job fills the reader with confidence that you know what you are doing. Along the same lines, the demands of a particular product may require divergence from the typical development process and hence introduce some uncertainty about how completely the plan can be charted. Again, your overt recognition of this fact in the proposal indicates your competence.

Whether and How Thoroughly to Evaluate the Product

Most dissertation advisors want you not only to do the development work, but also to show that you did indeed create a satisfactory product. This usually means a tryout, demonstration, and/or evaluation. In some instances, your committee will decide that the development work is enough for the dissertation and deem a trial as above and beyond what is reasonable to expect of a graduate student. This is more likely if your dissertation doesn't reach the product stage but is a formative step in the development process intended to guide next steps or to remedy problems in past work.

If your proposal includes an evaluation, it may best be described as a second phase separate from, and following, development. Suggestions for evaluation proposals in the previous section of this chapter are relevant to such a second phase.

Protection of Your End Product

Most institutions allow you to copyright your dissertation and publish it as you wish. Your abstract will appear in *Dissertation Abstracts International,* and interested persons can obtain the full manuscript from the same organization. In addition, most institutions encourage adaptation for publication in journal or book form.

There is a tradition that dissertations are intended to be a contribution to the field. Since they are done with faculty help and supervision, it may be difficult to establish sole authorship. Certainly, you will want to acknowledge intellectual debts in the dissertation. But are you using an institution's facilities? Their equipment? Are you on their payroll, perhaps as a graduate assistant? In some other way, are you in a position where someone may claim that the development process is a partial result of his or her contributions? It may be legally possible that the institution can seek partial ownership and/or royalties if you market your end product.

If you are at all concerned about protecting your rights, determine the implications of your institution's copyright, patent, and publication policy for ownership and for royalties. The university's policy may have provisions that uniquely apply to dissertations. Be sure you can accept that policy before development gets under way. If necessary, negotiate a waiver in writing with those who have the power to commit the institution and include a copy in your proposal. If you need help, consult a specialist in intellectual property law.

Do not let this discussion make you paranoid! The social sciences are typically free of such problems. Further, most institutions are generous with respect to ownership of intellectual property; they want to encourage creativity. Though extremely rare, it seemed important to call attention to what can become a concern.

Proposals for development dissertations may look considerably different from more conventional dissertations. Use Worksheet 9.3: Review of Proposals for Development Studies to ensure you have not omitted any important components.

SECTION 4: DEMONSTRATION AND ACTION RESEARCH STUDIES

Demonstration and action projects are similar in that they both involve field locations for their work and are intended to solve one or more practical (in contrast to theoretical) problems. They differ in that the focus in demonstrations is on showing a problem solution, and, in action projects, on working with those in the field to ameliorate a problem or, if possible, find a solution.

In the case of demonstration projects, you already have a presumed answer to a problem, and the intent is to demonstrate its effectiveness in such a convincing way that others will be persuaded of its efficacy and adopt it. In the case of action studies, you may or may not initially have a possible solution in mind; the focus is on working with those in a situation to find a way to improve it or solve the problem in that particular context.

Allowing demonstration and action projects to satisfy dissertation requirements is likely unique to professional schools. Where a graduate school or college controls graduate degrees, such studies may be acceptable only for a professional degree—an Ed.D. or Psy.D., not a Ph.D. Further, because they are not what is usually considered research, even many professional schools will not accept them. Check with your advisor to determine whether such a study is acceptable as a dissertation for your program.

We discuss demonstration projects first, and then, because they have similarities, add to it for action research projects.

Review of Proposals for Development Studies

How Well Does My Proposal Reflect the Special Concerns of This Particular Dissertation Approach?

How Well Have I Provided Strong, Detailed Descriptions of . . . ?	Strong	Acceptable	Weak– Improvements Needed	Not Applicable
Need for the new development including its significant benefits and relation to prior development work?				
Work plan charting the actual process of development including who will be involved?				
Plans for an evaluation (See e.g., Worksheet 9.2) of the development product?				
Agreements concerning copyright, patents, and royalties of any commercialization of the development product?				
Ethical concerns and accommodations?				
Study timeline, resources, and management issues?				

Demonstration Projects

Demonstration projects show that something works and works well enough to achieve some result. For instance, the new counseling center is expected to reduce teenage suicides by 50 percent. It is assumed that such a result would cause it to be copied by other institutions in the counseling communication network. A proposal begins with a description of what is to be done together with its rationale. This leads into how it is to be done, for whom, and when. Finally, you may or may not have to demonstrate evidence of its effectiveness—an evaluation. Therefore, important aspects of these proposals include:

- the problem statement and a discussion of the project's typicality and generality,
- a description of what is to be demonstrated and the process of getting it applied,
- an evaluation, if relevant,
- possible plans for dissemination, if relevant, and
- the nature of the dissertation write-up.

These topics form the basis for discussing demonstration proposals. Note that you are constructing a chain of reasoning, much as was described in chapter 3. The chain may be cut short if your committee considers installing the intervention in one or more settings enough for a dissertation. If they require evaluating its success and are concerned with its generality, then the whole chain of reasoning is involved.

Problem Statement

The problem statement should include:

- the nature and extent of the problem,
- what you will demonstrate and why it might be a solution,
- what the history has been of past efforts, and
- the progress that your project hopes to make in attacking, ameliorating, or solving the problem.

Demonstration projects usually attack a general problem with greater significance than its immediate application. Therefore, the proposal's problem discussion can follow the advice of chapter 3 in describing its nature, scope, and significance. To this, you will want to add a very general description of what is to be demonstrated (you do it again in detail later in the proposal), what evidence there is of a successful past track record for what you plan to demonstrate, how that evidence generalizes to your effort, and evidence of your own capabilities for carrying out the demonstration.

In some instances, the need for action and the readiness to adopt potential solutions are obvious and need not be documented. Where they are not obvious, and especially where readiness to participate is a question, a needs analysis can be important. The needs analysis shows both that the problem exists and that it is recognized as a situation in need of change by those whose cooperation will be required to change it. Such a survey may persuasively raise awareness of a problem, increase readiness to change, and ease adoption. It can be done as part of a pilot of the dissertation or as part of the demonstration. If the former, the results can be cited in the proposal. Facilitate understanding of analysis results by embedding statistics or other "hard" evidence in typical stories of persons affected; make the "facts" come alive, and include relevant quotations from stakeholders. Append letters of support from officials whose cooperation would be needed to bring change about. For references on needs analysis, see the section devoted to it in "Development Studies," the previous section of this chapter.

The literature survey for demonstrations usually includes research evidence that supports whatever basis exists for presuming the intervention might be effective and evidence of previous instances of use. This takes one into the realm of "fugitive literature," that is, literature not usually indexed or published in the major journals. Sources include government reports, dissertations, ERIC, professional association publications and convention programs, and sometimes organizations especially established to facilitate the spread of a certain program. Don't forget to also query other faculty, not just those on your committee.

Government reports and ERIC are both accessible through indexes and the Web. Convention programs are increasingly online at the professional association's Web site. Use various search engines to search the Web; each picks up different sites. School system Web sites may contain mention of the intervention that can then be followed up by e-mail or letter. The Web has made the accessibility of "fugitive" sources greater than ever.

If you have relevant experience that would contribute to your ability to do the demonstration, cite it. Your experience with individuals at the site, your connections to that staff, prior evidence of your personal concern with the problem, and prior experience with what is to be demonstrated are all examples of evidence that should be cited.

Indicate what progress you hope to achieve through the demonstration. This gives an idea of the scope of the project and provides a reasonable termination point toward which you can strive. It also makes clear whether evaluation and dissemination are or are not to be part of your effort.

Finally, summarize this into a statement of why you think whatever is to be demonstrated is applicable to the situation in which you propose to work, what arguments you can marshal for why it should succeed there, and why succeeding there might have some significance for its application elsewhere.

The What and How of the Demonstration

Although you have described what you hope to demonstrate in general terms, a section is required where you describe in detail the process of application to the chosen situation. The discussion of chapter 3 is useful in this regard. Here you are into the design phase of the chain of reasoning and will want to cover all six rings at that level. However, the "Comparison and Contrast—The Basis for Sensing Attributes and Changes" ring is relevant only if you plan to evaluate the results. Elimination of alternative explanations is of concern if you are interested in why the intervention works, rather than simply that it does. Knowing "why" gives information regarding what to change to make improvements. Describe the scope of the project and make the design section consistent with what you promised in previous sections.

Evaluation

The termination point for a demonstration is fuzzy unless agreed upon in advance. For this reason, whether an evaluation will be required should be noted early in the proposal, usually in the problem statement. Some chairpersons and committees will consider getting the intervention applied as accomplishment enough for a dissertation. Others may require an evaluation to determine if it is effective enough that others will want to copy it.

If providing convincing dissemination is a goal, it will be facilitated by a solid, unbiased evaluation. Such evaluations are best done as an integrally planned part of the project, not as an afterthought. Consider the suggestions in this chapter's discussion of evaluation proposals. They give perspective on the problems likely to be encountered by the demonstration proposal writer who must include an evaluation.

If an independent third party can gather and interpret the evaluation data, the evidence may be more compelling. Whereas you and your client may have an interest in gathering positive data, an outside evaluator is less suspect. Bring the evaluator into the proposal writing process as soon as you have identified her and ask her to participate in the writing process. Not only will that improve the evaluation part of the proposal, but typically, you'll also find the evaluator helpful in the formulation of the proposal itself. Above all, resist the tendency to do the whole proposal and then call up someone and ask her to write a few paragraphs regarding the evaluation that you would like her to conduct.

Dissemination

Dissemination efforts are less likely to be considered an appropriate part of a dissertation than evaluation. Nevertheless, because demonstration projects are to show others what can be done, the generalizability of your demonstration should be indicated. You probably have done so in previous sections, but if not, make sure your proposal has answered such questions as: Why is yours a good site for the demonstration? In what way is your site typical of those to which transfer is intended? Would installation problems be the same? Different? In what ways? Help reviewers see the generalizable aspects.

If dissemination is part of your dissertation's scope, here are some things to consider. Dissemination requires defining one's target group and determining how best to reach it. Most demonstration projects fail to define this group, to set up a means for determining its needs in relation to the demonstration, and to show how the demonstration will relate to those needs. Further, they often fail to consider how the target group's adoption decisions are part of the dissemination problem. For instance, if the intervention involves considerable expense, it is unlikely that users alone could make the decision; therefore, dissemination must involve the critical portions of the decision-making structure—members of the administration and possibly board members or trustees.

Further, it must reach these people in ways that are realistic in view of their workload and possible interest in the intervention. Answer such questions as the following: If people are expected to visit your site, is it easily accessible to those who are the dissemination targets? Who will be invited? An open house? Individual tours? If visits are not involved, how will the results of the demonstration be convincingly portrayed to the target audiences? Newsletters? Films? An evaluation? How will you facilitate transfer? Will you send staff to other institutions to assist? Invite regular consultation?

The Nature of the Dissertation Write-Up

Of what will the writing of the dissertation itself consist? A narrative of what you did? The demonstration as seen by staff? By other stakeholders? Mainly the evaluation and lessons learned? What you would do differently next time? The nature of what the final dissertation report itself should include will determine what data you gather as the demonstration progresses. This must be part of the proposal and agreed upon in advance. Otherwise, opportunities for data gathering will be lost. As indicated earlier, a dissertation can be whatever the chairperson and committee agree it should be. Get agreement on what their definition is for your demonstration.

Use Worksheet 9.4: Review of Proposals for Demonstration Studies to double-check that you have covered the special aspects of this kind of dissertation.

Action Research Projects

Action research studies range widely in nature. On the one hand, one may do what might be considered a research project in a field setting with the intent of having some impact in that setting, much as a conventional evaluation is intended to do.

At the other extreme, the project may be a collaborative one in which the graduate student acts as advisor. He is helping others to learn how to do the study, learning with them how best to gather relevant data and interpret it. He

Review of Proposals for Demonstration Studies

How Well Does My Proposal Reflect the Special Concerns of This Particular Dissertation Approach?

How Well Have I Provided Strong, Detailed Descriptions of . . . ?	Strong	Acceptable	Weak–Improvements Needed	Not Applicable
Problem statement describing the demonstration's importance and potential impact on the problem of concern?				
Procedural details of what is to be demonstrated and how the demonstration will be accomplished?				
Plans for an evaluation if one is called for (See e.g., Worksheet 9.2)?				
Plans for dissemination, if relevant, including target audience needs, resources, and adoption patterns?				
Nature of the demonstration project write-up as a dissertation report?				
Ethical concerns and accommodations?				
Study timeline, resources, and management issues?				

is sharing with them his knowledge, but encouraging their comments and contributions and helping to form them into an integral part of the project. He is seeking with them the best interpretation of the data to form some basis for further action. Through all this, he is particularly sensitive to ensuring that all those who wish to be included find an appropriate role in the activity—he seeks to give voice to the powerless. Yet, he ensures the project has some momentum of its own and keeps moving forward in directions that are mutually determined by the participants. For example, this is the stance of many evaluators in the newer collaborative, participatory, and empowerment forms of evaluation. And of course, there are an infinite number of positions between these two extremes of "doing to" and "doing with." Your proposal will usually bear the characteristics of whichever extreme is closest.

Clearly, proposals from these two extremes will be quite different. That of the "doing to" type will be closer to a conventional evaluation type of proposal. But it will have the added emphasis of moving beyond some kind of conclusion from the data into some kind of action steps taken by those at whom the research is aimed. Just how that will be achieved without their participation will be of considerable importance to discuss in some detail. Include the basis for your belief that what you propose will be feasible and have the intended consequences.

In "doing with" proposals, you will want to lay the groundwork for understanding from what philosophical position you are undertaking the study—e.g., the empowerment of those with whom you will be working. This should probably involve reference to the literature that discusses your position and perhaps to examples of similar work.

Problem Statement

Like other emergent proposals, you don't go in as a blank slate to see what will happen. You choose the site for some reason. You enter it because you have something to offer. You have in mind, if not one solution, a variety of possibilities. So you have much grist for the problem-section mill. Some of the suggestions in the problem section of demonstrations above may be relevant here.

Particularly relevant is the discussion of dissertation termination. If demonstrations have fuzzy end points, those of collaborative action programs can be utterly amorphous. To avoid disagreements with your chairperson and/or committee regarding how much is enough, include the best statement possible regarding when you will stop. *Even if you think everyone would agree, remember to update your committee in writing as conditions change.* The latter is very important and, in the heat of activity, often overlooked. You may decide the end has come, only to find your decision questioned and end up contemplating an ABD rather than a doctorate. *Regularly update!*

Describe the What and How of the Project

Assuming it is a collaborative enterprise, not one you have preplanned, describe what you will do to start the project, where and what actions this involves, and, perhaps, what you hope to accomplish. These may be in general terms, so as not to violate the spirit with which this research is undertaken. Similarly, anticipate what you might do in the situation and explore some alternative "what ifs." Give your committee as much tangible hope as is reasonable that something positive may arise from your activities.

Like demonstration projects, a needs analysis may be very helpful in an action research project, particularly if the group you will be working with is divided in terms of which direction to take. It can help establish priority for certain directions over others; this may unify the group's sense of purpose. But in contrast to a demonstration project, where the needs analysis is likely conducted by the researcher, here it will more likely be developed collaboratively with those in the field. Anticipate this in the proposal if you think it a likely possibility.

Evaluation

As with demonstrations, evaluation may or may not be a part of the project. Whether it is or not will depend on several factors. If the project is successful, and the results are obvious, there may be no need for a formal evaluation. If it is not obviously successful, it is not inconceivable that you will be asked to add an evaluation to your end point. You may want to discuss that eventuality with your committee before reaching this point. If possible, get everyone to agree regarding what is required in your dissertation. A formative evaluation could help determine where it went wrong. That may help salvage the project. Where results seem equivocal, or there are many outcomes and it is difficult to get an overall assessment, evaluations may provide a basis for showing what is working and what isn't so the group can move forward from that point.

You may want to indicate how you would help the group conduct such an assessment. Then, when you get to that point in the project, you will have given some thought to how you may be most helpful in guiding the group through it.

Dissemination

In action projects, your intent is usually to find a solution for *this* group in *this* situation. Unlike demonstrations, one is not particularly concerned with generality and typicality, or with dissemination. This is an application study in which the utility of local findings is of greatest importance (see chapter 2). If your results appeal to others, so much the better, but that is not usually the prime goal of the project. On the other hand, your committee may be more interested in gaining what knowledge they can from the project. They will likely ask you to speculate on the implications of what you have done for other situations and how atypical or typical yours was. Again, determine early if your chairperson and committee want this included. Although it may be outside your focus of attention, it may be more central to theirs.

The Nature of the Dissertation Write-Up

Action projects have the same problem as demonstrations in terms of what to include in writing the final dissertation document itself. Further, as is clear from the previous paragraph, although your main interest and motivation center is the situation you worked in, your chairperson and committee's are more likely to be in what was learned that could apply elsewhere. As with demonstration projects, make clear in the proposal what you intend to include in your writing so that discrepancies in expectations between you and the faculty, and the faculty with each other, can be ironed out before the project is started.

As a starting point in the development of your action research proposal, the materials of the Grantsmanship Center (http://www.tgci.com [accessed February 12, 2004]) are oriented toward action projects for nonprofit organizations and are excellent. See especially their product *Program Planning and Proposal Writing*.

Finally, once you have a draft of your proposal, Worksheet 9.5: Review of Proposals for Action Research Studies will help you check that you have attended to the special aspects of action research dissertations.

Review of Proposals for Action Research Studies

How Well Does My Proposal Reflect the Special Concerns of This Particular Dissertation Approach?

How Well Have I Provided Strong, Detailed Descriptions of . . . ?	Strong	Acceptable	Weak– Improvements Needed	Not Applicable
Problem statement describing the concerns being addressed and why action research is an appropriate approach?				
Procedural details of how the action research will be accomplished including anticipated collaborative relationships and emergent procedures?				
Plans for an evaluation if one is called for (See e.g., Worksheet 9.2)?				
Decision rules for "completion" of the study as a dissertation requirement?				
Nature of the action research write-up as a dissertation report?				
Ethical concerns and accommodations?				
Study timeline, resources, and management issues?				

PART FOUR

Additional Considerations

This section contains a single, but important, chapter on moving ahead in the preparation of your proposal—from getting started to getting your proposal accepted.

CHAPTER 10

Other Things to Consider

CHAPTER CONTENTS

WHAT IF THIS BOOK'S ADVICE AND THAT OF MY COMMITTEE DIFFER?

No question, follow your committee's advice—a dissertation is what your chairperson and committee say it is! That doesn't mean you can't disagree and, where you are convinced you are right, do your best to try to persuade them. And while we authors provide our best advice, it is just that. What it eventually comes down to is that you must make the final decisions, and the people you are working with make the final judgments about whether your decisions are acceptable to them.

Two places where some faculty may differ from what is suggested here are the literature review and the statement of hypotheses in quantitative studies.

Literature Review

Faculties tend to split along two lines in advising how to do the literature review; they either want:

    1. a very thorough review of your dissertation field's literature, including all of the aspects involved, or

    2. a highly selective review of such literature as bears directly on what

you plan to do, critiquing that literature and showing its relation to your study.

Why the difference? The first represents the traditional approach to the dissertation. The faculty want to be sure that you have read and digested all literature that is relevant to your study, including a thorough understanding of each of its separate aspects. Writing such a review will help you understand the field broadly, giving you perspective on where your study fits. It makes for a lot of reading, but it can be worth it as a way of ensuring you have a grasp of your area.

The problem with this argument is that the format in which they ask you to write it up, like the traditional dissertation format itself, is something of an anachronism. Only if you write for one of the review journals or annual review volumes will you use such a format, and even then, it must to be more targeted and more critical of flaws and weaknesses. Further, the tendency in traditional reviews is to emphasize coverage, and those few studies that contribute to your research tend to get buried with the rest.

As indicated earlier, we advocate the second position, limiting the review to those references bearing on the problem in hand, commenting on their quality, showing how they fit together, how they advance theory, and how they bear on your study. But if your committee wants the extended literature review, do it! If they agree to let you use the article format, simply put the long review in the dissertation's appendix. You may be able to edit it for publication if you prepare it so it will fit the style of the journal to which you plan to submit.

Statement of Hypotheses

Another place where the advice of this book and that of your committee may diverge is the statement of hypotheses in a quantitative study. Some advisors will insist that the hypotheses be stated as null hypotheses. Such hypotheses are part of statistical logic. Include them if you are required to do so. But also include directional hypotheses if reasonable predictions can be made—the most precise hypotheses that prior knowledge allows.

An astronomer can ask you to look at a certain point in the sky at a given time and know that you will see three stars in the shape of a cross. He tells you the magnitude of the stars, that some are actually galaxies, etc. This impressive performance indicates a strong base of knowledge.

The social sciences aren't there yet; to get there we must stretch to make and confirm the most precise hypotheses that one's understanding of phenomena permit. This means not only anticipating a difference between groups, but hypothesizing which group will be superior, the size of the relationship of treatment to effect, the shape of that relationship in relation to other variables (e.g., class size), how long it will last and how it will decay, etc. The more we can hypothesize about the phenomena, the greater our understanding if the prediction is borne out. If it is disconfirmed, perhaps we can use our data to find the basis for a more precise prediction in the next research.

I'M HAVING TROUBLE GETTING STARTED, WHAT DO I DO?

Getting started is often a serious hurdle. The pressure of other duties often leads to procrastination and to giving proposal preparation too low a priority. Time management specialists agree that it is critical to give "getting started" your highest time priority! Set aside a time period long enough to get something done, and don't let anything else interfere. Find a place where you can hide and won't be distracted—NOT where you typically work and will be surrounded by reminders of other demands. Then spend that time writing!

Write what you know about your dissertation topic even if you haven't formulated your problem. Stay with it for the whole time you have set aside, writing even when you don't think you are getting anywhere. You'll be surprised. Writing organizes your thoughts and helps you understand what you know and don't know. It may take several such sessions, but each will put you closer to your goal; you'll notice the progress, and nothing is more encouraging. Once you get a draft, revising is easier.

IS THERE ENOUGH DETAIL?

Proposal writing is a fine balance. You should describe the study in sufficient detail that any reviewer will be convinced both that the problem is worth investigation and that you have the ability to handle it. It is not necessary, however, to give so much detail that every single possibility is explored and all flexibility eliminated. Half the excitement of doing research is in exploration. The secret of success is to find the appropriate balance.

The balance between expected detail and ambiguity shifts toward detail as the nature of the project involves less exploration and more known territory. It shifts toward detail for projects that, using familiar techniques, engineer a new curriculum or tool. It shifts still more toward detail for demonstration or dissemination projects.

When deciding how much detail to give, it is usually better to include important information than to omit it. Putting it in an appendix permits a reviewer to have on hand such information as she may need. Ask your chairperson for two or three well-written proposals by former students—how much detail did they include?

IS THE HASTY READER SIGNALED TO CRITICALLY IMPORTANT PROPOSAL PARTS?

It is always safest to assume that your proposal might have to be reviewed under time pressures or where there are distractions (reading on weekends when the children, dog, or spouse want attention, for example). The reading load of faculty varies, in part with the rhythm of the school calendar. Once classes are under way and before midsemester exams is probably the best time to present your proposal.

Good writing, like good acting, uses nonverbal gestures:

- Use punctuation, underlining, spacing, and paragraphing to command the reader's eye.
- Use diagrams, flowcharts, tables, and other graphic devices to present overviews of content, to put details in perspective, to provide a succinct summary of important aspects, and to provide a road map of the important concepts and their relationships.
- Signal upcoming content with topic sentences at the beginning of paragraphs.
- Try skimming your proposal, reading it very rapidly, jumping from topic sentence to topic sentence. Does it convey what you intend?

Be careful, however, to avoid jazzing the copy with jargon or with more gesture than sense. Remember that research is essentially a scholarly activity.

The reader should be able to easily find essential substance within certain parts of the proposal. For example, place a succinct statement of the purpose of the research in an obvious position in the problem section. Similarly, list objectives in order of importance in the objectives section. The spiral pattern of newspaper writing is a good one, starting each new section with a summary of the essentials, then follow it with development of the detail.

The initial emphasis should be on legibility, lucidity, and clarity of presentation. Then make the proposal look as though it wanted to be read! Use white space to lighten the text and to surround points that you want to stand out. Avoid solid, massive blocks that repel rather than invite reading. And don't forget a succinct abstract and well-designed table of contents to guide the reader through the proposal.

HOW SHALL I SHOW MY COMPETENCE?

Your chairperson and committee want you to succeed. But unless they know you well, they may need evidence that you have the competence to undertake what you propose. There are several places in the proposal where you have a special opportunity to show your skills:

- The conceptualization of your problem is the first of these. Your ability to conceptualize your problem in a framework that places it in a position of importance in its domain is the first sign that you have a good grasp of the field and an understanding of what you intend to do in it.
- Your handling of the review of the literature is the second place. Your ability shows when you present your project in appropriate perspective

in relation to the other relevant work. Your capacity to master others' work, appropriately critique it, and show how your study will not repeat their mistakes but will move beyond them all indicate you are on top of your problem. If you are also able to include as yet unpublished work, it shows you are well connected with the "invisible college" of researchers already working on your problem, a very positive sign.

- Your ability shows when you present a study design and procedure that appropriately eliminates alternative explanations of the relationship you wish to demonstrate, that explicitly recognizes those explanations that were not eliminated, and that tells why a compromise was developed and the basis for it.

Take pride in your work; submit drafts that reflect well on your talents and effort. Don't be backward about sharing your ideas. The encouragement and excitement of a lively interchange on ideas of interest and importance to you can go a long way in keeping you motivated and working on your proposal. Again, it is a matter of balance.

WHEN SHALL I GET MY CHAIRPERSON'S REACTION TO A DRAFT?

When to show your draft to your advisor or dissertation chairperson depends, in part, on your mutual relationship. Some advisors will want to see your very first stirrings of an idea and interact with you from that point on. Still others will want you to work on their research and either plant an idea, give you a part of their research, or ask you to find a part with which you want to work. Most of them will want to see your ideas early to ensure compatibility with the larger project. Still others will prefer to see your ideas when they are past the rough draft stage and are solid enough to withstand reaction and critique.

In part, it also depends on how much you want the ideas to be your own rather than the advisor's. You may feel the dissertation is a test of your ability; you may want it to be an original piece of your own work. The earlier you show it to an advisor, the more input she is likely to have and the less you may feel it is your own. The further along it is when you test the waters with it, the more you are likely to feel it is really "your baby." That possessive feeling can be important to the commitment necessary to see the dissertation through to the very end.

Finally, remember not only are you building a relationship with your chairperson and committee in terms of your dissertation, but you are also creating a lasting impression in persons from whom you will later want to request recommendations and, perhaps, help in job placement.

Forming a group with other individuals who are also working on their dissertations can be very helpful in many ways—clueing you in on what to expect from certain faculty, helping you move on when you get stuck or disheartened, and, most of all, giving you perspective on the process. It is in this latter role that the group can help when you try out your drafts on them; they'll help you realize when the proposal is ready.

For these and other reasons, once you have a rough draft, at least consider holding on to it for a bit. At a minimum, if time allows, put the proposal aside long enough for your ardor for your own words to have cooled. If possible, wait until you can gain a fresh perspective on it. You'll be surprised at what you see!

A FINAL REVIEW

Before sharing a draft of your proposal with your chairperson, give it a final review. If you use the worksheets provided in the prior chapters, you can check how well the proposal fulfills the chain of reasoning information requirements discussed in chapter 3. You might also want to use Worksheet 10.1: Checklist of Sections of a Dissertation Proposal, provided below, which suggests a comprehensive structure with headings and content that covers many, indeed most, dissertation proposals.

Finally, congratulations on having a draft of your dissertation proposal ready for review. Undoubtedly, many revisions and alterations to your study plans lay ahead, but writing the first draft is always the most difficult part. You are well on your way to a carefully thought through and important dissertation study!

We wish you the very best! Good luck.

Checklist of Sections of a Dissertation Proposal

Note: Some of these checklist items may not be required or typical at your institution, and some may not fit what you propose to do; the list is very broadly drawn to try to anticipate the variety of items that might be relevant. Don't assume that because it is listed, you must have such a section. Include only those that are appropriate, as well as those likely to be expected at your institution. If you've looked at the proposals of others who have gone before you, you'll quickly know which they are.

INTRODUCTORY MATERIAL

☐ **Cover Page**: Cover Page or Approval Sheet if required for submission of proposal, or to record acceptance and approval of proposal.

☐ **Title**: Concise, jargon-free, descriptive title of proposed study that communicates clearly to the nonspecialist reader and serves as an accurate index to your work for information systems such as *Dissertation Abstracts International*.

☐ **Abstract**: Abstract succinctly summarizing problem and phenomena of interest, method of proposed study, and study significance based on anticipated results.

☐ **Table of Contents**: Table of Contents of dissertation proposal, including lists of tables and figures if appropriate.

☐ **Acknowledgments**: As a "thank you," a statement recognizing important assistance and support provided during the preparation of the proposal.

PROBLEM STATEMENT

☐ **General Problem**: Description of general problem and relevant context (e.g., social, historical, theoretical background). The *what*, broadly described.

☐ **Study Focus**: Description of nature and importance of specific phenomena of interest. The *what*, in terms of specifics to be studied.

□ **Study Purpose**: Description and justification of study purpose and rationale. The *why*, in terms of study goals or intents.

□ **Study Importance**: Statement of the importance of likely study results, e.g., theoretical, social, or practical significance of the study. The *why*, in terms of possible beneficial consequences of the study.

□ **Inquiry Framework**: Presentation of theoretical, technical, or practical framework within which the study has meaning (e.g., experimentation, qualitative-ethnographic, etc.). The *how—conceptually*. This leads to an appropriate conceptual basis for the study.

□ **Inquiry Statement**: Explanation of phenomena to be described, issues to be examined, questions to be answered, hypotheses to be tested, theories to be investigated, interventions or treatments to be compared, causes to be assessed, or models to be developed. The *how—procedurally*. This leads to appropriate methods choices.

□ **Study Boundaries**: Statement of study boundaries, presuppositions, trade-offs, and limitations, including what the study will *not* do.

□ **Terms**: Definition of key terms, constructs, technical language, and abbreviations used in the proposal that readers might not be expected to know.

□ **Summary**: Summary of problem statement and transition to literature review.

LITERATURE REVIEW

This section may become a complete review, much as it will appear in the final dissertation document, or it may be a progress report which covers enough of the literature to justify proceeding with the investigation as planned. Which it becomes depends on the expectations of your chairperson, committee, and institution.

□ **Overview**: General description of available, relevant substantive and methodological literature.

□ **Selection Process**: Statement and justification of procedures for identifying and selecting relevant literature, including databases consulted, review criteria, and selection criteria.

□ **Review Process**: Description and justification of literature review procedures, e.g., narrative analysis or meta-analysis procedures and/or use of qualitative computer software for analysis.

□ **Literature Quality**: Assessment of scope, relevance, and methodological quality of literature reviewed.

□ **Major Works**: Presentation and critical analysis of the most significant empirical, theoretical, and practical writings, indicating relevance to the proposed study.

□ **Substantive Findings**: Summary of major findings concerning the phenomena of interest, including what is known, what is not known, and what needs to be known about the phenomena.

☐ **Methodological Findings**: Summary of major findings concerning the methods chosen, including how others have studied the phenomena, what methods have been used, what has worked, what has not worked, and what adaptations need to be adopted or developed.

☐ **Implications**: Summary of implications from the literature review (including theoretical positions and their support, empirical evidence, policy statements, and practical knowledge and experience) for (a) understanding the phenomena of interest, and (b) studying the phenomena of interest.

☐ **Contributions**: Brief statement of the contributions that the proposed dissertation study will make to the literature on (a) understanding the phenomena of interest, and (b) studying the phenomena of interest.

☐ **Summary**: Summary of literature review and transition to Method Statement.

METHOD STATEMENT

☐ **Research Approach**: Statement and justification of general study approach and general study design (case study, experiment, evaluation, development project).

☐ **Study Design**: Description and justification of study design and basic procedures, including setting characteristics, use of controls or comparisons, interventions, debriefings, elimination of alternative explanations, etc.

☐ **Interventions/Treatments**: Description of any interventions or treatments to be used, including their design, development, testing, and validation.

☐ **Data Collection**: Description and justification of data collection procedures, including information sources, study populations, sampling procedures, data collection activities and timelines, data storage, and quality control.

☐ **Instrumentation**: Description and justification of instrumentation selection, development, testing, quality (e.g., reliability, validity), and protocols, including sample instrumentation, sample directions to participants, sample participation consent forms, and sample instructions to train others collecting data (samples may be included as appendices).

☐ **Data Analysis**: Description and justification of data analysis and interpretation procedures, including analysis software, sample data displays, interpretation procedures, quality control procedures, and nature of expected results.

☐ **Work Plan**: Management plan with timeline of major study activities, interim reports or products, key field events, names of other individuals involved in study procedures (e.g., expert reviewers, data collection staff, data analysis support), etc.

☐ **Resources**: Description of resources needed, including financial support (study budget), laboratory equipment, facilities, computer technology (software, hardware, data bases, etc.), field access, permissions, expertise, library collections, time, etc.

☐ **Pilot Studies**: Description of the purpose, design, and results (if already completed) of pilot studies, including implications for modifications to study procedures.

☐ **Limitations**: Overall summary of study method including study limitations, alternatives considered, and justification for choices made.

APPENDIX

☐ **References**: List of references cited in the proposal.

☐ **Bibliography**: List, possibly annotated, of related reading on phenomena of interest, prior research, or study methods.

☐ **Dissertation Outline**: Annotated outline of final dissertation report, especially if it will not employ a conventional format.

☐ **Sample Instruments**: Copies of instruments unfamiliar to the committee, sample items of instruments to be constructed.

☐ **Amplification of Procedures**: Directions to be read or spoken to participants, details of software, qualitative or statistical procedures unfamiliar to the committee, etc.

☐ **Copies of Key Documents**: For those unusual cases where there are documents absolutely critical to your presentation that committees members are not familiar with and are unlikely to otherwise see, you may wish to include them in the appendix.

☐ **Institutional Review Board Clearances**: Human Subjects Review application and/or approval notification; Animal Subjects Review application and/or approval notification.

☐ **Letters**: Copies of letters confirming participant or collaborator cooperation, assuring field access, documenting approval to conduct treatments or interventions, guaranteeing commitment of resources, verifying permission to use copyright materials, etc.

☐ **Support Requests**: Copies of grant or financial support applications, anticipated required expertise not yet located (e.g. computer or statistical consultants), etc.

☐ **Résumé**: Copy of the student's professional résumé or curriculum vita.

PART FIVE

Annotated Proposals

This section contains three annotated examples of former student dissertation proposals, each differing by method and topic. These proposals were successful proposals that served as the basis of a dissertation. Because of the limitations of space, some parts have been omitted from some proposals, but the main parts needed for instructional purposes are reproduced. Because these were successful proposals, certain errors could not be illustrated unless the proposals were altered. Therefore, in some instances the material has been modified to illustrate particular errors in proposal preparation. Each proposal is used with the kind permission of the author. Where errors were introduced, the author agreed the proposal could be modified for instructional purposes.

Chapter 11 is an example of a dissertation proposal using qualitative methods, *The Change Process in Men Who Batter Women,* by Bill Warters.

Chapter 12 has a quantitative methods proposal, *A Study of the Effectiveness of Concept Mapping in Improving Problem Solving,* by Katherine L. Beissner.

Chapter 13 is a mixed methods-study example, *Self-Directed Learning's Impact on MBA Students and Their Attitudes Toward Personal Development,* by Thomas D. Phelan. This last example includes not only our annotations, as do the first two examples, but also comments by other doctoral students learning to develop their own proposals. These students make excellent observations about the strengths and weaknesses of this proposal—a skill you, too, can develop by studying these three examples carefully.

CHAPTER 11

An Annotated Dissertation Proposal Using Qualitative Methods

Approval of the "open-ended hunting licenses" requested by many qualitative proposals comes easily neither to dissertation committees nor to funders. Avoiding such a request is an early problem of qualitative researchers. This proposal by Bill Warters does so. While Warters makes it clear that he is open to what will be found, he has targeted the groups from whom to collect data (batterers of women who have been through treatment programs and the staffs of those programs), what he wishes to talk to them about (the perceptions of batterers of their problem and of treatment staff of the batterers), and where he anticipates there is a problem (the incongruity in perceptions of the two groups).

Warters's problem may seem more structured from the outset than many qualitative dissertation proposals but that is only because he has done more work on the problem before formulating his proposal. Pilot work solves the "hunting license" problem, for as the piloting proceeds, one can usually shape the study into a structured form that becomes the proposal's basis—the focus of activity becomes clear and the choice of method, persons, and places of data collection all fall into place. Those may indeed change as the study proceeds; indeed, they often do (just as, if something of greater interest appears, they might have with Warters's study—targeted as it was). Such changes occur regardless of method. But the proposal provides grounds for agreement between doctoral committee and student as to how to proceed and what to expect, as best that can be anticipated.

Unless obliged to by a funder's form or an institution's requirements, writers of qualitative proposals are much less likely to follow a common format or structure. But one can provide a checklist of aspects that should be included in all such proposals:[1]

1. An initial focus or question that provides boundaries for your inquiry and a rationale for doing the study that includes:

1. Adapted from Egon Guba (undated), *Essential elements in a naturalistic thesis proposal,* unpublished manuscript, Indiana University, Bloomington.

2. who will be studied and what they represent and what contexts will be studied and what they represent,

3. the approach used such as symbolic interactionism, ethnography, etc.,

4. your qualifications and experience with this approach,

5. the methods of data collection,

6. the methods of data analysis, and

7. anticipated ethical problems and how they will be handled.

Comments in italic below will note how these aspects are covered in this proposal and discuss, as well, other aspects. Paragraph numbers have been added for ease of reference. The original proposal's list of references was omitted to provide more space for comments.

THE CHANGE PROCESS IN MEN WHO BATTER WOMEN

A Dissertation Proposal
by Bill Warters

1. I am proposing to conduct a qualitative study with participants of several treatment programs designed to change men who batter their wives and women friends. The emphasis will be on the experiences of men who have gone through these programs in attempts to end their violence. Also central to the research agenda will be an examination of the interaction between the contemporary social construction of domestic violence by program staff, and the way the issue is understood and explained by the program participants/clients themselves. I contend that the ways in which program staff "construct" and define the problem of domestic violence clearly affects the design and delivery of services to abusive men, and ultimately affects the messages that men receive from the programs about their violence. If program coordinators understand and define the problem in ways that are very different from the men in the programs, it may lead to fewer effective interventions, or at least to significant struggles with the men over the meaning of their experience. To assist in the possible improvement of treatment programs for men who batter, I will try to provide much lacking insight into the world view of the male participants in batterers treatment programs. The research will incorporate interviews with program staff, observation of group sessions, and surveys and in-depth interviews with men's treatment program members and "graduates" at 3–4 different batterers treatment programs located in the State of New York.

Paragraph 1. An excellent introductory paragraph! It covers many of the required items: question, significance, context, and sample and describes the methods of data collection. Thus, several critical parts of the required set are already covered well enough to set a framework in the reader's mind that can be filled in by succeeding sections—all this in 240 words!

Significance

The significance of the problem briefly noted in the introductory paragraph is "driven home" in this section that places it in a broad context.

2. There is now ample documentation of the widespread nature of domestic violence and of its costs to individuals and society. National studies indicate that at least 1 in 10 American women each year are beaten by the men in their lives and that at least 1.8 million women are severely beaten every year. The National Center for Disease Control recently reported that attacks by husbands on wives result in more injuries to women requiring medical treatment than rapes, muggings, and auto accidents combined. Other studies show that 40% of all murdered women are killed by their husbands or lovers (NCADV 1985).

3. While clearly the social and political movements to establish shelters for battered women have provided a significant reprieve for many abused women, it is estimated that more than 30–50% of women using shelters return to battering relationships (Martin, 1976; Roberts, 1981). Even if the abusive relationship is severed, the male frequently finds another mate that he also abuses (Shainess, 1977). Because of these concerns, practitioners, politicians and researchers on family violence have increasingly advocated counseling and reeducation programs for the abusive men.

4. Programs to treat this population are proliferating. Current estimates show close to 300 programs in existence in the United States and over 140 in Canada. One indication of the growing trend of interest in treatment programs for men who batter is that there have now been at least four annual midwest regional conferences, three west-coast regional conferences, and two national conferences all focused specifically on working with "batterers." Domestic violence is also clearly growing as a distinct area for scholarship and research, with at least three national research conferences having now been hosted, and since 1986, three new national scholarly journals have been devoted to the subject.

5. My project, as currently conceived, will begin filling a void of theory and information regarding how contemporary social service representatives, particularly those working directly with abusive men, are personally conceptualizing the problem of domestic violence by men and seeking to address it, but more importantly, the study will directly address the even greater lack of data on battering and the responses to it as perceived by the male perpetrator.

Paragraphs 2–5. Note how these paragraphs use a "funnel" approach, starting with the problem of abuse of women broadly, moving to treatment programs, their growth, their study, and, finally, his study. This is a common and very effective way of placing one's study in its larger context.

6. In my review of the literature I have found little qualitative or context-specific research on batterers in which men tell of their experiences and perceptions. I have come across one conference paper (Adams 1985), one Master's thesis (Ptacek 1985), one published dissertation (Stets 1988) and four published journal articles that use the words and perspectives of male abusers as their primary data (Harris and Bologh, 1985, Gondolf and Hanneken 1987, Gondolf 1985, Coleman 1980). While some valuable qualitative work has been done on men who rape, and on men incarcerated for violent crimes (Amir 1971, Athens 1974, 1986, Beneke 1982, Groth 1979), there apparently remains a lack of insight into the more commonplace reality of domestic violence from the male perpetrators point of view.

Paragraph 6. Simply citing studies doesn't do it! The implication of the writer is that although there are six items that "use the words and perspectives of male abusers as their primary data," none has any findings that would be helpful to this study. Doesn't sound reasonable, does it? We'll bet the doctoral committee wondered about this too and the final write-up included some comment on this aspect. The proposer must show both that the literature is understood and how that understanding leads to implications for the current study—or if there are no implications, why there are none. Showing how one is "standing on others' shoulders" is important in the literature review. That isn't demonstrated in this proposal yet; one knows mainly that he's been to the library.

7. As an indication of this gap, Edleson et al. (1985) in their article "Men Who Batter Women: A Critical Review of the Evidence" stated that,

> In the past decade the issue of battered women has come to the center of public attention. However. the men who batter and their perceptions of such violence have been largely overlooked. The published research presents a view of battering largely from the victim's perspective, in contrast to research on other kinds of social deviance. (emphasis added)

8. In his 1987 article, "Evaluating Programs for Men Who Batter: Problems and Prospects," sociologist Edward Gondolf indicates that

> The review of the research on batterer programs indicates the need for evaluation studies that address the following questions. 1) Which treatment modalities are most effective in reducing wife abuse? 2) What contribution does the participation in a group process make to the reduction of wife abuse? (p. 101)

My research could begin to address these important and elusive questions.

9. In his recent book, Stopping Family Violence: Research Priorities for the Coming Decade, David Finkelhor (1988) lists 11 areas of "high priority research on spouse abuse." First on his list is research on what stops wife abuse. He strongly recommends a study that would "elicit ideas directly from perpetrators and victims

about what works to end abuse." Criminologist Lee Bowker (1983) has already conducted a study of women who have escaped wife abuse, which was published under the title Beating Wife Beating, but no major study has yet examined men's strategies for ending abuse. According to Finkelhor, "the abusers need to be asked what were the considerations that lead them to stop, what did they see as the 'costs' to their behavior. (p. 91)"

Paragraphs 7–10 nicely marshall evidence from the literature to support his approach.

10. Finally, the study represents a significant addition to the growing body of work in the relatively new area of research known as "men's studies" (Brannon 1976, Pleck 1981, Gerzon 1982, Doyle 1983, Gondolf 1985, Kimmel 1986, Brod 1987). I believe that the growth of work to end domestic violence is spurring important symbolic struggles over the public and private imaging of appropriate masculinity, and in many ways, I see the groups for men who batter as being both theoretically and practically in the forefront of this struggle over redefinition.

Paragraph 10. Not one to miss a possibility to show the importance of his study in another light, here the problem is put in still another context.

By this point in the proposal, it has become clear that the author plans to compare batterers' perceptions of the problem of men battering women with the perceptions of batterers by staff who structure and administer treatment programs for them. If the two views are incongruent, he anticipates this may provide insights that may lead to improved treatment programs. But, the reader may be asking himself, "What are the proposer's reasons for thinking they may be incongruent?" And, "If they should turn out to be different, may this be because it is a function of the treatment programs to change batterers' perceptions of the problem (especially if they think their emotions are uncontrollable)?"

An answer to the former appears much later in paragraph 23 under the heading "Data Analysis." It might well have been cited in this section as well. But the latter question is not addressed. While it seems likely this aspect will be picked up in the study itself, we suspect that many critical readers would expect it to be covered in the proposal. It is important that the proposal be used to discuss aspects that readers expect to be covered. How well the proposer anticipates their questions determines in large measure their evaluation of the proposal.

As you create any proposal, but doctoral ones especially, keep in the front of your mind that the proposal is a demonstration of your scholarship. Readers already acquainted with your problem, but even those who are bringing their wit and logic to bear on it for the first time, will be thinking of aspects of which they would expect you to be aware. If you don't discuss them in the proposal, it raises questions about how thoroughly you understand your problem, and how competent you are as a researcher.

Methods

Paragraphs 11–17. Here are more of the essentials, details of methods, qualitative orientation to be used, and schedule. While the discussion is begun here, important aspects of it are handled in the section on methodological and theoretical issues that follows.

Lacking here and throughout the proposal is some sense of the schedule on which the activities will be pursued. A proposal for funding requires a time schedule since budget is heavily dependent on the number and length of the activities. Because dissertation proposals usually have no budget, they generally also lack a schedule. This is unfortunate for several reasons:

1. *Working through a schedule gives the proposer a clearer idea of how well the method section has been thought through and whether some items have been omitted. Schedules that go together easily indicate the proposal is well written—and vice versa.*
2. *The schedule facilitates judgment of the project's feasibility.*
3. *Scheduling helps anticipate problems early so one can do something about them, e.g., planning data gathering during a holiday period when staff and others are likely unavailable.*
4. *In a dissertation proposal, scheduling helps committee members anticipate when you may be needing their attention so they can warn you of conflicts with their calendar.*

Adding a project schedule in at least minimal detail is important!

11. I intend to use qualitative research methodology (Bogdan and Biklen, 1982), in particular in-depth interviewing, to gather and examine accounts given by abusive men of their behavior and the subsequent treatment they receive from third party intervenors. To a lesser extent I will rely on participant observation techniques as a temporary member of the groups I am studying. The study also will include a short survey given to program participants to gather demographic and anecdotal information.

Paragraph 11. It is reassuring that the researcher already has considered the necessity of using three different approaches to gathering qualitative data, thus providing for triangulation of findings—a research quality aspect. A slight question is raised by the very last phrase, "anecdotal information." Either here, or somewhere in this section, it would be helpful if a sample question were given so that we could see what kind of "anecdotal information" is to be sought here and how it bears on his approach to the problem. Indeed, this is just what he does in paragraph 17, the last in this section. Make your references to data-gathering instruments as concrete as possible—sample questions, names of established instruments, etc.

12. The symbolic interactionist tradition I locate myself in as a researcher assumes that behavior is largely self-determined (i.e., neither biological/ psychological nor social structural factors alone pre-determine behavior) and is observable at both the symbolic and interactional levels. Within this theoretical framework, it is understood that objects in the social world do not have intrinsic meaning but are defined by an individual's plans of action and are in constant flux. Meanings are negotiated and renegotiated during interaction with others. Typically a consensus of meaning is reached in social networks so that people can communicate using shared symbols, and an attempt to understand a particular milieu (such as the one developed within a men's treatment program) fully requires firsthand observation.

Paragraph 12. Note how the phrase in parenthesis in the last sentence brings this highly theoretically oriented paragraph down to earth as it bears on his study. Too many proposals leave the implications of the theoretical material to the reader to infer. Tie it down! It shows you know what you are talking about and not just spouting some professor's rhetoric.

13. I hope to be able to do a substantial amount of my data gathering by observing and talking with men "in situ," which means finding men who are identified as batterers and staying with them in some way that, while acceptable to them, would allow me both intimate observation of certain aspects of their behavior and enable me to report it in ways useful to social science and yet not harmful to them or their partners. My goal is to identify several research settings where I can observe, interview, and casually interact with men who have battered, in a setting that is unique to them, and in which I would present little or no threat. At this time, it seems that batterers' treatment programs are one of the few places where men identified as domestically abusive gather together, and thus these sites are where I will begin my research.

Paragraph 13. Recognition of the importance of ethics need not be reserved to the section on clearance by the Committee on the Protection of Human Subjects (paragraphs 45–52). Indeed, it is much more convincing that you are a mature researcher and genuinely concerned about subject protection if, at appropriate points in the proposal (e.g., see also paragraphs 15, 22, and 24), you mention your anticipation of an ethical problem, explain your concern, and indicate how it will be handled. The first sentence here does this well.

14. Herbert Blumer, (1969) one of the founders of the symbolic interactionist tradition within sociology, suggests using "sensitizing concepts" to help us decide where to look while we are gathering and analyzing our data, while avoiding the temptation to too narrowly predetermine what it is that we hope to find. In this spirit, some concepts I am interested in exploring as the study proceeds include the notion of a "moral career" of program participants, the idea of how they are negotiating a stigmatized identity, the idea of a developmental or stage process for change in men who batter, and the impact of perceived "threats" to their core constructs of

masculinity. Analysis of the gathered data will probably include examination of the distinctions between men who report no more abuse, and those who report reoffense. I also will be probing for strategies for staying nonviolent that the men report to have adopted, and what kind of support systems, if any, they claim to rely on. Also subject to analysis will be examples of self-labeling by the men, i.e. "I am a batterer," or "I've been framed," or "It was just a minor incident."

Paragraph 14. What a great way to avoid the open-ended "hunting license" problem of the qualitative researcher; one wants to start focused, yet not too much so as to be closed to what is important. Use of this device, and especially the concrete implementation of it in this paragraph, marks the researcher as knowledgeable about both his method and his problem— a model worth copying!

15. Gradually, as my understanding develops, I will begin to be more focused, and will test assumptions and check out meanings with the men. Eventually I intend to construct an interview schedule based on my developing insights, for use in one-on-one interviews with the men, perhaps in their homes, or at the program site office, or some neutral location that I can secure in the area. I would prefer to interview the men in their homes because it would give me more insight into their worlds, but it may be awkward or impossible if other family members are present.

16. At this time I have but a very general sense of the type of interview schedule I want to use with the men from the programs. It builds on Ed Gondolf's qualitative work with Jim Hanneken on reforming batterers as reflected in their article "The Gender Warrior: Reformed Batterers on Abuse, Treatment, and Change" (Gondolf & Hanneken, 1987), and Jim Ptacek's work as reported in his 1985 Master's Thesis, *Wifebeater's accounts of their violence: Loss of control as excuse and as subjective experience.* The areas of inquiry I am interested in include: recollections of where and when the men first recognized that they had a problem with abuse or were being labeled as an abuser; accounts of their abusive behavior from their perspective; the process of affiliation with the men's program, i.e. first contacts, expectations, impressions of other members, degree of involvement; help seeking behaviors related to abuse before or during the program; the nature of their changes, i.e. what things have stayed the same, and what has changed since contact with the program; onset of the change as related to particular events or insights; turning points for them; motivations for change; maintenance strategies to maintain change; payoffs, if any for ceasing or avoiding abuse; self-labeling and self-concepts regarding themselves and their behavior; the role of the program in their changes and self-definition; and recommendations for other men. Naturally, this list will be modified as the study develops and other relevant categories emerge based on the results of my observations and preliminary interview experiences.

Paragraph 16. Instead of simply stating that he would construct an interview schedule, again, the proposer shows his grasp of his problem by citing very specific topics that will be included, "standing on the shoulders" of researchers who have gone before. This kind of mastery and use of the literature is just exactly what readers want to see—a person who has mastered the contributions of previous research to his study. It provides a strong counteraction to the impression left earlier in paragraph 6, where he merely mentions studies.

17. To maximize the diversity of types of men I get, I will employ theoretical rather than random sampling procedures to try to interview men from the range of categories of participants that emerge during my initial explorative work. The proposed focus of the study on participants of three or four different programs allows the opportunity for some comparison of treatment modalities, and the identification of specific aspects of group process thought useful by the men themselves in eliminating abuse. After the formal interview(s) I will be asking the men to self-report their level of current abusiveness on a survey instrument that will gather minimal demographic information and abuse self-reports, and that invites them to complete a brief essay on their strategies for remaining nonviolent.

Paragraphs 17, 20–22, 48. Here are further details regarding sample and context (the two are intertwined in this, study as is often the case). As the reference to paragraphs 20–22 and 48 indicates, further information on sampling is to be found at several points in the document. It would have been better to bring it all together at this point to provide the complete picture. We'd also include here paragraph 23 on Wiseman's study that provided a model he is following.

Data Analysis

18. The approach taken to gathering and analyzing the data will be an inductive one (see Glaser and Straus, 1967), and will necessarily be adapted as the study proceeds and relevant categories emerge. My data analysis and data collection will be done sequentially with preliminary data analysis informing future data collection. In addition to regular fieldnotes and interview transcriptions, early in the data collection process I will begin to write theoretical notes in which I can play with the data, relating observations to one another, developing new concepts, and linking these to ones in the treatment program literature. Gradually I will integrate these theoretical notes into longer analytic memos that will help further focus my study. This data analysis process should continue during and after data collection until I have developed some kind of guiding metaphor, general scheme, or overall pattern for data analysis that accounts for all the phenomena observed.

19. In addition to the use of memos, the ongoing process of coding my observations and interview transcripts will be central to the data analysis. This will require reading and rereading the data to highlight and label important, descriptive, or informative issues that emerge, for later sorting and categorization. I will be looking at the data with an eye for identifying and discovering classes of things, persons and events and the properties that characterized them. The ultimate goal will be to develop theory that accounts for the men's violent behavior and their subsequent

changes, although at this point, relatively rich description that elegantly describes the experience and the meanings of events for the men in the programs would in itself be a significant contribution to the literature. I will know that I am done when no new ideas or concepts seem to be emerging, and when no negative cases can be found that disconfirm or invalidate the proposed framework of analysis.

Paragraphs 18–19. These first two paragraphs nicely cover another of the essentials, the methods and timing of data processing. They are an excellent two-paragraph summary of the generic data gathering-analysis process! We doubt that his professor could have done any better. Now he must bring it down to earth by showing how it applies to this study— which he does in the next paragraphs.

20. I will begin by exploring five or six possible program sites I know of that are within driving distance of Syracuse. I will meet with the program coordinators and facilitators, explain my project, and then seek permission to interview them and to observe a few groups and conduct interviews with men from the different program sites. Gaining entrée into these sites and to the men who have been through the programs will certainly represent a significant challenge and is an important piece of methodological work in its own right. Still, based on my preliminary explorations and discussions with contacts, and the number of potential programs in the state, it appears at this time I will have no trouble gaining the necessary access to proceed with the study.

Paragraph 19. Recognition of the problem of gaining entrée shows maturity as a qualitative researcher. Citing preliminary positive results adds to the favorable impression.

21. As part of the study, I will interview a total of at least 10 program coordinators and/or counselors drawn from the different batterers programs. The interviews will explore their ideas about and attitudes toward the men they treat, and examine their perceptions about the change process for men in the groups, and finally, solicit their support in contacting former group members.

22. Using an initial introductory letter sent to former group participants by a program coordinator, potential subjects will be requested to return a postcard if they are willing to participate in the study, or also if they have strong objections to being contacted. I will then interview a group of former program participants about their experiences with the domestic violence program and their attempts at changing their abusive behavior.

23. One potential model for my research is provided by Jaqueline Wiseman in her book *Stations of the Lost: The Treatment of Skid Row Alcoholics.* Wiseman takes a qualitative approach to the study of both the alcoholics and the various organizations that treat them, and focuses on the interactions between them. Wiseman found much disparity between the interpretations of events and interactions when described by the alcoholics and by the program staff, despite the program

staff's assumptions that they knew what the alcoholics were thinking. I would hope to gather enough data to conduct similar comparisons regarding men's treatment programs.

Methodological Issues

24. Sensitivity of the subject matter will make rapport building important for successful interviews. I believe that my experience over the years of working in two different batterers programs has given me some insight into the worlds of these types of men, and should help me be an empathic listener. The issue of establishing interviewees trust in me will be a challenge. I will make it clear that in my final writeup, the participating programs and the men who have been through them will have their identities and locations disguised. I have already conducted several interviews with men who have battered their female partners, and based on these experiences I believe it will be possible to get these men to open up to me about their experiences.

25. One of the important things I have learned in my own group work is that there is not always a good correlation between the men's self-report of their behavior and their behavior when it is described by their spouses. It should be understood that I will be attempting to understand and use the men's stories as their representations of a domestic violence related experience, and not as verbatim depictions of physical reality. There is already research on reliability of self-report data by men that I can build into my discussion of the survey results.

Paragraphs 24–25. We noted earlier the need to discuss issues readers might expect a good researcher to address. The two paragraphs above are excellent examples of the writer's doing so! Indicating awareness of the sensitivity of the subject matter and ability to handle it undercuts concerns readers may have had about this issue. Similarly, noting the likely disparity of perceptions of battering between spouses anticipates this issue and shows he is not naive about it. Over and over this graduate student is providing evidence that he is well prepared to take on this dissertation.

Theoretical Issues

In this and the next section the proposer explains the theoretical framework from which he is approaching the problem, an important aspect of qualitative research. We are not sure this discussion is as clear as it might be and may have caused some discussion among his doctoral committee members. How does one catch such sections ahead of time? Have an intelligent friend who is unfamiliar with your problem read your proposal and ask questions about it as he or she goes through it.

26. Theories about the "social construction" of social problems have been developed in sociology that can be used to explain the relatively recent reemergence of wife abuse as a social problem deemed worthy of a public response. (Fuller and Meyers 1941, Blumer 1971, Mauss 1975, Spector and Kitsuse 1977, Pfhol 1977,

Conrad and Schneider 1980, Gusfield 1981, Nelson 1984, Schneider 1985) These theories help us to understand the impact of conditions under which a problem rises to prominence, and to examine some of the other potential ways in which the problem could have been framed had it taken a different route or emerged in a different domain.

27. Public interest in wife abuse is certainly not new. There have been several earlier historical periods during which domestic violence was acted upon collectively through social and legal channels. Elizabeth Pleck, in her book *Domestic Tyranny* (1987) describes several significant domestic violence prevention efforts during three distinct periods of American history. She outlines wife abuse prevention efforts in the early 1600's (among the Puritans in Massachusetts), again in the late 1800's (as an off-shoot of the "child-saving movement") and finally during the recent period beginning in earnest around 1972. For a time (in the early 1900's) there were even reports of vigilante groups, including the Clan and the White Caps, who went out and punished men in the community who were known to be beating their wives. The White Caps were quite different in their ideological outlook than modern feminists, and yet they too took action around the issue of domestic violence.

28. When one steps back and looks at these historical accounts of social and legal responses to domestic violence, one can see that there have been wide-ranging and at times dramatic changes in the way in which the same type of behavior, a man hitting his wife, has been labeled and dealt with by members of society. The definition of an act as violent, its evaluation as socially tolerable or not, and even its emergence in the public consciousness at all, seems to depend on a complex interplay of factors. My intent in this dissertation will be to focus on the impact of the ways in which the problem is being structured in the contemporary period, using historical accounts primarily as a point of comparison.

29. My use of a social constructionist framework is not meant to imply that I believe that domestic violence is really only a problem because of some social fabrication in the media or by social service experts. My work in the field has lead me to believe that the putative conditions of men hitting and hurting women exists. I also believe that there are significant social costs resulting from violence in intimate relationships (for example, medical expenses, runaway or homeless women and youth, increased levels of substance abuse, police and court costs associated with protecting victims, loss of life, etc.) and that reducing the level of violence and its costs is a worthy investment of time and attention.

30. Recently some existential/interactionist sociologists (Erchak, 1984, Ferraro & Johnson 1983, and Denzin, 1984) have begun to look at aspects of the sense of self and the situation of interaction that the self confronts in domestic violence. Their work is somewhat abstract, but it represents an important theoretical basis for future work like my own using a symbolic interactionist perspective on abuse. It represents efforts to tie together different levels of reality, from the individually interpreted meaning of face-to-face situations to the more objectified cultural and

historical meanings of domestic violence. The meanings men give to events, in this case, are essential data. I hope to draw upon these theoretical works as I conduct my data analysis.

Paragraph 30. What do you include and what do you leave out? Here is another instance of this—the researcher holds out hope that these authors "are on to something." But, if it is important enough to include, then use enough space to explain it clearly; don't merely allude to it. The sentence beginning "It represents efforts . . ." tantalizes readers without going far enough to help them see for themselves there is likely something there.

Qualifications of the Researcher

31. Ethnographers and qualitative researchers are often encouraged to disclose their personal perspectives on the groups they are studying with readers of their research so that these readers can be conscious of potential bias in the work. I would describe myself as coming from a pro-feminist background and ideology, beginning with my work with Men Against Rape in Santa Cruz, CA in 1980. I have worked as a counselor at two different programs for men who batter, one in Santa Cruz, CA, and now one in Syracuse that I helped to found. I have served as network coordinator for a California network (MATV) of 11 men's anti violence programs, and now serve as co-coordinator of the Ending Men's Violence Task Group of the National Organization for Men Against Sexism (NOMAS, formerly the National Organization for Changing Men). As a result of these experiences, I've been exposed to a wide range of possible treatment models and to many ongoing debates in the treatment field. I currently edit a small publication, The *Ending Men's Violence Newsletter,* as part of my work for the Ending Men's Violence Task Group. I have worked as a classroom educator on domestic violence prevention and child assault prevention, and have helped host four annual men's public actions known as BrotherPeace, where men speak out in favor of nonviolence. I have received media attention for my work and get paid for my part-time facilitator role. I am clearly currently functioning as an advocate of social intervention to reduce men's domestic violence. This perspective will most certainly affect my interpretation of events and discussion during the course of my study. I will say that I am not wedded to the idea that treatment programs for men who batter are necessarily the best or most efficient form of social intervention to reduce violence against women, and I remain open to other ideas and approaches.

32. I hope that by continuing to read historical accounts of the wide variation in ways that social problems get dealt with, and by maintaining a critical stance toward my own current work in the field as a counselor in a men's program, I can see beyond my own ideological and practice assumptions. I am interested in describing how the "social construction" of domestic violence adopted by counselors in treatment programs for men who batter gets passed on to the men who go through their programs, and what some effects of these definitions may be on the men who are supposedly there to end their violence. I am interested in as wide a range as possi-

WARTERS

ble of batterers treatment program participants' experiences. The lived experience of the participant in a batterer's program remains central to my analysis.

Paragraph 31–32. Here the proposer covers his qualifications, another of the essentials of every qualitative proposal. From the standpoint of the researcher being a person on top of his problem, one can hardly ask for more impressive credentials. But, as he himself notes, this makes it more difficult to believe that he will be open to "what is there" without preconceived opinions. In a funded proposal, some additional evidence other than his own claims would be needed. This could be evidence from his previous research or letters of support by other researchers of this person's ability to seriously consider other than his own perspective. In a doctoral dissertation, this isn't as much of a problem, and one's own claim may be all that is available. But any evidence of open-mindedness, such as excerpts from his newsletter indicative of other than a strictly crusading mind, would be helpful.

Contribution to the Field

33. I believe that this project will be an important contribution to the field. If effective systems for reducing domestic violence are to be developed, more information will be needed on how interventions impact on abusers and affect their attitudes and beliefs about the use of force and violence in relationships. We have a growing body of descriptive (primarily demographic or psychological test profiles) information on men who participate in batterers treatment programs, but *very little* information about how these individuals see themselves and their role in the activity. Nor do we have much information on the particular aspects of treatment programs that the men believe support their being nonviolent. This work may in some way help to improve our understanding of the impact of one of the predominant societal responses to men's violence in relationships, batterers treatment programs. By learning more about the change process for men who batter, efforts to coordinate criminal justice intervention, treatment programs, and self-help groups for batterers may be enhanced, and there is hope that more men may cease to be violent as a result of these enhancements. It is a goal I believe is worth working toward.

Paragraph 33. It is unusual for such a statement to end the body of the proposal. Usually, the statement of contribution is near the beginning to convince reviewers "this is a worthwhile proposal." Here, it is a bit redundant of what was said previously, though it does serve as a kind of summary of the hoped-for outcomes. All proposals are "works of art" with the proposer adapting format to achieve the desired impression. In this instance, it is ending the proposal on a very positive note—good strategy!

(The following sections appeared each on a separate page as a series of appendixes. To save space, they have been put in run-on form.)

Summary of Progress Toward Completion
of Dissertation Research, 1/24/91

Paragraphs 34–42. This "Summary of Progress . . ." is an unusual but excellent addition to the proposal. Such information is usually worked into the body of the proposal. Maybe that is best if the evidence is meager. Where it is extensive, however, putting it in a separate section, as done here, calls attention to it and makes an impressive display. (If you've got it, flaunt it? Not always, but in this instance, yes!) It indicates that the researcher is a mature student who is serious about getting on with the work. Note how the description touches on nearly all the things someone concerned about the progress of the student would hope to hear about:

- *Contacted authorities who have a need to know about the project and might be helpful,*
- *Gained access to one of the programs he plans to use,*
- *Observed in that program and also started interviewing,*
- *Contacted two other programs and gained approval "in spirit,"*
- *Applied for research support,*
- *Had an article on theoretical aspects accepted for publication,*
- *Freed up time for the research by retiring from his position,*
- *Began interviewing persons in the social system network that surrounds these men in the community, and*
- *Continued to read broadly about the problem.*

34. I have applied for and gained clearance from the human subjects review board to conduct my research on "The Change Process in Men Who Batter Women."

35. I have made contact with the Governors Office on Domestic Violence that helps to coordinate the activities of several of the programs I am interested in, and talked with the research officer there about my proposed work. I informed them of my intentions and gained their support and approval to proceed, contingent, of course, on the approval of the program coordinators at the proposed sites.

36. I have met with the program coordinator of one of the three main programs I am interested in gaining access to and have gained permission to sit in on group sessions and conduct interviews with current participants in the program. I am working on a sample letter and postcard to be used in recruiting former group participants. This letter is still subject to some review and revision prior to approval for mailing by the program coordinator. The program coordinator himself has also agreed to participate in in-depth interviews.

37. I have observed for 3 months now at a batterers program and have begun to do some very preliminary interviews with men who have battered to begin to develop my interview schedule and procedures. To date I have conducted 4 formal interviews and several more are currently being arranged.

WARTERS

38. I have made phone contact with the directors of two other programs in the state that would make appropriate sites for my research. I have gained approval "in spirit" to conduct the research at their sites. I have arranged to meet personally with each of them before the end of February to discuss the specific details of the study and to gain their input and final approval.

39. I have developed an application for a University Graduate Research Award (a maximum award of $1500, primarily designed for summer support) that I will submit as soon as the competition is formally announced, with the hope that it will support my planned summer research activities as a participant observer in the men's groups. My plan is to conduct at least the first 25–30 formal interviews with men who have battered during the months of June, July, and August.

40. I have had an article pertaining to some of the theoretical aspects of this research accepted for publication during 1991 in the *Men's Studies Review.*

Paragraph 40. Having one's work published prior to completing the dissertation has been unusual, but is becoming more common. It looks good on the vita and gives one an advantage since employers know that those who have already published are more likely to do so in the future.

Having done the literature review and researched the theoretical positions of a problem, any good graduate student is likely to be more up-to-date on that topic than most professors. Those planning a career in higher education would do well to capitalize on this effort by putting their knowledge in writing and publishing it. Not only is this good self-discipline, but it also starts a habit of making use of what has been learned. Remember, science is a communal enterprise; we are not in it just for the personal pleasure (though that is considerable and may alone be worth it) but must all contribute if the community is to grow and thrive. Though satirized by the phrase "publish or perish," good scientists take seriously their responsibility to others to communicate what they have learned.

41. I have made arrangements to "retire" from my role as Program Coordinator for the Campus Mediation Center at the end of this academic year. This will free my time up to completely focus on the dissertation research.

Background Research Activities

42. Since completing the advanced qualitative methods seminar that laid the foundation for my proposal, I have engaged in background research to familiarize me with the possible points of contact a man identified as domestically violent might have with other members of the community. I have been documenting these "points of contact" where men might interact with social systems as a result of their identification as domestically abusive, so that I can intelligently talk to the men about these experiences later during the interview process. To this end, I have interviewed almost two dozen people, usually in an audio-taped interview of over one hour in length, about their contact with and impressions about men who batter. I have cast a rather wide net, using a snowball sampling method, in order to get a

brief taste of the thinking of key people in various local social service agencies. My intent has been to gain a general understanding of how various agency personnel think about the men's violence, and learn how an abuse case would typically move through their systems. These interviews were done as background preparation for the dissertation study which remains focused on the abusers' change experiences while involved in a batterers treatment program.

43. The people who I have interviewed in the preparatory and exploratory stage have included:

Public Health Social Worker
Battered Women's Shelter Worker
Shelter Director and Coordinator of DV Coalition
Volunteer Center Helpline Coordinator
Victim Witness Assistance Center Staff Members (2)
Senior Assistant District Attorney
County Social Services Administrator
Mediation Program Coordinator
Sheriff s Dept. Chief Administrator (formerly of Abused Person's Unit)
Assistant District Attorneys (2)
Director of Legal Aid
Assistant Director at Probation Department
Chief of Local Township Police
On-duty police officer in an outlying suburb
Director of a program for batterers

Paragraph 42 and 43. In a dissertation proposal, just as in a funded proposal, there should be no surprises; it should flow logically, unfolding with additional details of what has been anticipated in the foregoing. This is a surprise and one that has involved a significant amount of work. It deserves better than to be an add-on to an appendix. Interviewing those in the social network that surrounds batterers and who therefore have both a perception of them and some knowledge of how they perceive themselves is an excellent idea. Further, including it in the body of the proposal would have strengthened it.

Placed in what was obviously a section that was written after the proposal was constructed, it probably did little harm in this instance, nor might it in any dissertation proposal. But in a project submitted for funding, where the proposal is usually all that informs reviewers about the applicant, the proposal should be an integrated package without unanticipated add-ons like this.

Related Readings

44. In addition to successfully completing my comprehensive exams, and my initial literature review on treatment programs for men who batter, I have also continued to read materials that apply in a more broad sense to my topic area. Recent books have included the following.

Domestic Violence and Control by Jan E. Stets (a qualitative dissertation turned into a book
    that interviewed couples involved in domestic violence)
Violent Transactions, edited by Anne Campbell
Domestic Tyranny by Elizabeth Pleck
The Male Batterer: A Treatment Approach by Sonkin, Martin, & Walker
Child Abuser: A Study of Child Abusers in Self-help Group Therapy by M. Collins
Heroes of Their Own Lives: The Politics and History of Family Violence by Linda Gordon
Anger: The Struggle for Emotional Control in America's History by Carol and Peter Stearns
Social Psychology of Aggression: From Individual Behavior to Social Interaction edited by
    Amelie Mummendey
The Domestic Assault of Women: Psychological and Criminal Justice Perspectives by
    Donald Dutton
Images of Issues: Typifying Contemporary Social Problems edited by Joel Best

Paragraph 44. The first entry is annotated. That good idea isn't carried through with the rest. Annotation isn't necessary by any means, but it is likely that not more than one or two, if any, of the reviewers will be experts about a specialized problem. Therefore, a set of readings, especially if it includes recently published material, is not likely to be familiar to them. Providing annotations is a courtesy that is likely to be appreciated and make the reader more favorable toward the proposal. And more than that, they indicate a familiarity with the literature, not just knowledge of the right titles to cite. If they include opinions about the quality of the entry in some way, they contribute to the perception of the proposer as a scholar. After all, that is one of the main characteristics that the proposal is intended to convey, and one on which the reviewers are continually making judgments as they read through it. Here is a way to contribute positively to it.

Protection of Subjects

Paragraphs 45–52. Although ethical questions are addressed in the body of the proposal, this is the section dealing with it most completely. Ethics is another of the essential topics. Note also the comment made earlier on paragraph 13.

Approval by a human-subjects review board is mandatory for federally funded projects, but most universities require it of any research by faculty and students involving humans (or by a similar board for animal research). Since this is such a critical aspect of this project where considerable harm to the participants could result if not carried out properly, further discussion of this aspect as done here is particularly apropos. However, the essential material could have been included as part of the proposal and been less redundant. It appears as though the proposer included the statement sent to the human-subjects review board verbatim. Material such as that in paragraph 48 with regard to the security of the data and 50 regarding the risk to participants and the problem posed by inadvertent knowledge of threats to potential victims properly belongs in the proposal; they are important topics. There are also details here (e.g., one—to two-hour audiotaped interviews later destroyed) that belong there as well.

45. In keeping with university regulations, the research plan for this study "The Change Process in Men Who Batter Women" was submitted to the Syracuse University Human Subjects Review Board. The proposal has been approved and permission to continue the research has been granted.

46. The study will adopt a qualitative, symbolic interactionist approach in its examination of the subjective world of the men who batter. I will use interviews with the various cooperating program coordinators and participant observation at counseling/reeducation group sessions (when access is granted), but the bulk of the data will be gathered through completely voluntary in-depth interviews with both current men's treatment program participants and formerly involved "graduates" from several batterers treatment programs located in the State of New York. I will ask the subjects to participate in a short phone interview, which will be followed up by a 1–2 hour audio-taped face-to-face interview.

47. None of the subjects are to be identified in the data collection. The security of the data is to be supervised by the principal investigator throughout the course of the research. The tapes and field notes gathered during the course of the research will be kept in a securely locked metal cabinet. All written materials resulting from the research will disguise the identity of the subjects and the location of the interview. After successful transcription, the original audio tapes will be destroyed. The field notes, stripped of any identifying information, will remain in the custody of the researcher. None of the interview data or documentation will include identification of the subjects. The data is not likely to be of use to courts in the case of legal prosecution, since it identifies information about the man's attempts to cease his abuse rather than information about the man's incidence of abuse.

48. The sample of reforming batterers will be derived from personal contacts the investigator develops with program participants he meets and from a phone survey of batterers listed in the cooperating programs' records as having attended the program 6–18 months ago. A letter introducing the survey and the right of refusal will be sent from the batterers' former counselors to those to be surveyed. A self-addressed postcard will be provided to indicate that the man does not want to be contacted in any way.

49. Perhaps the primary risk for the subjects posed by the research is the possibility of embarrassment or loss due to a public or private breach of confidentiality. In addition, the subject may consider it an intrusion of privacy to be contacted about the research in the first place. The subject may also experience some temporary discomfort when asked to discuss troubling personal experiences. It is highly unlikely, however, that any of the men's confidentiality would be threatened in any way. The exception would be if a subject mentions that he has battered someone immediately prior to attending the interview or that he intends to harm someone directly after an interview. While confidentiality is important, the subject's victim also needs to be protected from potential harm. In the unlikely event that a life-threatening situation appears, the subject would first be encouraged to obtain the appropriate help for himself and victim. This might entail the subject's setting up a counseling ap-

pointment with a staff program member and assuring that his victim receives shelter aid. If he is totally unresponsive, the interviewer would consult the program staff about the proper steps to warn the victim of imminent danger.

50. The men who participate in this study may not benefit directly from the research, other than that they will have a chance to talk with someone interested in what they have to say, and they may feel reinforcement for their efforts to curb their abuse. Articles and publications resulting from the study may indirectly lead to changes and improvement in treatment program practices. Men who batter are participating in an activity that is dangerous to both their partner *and themselves.* The information gathered in interviews with men who have been successful in ending their physical violence may be very useful for men who are currently battering and want to change their behavior.

51. Domestic violence is a well-documented and costly social problem. Treatment and reeducation programs for men are proliferating to address this problem. A significant amount of time and resources is being devoted to efforts to curb and eliminate this form of violence, and yet little research has been done on the efforts of perpetrators to end their abuse. This research should help develop a theoretical model of the change process that may lead to improved program practices and subsequently reduced levels of violence and abuse in the home.

52. The risks posed to subjects of this research is minimal. The subjects are all healthy, informed, consenting adults, and the research is very unlikely to harm them in any way. The potential fruits of the research, however, may be great, and may help reduce the level of violence in our society by providing us with new tools and perspectives on eliminating abuse in the home.

Other Support

Paragraphs 53 to end. Every reviewer is concerned that good projects be carried to conclusion. Lack of adequate resources is probably the most common cause of many graduate students leaving the institution ABD but with firm intentions of completing the dissertation on the new job—we all know horror stories about that. Thus, it is good to see the many pathways to funding this student is trying. In a way, this is an implicit appeal for help; should any of the reviewers know people involved in these various agencies, they could put in a good word, and an impressive proposal such as this might well lead to such an action. Excellent strategy on the part of this student!

53. I am prepared to do the bulk of my data processing on my own Macintosh personal computer. I hope to be able to borrow a university owned cassette tape transcription machine to assist me with the transcription process.

54. In terms of financial support, I intend to apply for a Graduate Student Research Grant from the Graduate School here at Syracuse University. I have been told that the grants will be given primarily to support summer research projects and are likely to have a maximum award of $1500. Although I was told to expect a Jan-

uary 30th deadline for proposals, the release of an official RFP has not yet occurred. If a grant was awarded to me, it would most likely start June 1, 1991.

55. I will also apply to the Program on the Analysis and Resolution of Conflicts at Syracuse University for a small graduate research grant to pay for a software package to assist me in the management of qualitative data, to pay for materials such as blank tapes, and to provide a small amount of money for travel and postage. In the past, grants have ranged from $300–1500 for graduate students. The requests are handled individually, and I will apply in time to get an answer in May of this year.

56. I am also exploring the possibility of applying for a National Institute of Justice fellowship for dissertation support in policy-relevant areas of criminal justice. The maximum award is $11,000, which would provide for a stipend of no more than $5000, major project costs and certain university fees. In the past, the deadline has been March 1, although I was told in a call on 1/7/91 that the RFP has not yet been released. I will continue to contact them and will apply if my work seems to fit within their guidelines.

57. Currently I am funded as a Graduate Assistant in charge of the Campus Mediation Center. This position will only be funded through May of 1991. After that, I will rely as necessary on my part-time job (approx. 6 hrs./week) as a facilitator with a local batterers treatment program.

58. The Harry Frank Guggenheim Foundation clearly represents my best hope for primary funding for this research project. I feel that my work on men's violence fits well within the mission of the Foundation, and I certainly would be honored to be chosen for such a prestigious award.

Supplementary Supporting Material

59. Attached are two issues (Vol. 5, No. 4 and Vol. 6, No. 2) of the *Ending Men's Violence Newsletter* that were edited by the applicant. The purpose of including them is to give the selection committee a greater familiarity with both the editorial ability and some of the values and beliefs espoused by the applicant.

Final comment. Notice what this student has done—this proposal is presented for approval by his committee, yes, but it is much more than that. The student, almost aggressively (but not overtly, only very subtly so), is working to convert the reviewers to his side—nay, more than that:

- *to win them over to the point of view that he is an unusual student with special capabilities and values (paragraph 59),*
- *with special expertise in the area in which he plans to work,*
- *with a mission, but with the capabilities to make science paramount in pursuing it,*
- *as one who had done everything possible to make the dissertation a success and therefore as a student especially deserving of their active support. Nice job!*

But he was not only looking for support from his doctoral committee, his project was also funded. We wrote Bill Warters for information about this. He replied as follows: "[T]he dissertation was funded by the Harry Frank Guggenheim Foundation on the basis of my proposal. I found their name through searching PRISM on-line at Syracuse [in a] . . . category . . . specifically for doctoral research. I approached them directly by phone after having read up on their previous grant-making activities. With minimal direction other than what I found in the application materials, I wrote the proposal that you have now annotated" (Warters, 1994).

Note his process:

1. *Checking a database of potential funders (PRISM is a program that allows the user to search data files such as that of the Office of Sponsored Research at Syracuse, which keeps track of funding opportunities. Look for a similar service at your institution!).*
2. *Having found a likely prospect, he did his homework, finding out what they had funded to see whether his fit.*
3. *He contacted them by phone to discuss the appropriateness of his proposal and learn how to present it.*
4. *He wrote the proposal.*

Bill was a graduate student at that time, just as are many of you reading this. It took little extra work, gave him experience in working with a foundation and writing a proposal for them, netted him the funding for his work (it is always easier and you do better work when you have funding to help you survive), and learned to manage a project's funding—superb experience for a future faculty member, which he now is. "If the shoe fits," go thou and do likewise!

CHAPTER 12

An Annotated Dissertation Proposal Using Quantitative Methods

The choice of topic in the following dissertation proposal, a study of the effectiveness of concept mapping in improving problem solving, is typical of topic choice in doctoral dissertations. Undoubtedly, Kathy Beissner had an "itch to scratch." Since the improvement of problem solving is central to the work she does as a trainer of physical therapists, why not tackle it in her doctoral dissertation? One must give her credit for undertaking a difficult problem central to her work. Further, where researchers so often work on abstract problems primarily of interest to other researchers, Kathy's problem is for those on the therapist-training front line.

Now comes the "but," however. An individual's problem-solving skill is developed over a lifetime; in the case of Kathy's students, it was over the past eighteen to nineteen years. Her intervention, by the constraints on her own time and resources, must be comparatively small. Eisner, in Bracey (1994), noted that the length of an experimental intervention in 1981's American Educational Research Journal averaged only seventy-two minutes. So Kathy's intervention will probably not be atypical. But, as Bracey (1994) notes, "this is a minuscule amount of time when placed against the enormous blocks of time represented by a school year." And, one might add, it's even smaller in contrast to such a long-term developmental process as this! From just the title we don't yet know the length or the exact nature of the intervention, but Kathy has already set the problem in a context that, while a common one for graduate students, presents difficulties in designing a study sufficiently sensitive to show any effect at all, let alone one that would have any practical significance.

Kathy's choice is the dilemma both graduate student and faculty face: how does one define a topic with enough "bite" to be satisfying and interesting, to be more than an exercise by having practical ramifications, keep within the scope of the student's skills and resources, and avoid areas where even top researchers have not yet found a satisfactory approach? Kathy has chosen to err on the side of possible practical significance—assuming that even a small intervention effect could later be developed into something worthwhile. Her faculty

BEISSNER

chair and committee, in approving this proposal, apparently decided they could live with this choice as well.

Each doctoral student must make that topic choice: finding a problem within their competencies with a reasonable and feasible approach, yet significant enough they are not just content to work on it, but sufficiently committed to follow it through to the end. Then they must convince their committee of this choice as well.

A STUDY OF THE EFFECTIVENESS OF CONCEPT MAPPING IN IMPROVING PROBLEM SOLVING

A Dissertation Proposal
by Katherine L. Beissner

The introduction in paragraphs 1–3 follows the common pattern of spiraling through the proposal's topic, in this instance, three times: in its most abbreviated form in the title, in a general way in the first paragraph, and in more detail in the following two. A very useful format! It is used often in news articles because it plunges the reader into the topic immediately, but then supplies the details that create a more complete understanding.

Since opening sentences set the tone for the reader, it is important to frame them so they draw the reader in from the start. For example, compare this alternate beginning with the original: "Selecting the correct solution to the patient's health problem is the care professional's key skill; how do you significantly improve it? This project will investigate. . ." Is that better at putting the significance up front and making the reader want to read further?

1. Problem solving, the identification and resolution of patients' problems, is a primary responsibility of health care professionals. As an essential element of practice, attainment of problem solving skill is an important goal in the educational preparation of health professionals. This project will investigate the effectiveness of a study strategy in improving students' ability to solve problems in a physical therapy content area.

2. Prior research on improving health professional students' ability to problem solve has focused on instructional or curricular interventions. One method involves a restructuring of the professional curriculum into a problem-based format, using case studies to present necessary information within the patient-based context in which it will be used (c.f. Shahabudin, 1987; Schmidt, Dauphinee, and Patel, 1987; Norman, 1988). Another strategy is to teach the problem solving process in a step-wise manner (May and Newman, 1980; Olsen, 1983; Jenkins, 1985), providing students with exercises for practice of each of the steps in the problem solving method.

3. Each of these methods focus on the instructor or instructional materials to achieve improvements in learners' performance. In contrast, this project will focus on a study strategy that can be used by learners independently. Study

strategies, as the term is used here, are those techniques used by students to process information from text or other learning materials in an attempt to increase their ability to recall and use the information at a later date. As a learner-based intervention, study strategies can be used with any type of instruction.

Problem Solving

Paragraphs 4–8 are as neat an example of a "funnel" approach to describing the research problem as one could ask for. Note how Kathy starts with a broad, general definition of problem solving, applies it to the narrower medical arena, delineates within that arena what she calls "externally controlled" problem solving from what she intends to study, narrows further to that aspect of the clinical process that seems critical but amenable to change, and finally relates that aspect, the organization of knowledge, to the concept mapping strategy she intends to use to improve it. Like the format used in the introduction, this too is a useful one worth copying.

4. In general terms a problem is "a situation in which an individual is called upon to perform a task not previously encountered and for which externally provided instructions do not specify completely the mode of solution" (Resnick and Glaser, 1976, p209). This definition can be applied to the health care setting by considering a scenario in which a health care professional is confronted with a patient who has a combination of signs and symptoms that are unfamiliar to the practitioner. The patient presents the health professional with a problem, or a "task not previously encountered." The second aspect of the definition of a problem "for which externally provided instructions do not specify completely the mode of solution" is also met in this scenario. While a general series of questions may be asked of the patient, and a routine set of evaluative procedures performed, these questions and tests do not guarantee that the correct diagnosis is made, or that appropriate treatments will be selected. The health care professional must judge the significance of the information gathered, and integrate the information in order to derive a diagnosis and treatment plan. Problem solving in the health professions is the identification of patient problems based upon the patient's complaints, history and objective evaluation, and the development of treatment plans to resolve those problems.

5. Other applications of "problem solving" in medicine do not fit this general definition of a problem. For example, when expert systems or flow charts are used to specify which tests to perform and to identify the significance of the test results, providing a diagnosis and treatment plan, "externally provided instructions" do specify the solution to the patient's problem (c.f. Essex, 1978). When this type of system is used, for the purposes of this research, the process used is not problem solving, because the solution to the problem is generated by something outside the practitioner.

6. Problem solving in the health professions has received much attention in recent literature. The clinical reasoning process, the thought processes used when diagnosing patients and designing treatment programs, has been described in

terms of differences in the ways that experts and novices approach problems. Experienced clinicians appear to have mastered the diagnosis and treatment planning process by learning how to group, or integrate data from patient evaluations easily, and by selecting key questions throughout the interview process (Cutler, 1979). Inexperienced clinicians, on the other hand, tend to collect a great deal of data regarding the patient, and later try to piece together information to fit a particular diagnosis.

7. The need to integrate information is a key component of clinical problem solving. Therefore, study strategies that emphasize integration of content seem particularly appropriate for facilitating clinical problem solving. Spatial learning strategies are a method of representing content structure through the use of two-dimensional diagrams. When studying, these strategies can be used to depict the relationships between ideas. Learning concept interrelationships is speculated to improve learners' ability to draw inferences based upon those concepts (Mayer, 1988). This drawing of inferences is a skill necessary in problem solving. Additionally, spatial learning strategies allow one to represent the relationships between new information and prior knowledge. To do this, concepts from prior knowledge are included on the spatial representation as it is drawn. The linking of new information to prior knowledge is speculated to assist in the transfer of learning to new situations (Mayer, 1988), another skill requisite in problem solving.

8. Concept mapping is one type of spatial learning strategy that may be useful in improving problem solving. Concept maps consist of a hierarchical arrangement of concepts, with labeled lines depicting relationships between the concepts (Novak and Gowin, 1984). This project will examine the effectiveness of concept mapping in improving students' ability to select appropriate treatment plans.

Avoid abrupt transitions; make the write-up flow by adding sentences like this to smooth it: "The next section translates this goal into the operational terms through which the study will be carried out."

Study Variables

Dependent Variables

9. The dependent variable in this study will be scores on a test of problem solving ability in a physical therapy subject area. This researcher-generated test will consist of items requiring subjects to identify appropriate physical therapy treatment techniques for given patient problems and to describe their rationale for treatment selection.

In paragraph 9, the student adds the development of a measuring instrument to the work of carrying out the research study itself. Can she do both? The development of measures often merits a study of its own. Readers will want some assurance that the researcher is capable of undertaking this supplemental task and that its feasibility has already been tested. Sample items in the appendix that included a plan to pretest them would help allay these concerns.

Independent Variables

Clarity of organization is important since it helps the reader keep the parts in mind and shows their relation to one another. In this section, treatment is discussed at both the beginning and the end. Paragraphs 10–14 would be better organized if they were arranged into two subsections: (1) a subsection on treatment that includes paragraph 10 describing the primary independent variable, and paragraph 14, a measure of the treatment, and (2) a subsection on control variables that includes paragraphs 11–13. Further, the latter might be expanded a bit to discuss the variety of alternative explanations not eliminated by the control group and then indicate the most important ones chosen to be controlled in this study. Such a discussion section might well have resulted in the discovery of the tightened control suggested in the comment on paragraph 26 below.

Remember, the proposal indicates one's ability to handle the problem. A rather complete exploration here of possible confounding factors that might prevent one from attributing the effect to the treatment is an important way of doing this.

Paragraph 10. Is group assignment the primary independent variable? No, it is training in concept mapping strategy. Group assignment is part of the control strategy to eliminate alternative explanations, and paragraphs 11–13 are more of this strategy.

10. The primary independent variable will be group assignment. Fifty percent of the subjects will be trained in the concept mapping strategy prior to introduction of a text passage and testing. The other fifty percent will receive the text passage and testing, but no training in the concept mapping technique until after completion of the study.

11. An inability to recall requisite facts about a patient condition or treatment technique can lead to an inability to select appropriate treatments. Therefore, a second independent variable to be included in this study is a test of factual knowledge on the basis for physical therapy treatment selection.

12. While the use of concept mapping is speculated to improve problem solving ability, other factors that may influence ability to problem solve are also considered in this study. First, a subject's critical thinking ability may impact his/her ability to problem solve. Previously acquired abilities to draw inferences and to make judgments of evidence may influence a subject's ability to critically read draw conclusions from text. The Watson-Glaser Critical Thinking Appraisal (Watson and Glaser, 1980) will be used to assess critical thinking ability.

Paragraph 12. Good, a well-known test of critical thinking is being used. Use well-researched instruments, where they are appropriate; they make results more understandable and give readers more confidence in the results. Where new or obscure instruments are a better fit to your variables, give as much description of the measures and their psychometric characteristics as possible so as to give readers confidence in them.

13. Another factor that may influence performance on a problem solving test is the manner in which subjects normally process text. The value of the concept mapping technique is that it requires the map-maker to identify relationships between concepts within text. As used in this study, concept maps will also require that the new content be related to prior knowledge. Subjects who normally study in such a way as to identify relationships in text content can be described as "deep processors" (Schmeck, 1983), because they actively manipulate the content to inner meaning beyond that represented in the text. Those who, in their usual study methods relate new information to prior knowledge can be referred to as "elaborative processors" (Schmeck, 1983). As noted previously, relating new information to prior knowledge is expected to improve ability to transfer learning to new situations, and identifying relationships between concepts helps in drawing inferences (Mayer, 1988). Since both of these skills are required for effective problem solving, a measure designed to detect whether subjects routinely process in this manner is included in the study.

Paragraph 13. Here are two covert behaviors, elaborative and deep processing, which are going to be difficult to tap. How will she determine an individual's routine use of these behaviors? The last sentence is vague on this point. A bit more detail would help, such as: "The Inventory of Learning Processes (Schmeck, 1983) has scales that will be used for this purpose." Give your readers enough detail to keep them positive about your project; avoid vague phrases that may raise questions in their minds.

14. Concept maps generated by learners can vary greatly in their detail and degree of integration of content. Concept maps can be scored according to a standardized method, resulting in a score that indicates the complexity and integration of the concept map (Novak and Gowin, 1984). The concept map scores of the experimental group will be an additional independent variable.

Paragraph 14. Her reference to Novak and Gowin's method lacks indications of its validity, the interrater reliability of scoring, and any evidence of its acceptability by the research community—e.g., use in other studies, studies by other researchers, etc. Additional details are needed somewhere such as the literature review. Then include a sentence like: "As noted in the literature review, this is the most widely used and carefully detailed method of scoring concept maps."

Hypotheses

15. In light of the previous discussion, the following hypotheses are offered:

1. Subjects who use concept mapping to study a text passage on physical therapy treatment procedures will identify appropriate treatment plans for more patient simulations than subjects who do not use concept maps to study the test. H1: concept Map > Control on Problem Solving

2. If concept maps are valid representations of the study processes used when generating maps, experimental subjects (Exp) who develop more integrated and elaborated concept maps (High CM) should outperform subjects with less integrated/elaborated maps (Low CM) on tests of problem solving. H2: Exp: High CM > Low CM on Problem Solving

3. Control subjects who deeply process new information (High DP) should outperform control subjects who do not deeply process new content (Low DP) on tests of problem solving. H3: Control: High DP, Low DP on Problem Solving

4. Control subjects who elaboratively process new information (High EP) should outperform control subjects who do not elaboratively process new information (Low EP) on tests of problem solving. H4: Control: High EP, Low EP on Problem Solving

5. Subjects with high critical thinking ability (High CTA) should outperform subjects with low critical thinking ability (Low CTA) on tests of problem solving. Hs: High CTA, Low CTA on Problem Solving

Paragraph 15. Note how her hypotheses follow nicely, just as they should, from the discussion of problem solving and description of the variables. No surprises! Great, there shouldn't be!

Limitations

A limitations section, paragraphs 16–18, is often the place where the student seeks to forestall the readers' questions about the generalizability of the study. It often contains all kinds of disclaimers, many of which are so far-fetched as to be unnecessary. While not far-fetched, paragraph 17's disclaimer is probably unnecessary, since in many ways this study could be considered research on the improvement of problem solving in general; it just happens to use health professions material and students.

Paragraph 16, however, is an important limitation because only part of the clinical problem-solving process will be involved. Restrict a "limitations" section to similarly important caveats.

16. Since a major factor in problem solving is prior experience, and providing students with identical experiences is not feasible, it is necessary to select subjects with little to no experience in physical therapy treatment. With this lack of experience there is a concomitant problem in that the knowledge base upon which the subjects can problem solve is also limited. Therefore, only a portion of the problem solving process will be tested in this study. The full process consists of identifying the cause of the patient's problem, and then selecting an appropriate treatment. The subjects in this study do not have the background required to diagnose patients' problems. They can, however, be provided with the information required to select basic treatment techniques. Therefore, this study will be limited to an as-

sessment of the effects of learning strategies on the treatment-planning component of problem solving.

17. While elements of the clinical problem solving process are utilized in all health professions, for practical purposes students from only one profession will be used in this study. While there is no evidence to suggest substantial differences between students in the different health professions, if such differences between professions do exist the inclusion of only physical therapy students in this study may limit its generality.

In contrast to the abrupt transition earlier, note the nice transitional paragraph, number 18, that helps us anticipate what is coming and how it is organized. Transitional material helps keep readers oriented and integrate their thoughts about the proposal.

18. The next section of this proposal deals with the literature related to the proposed study. First, problem solving in the health professions is examined, and the research on instructional methods to facilitate problem solving is discussed. Since the cognitive processes that are activated when using study strategies may have an effect on the learning outcomes, the literature on cognitive processing is given an overview, and the cognitive processes required in problem solving are identified. This information is then related to the literature on learning strategies, focusing on strategies that represent relationships between ideas in graphic formats.

Review of Related Literature

19. Clinical problem solving requires "the ability to gather data from the patient by history and physical examination, integrate this information into a diagnostic formulation, select appropriate investigations to confirm the diagnosis, and institute efficacious management" (Norman and Feightner, 1981, p. 26). While the outcome of the problem solving process, the treatment plan, is the same for experts and novices, the thought processes that occur en route to a treatment plan may differ. When attempting to diagnose a patient's problem, experts often rely on prior experience with similar patients to generate hypotheses about the source of the patient's problem. These hypotheses, which are generated early in the evaluation process, are then used to guide the remainder of the evaluation, as information is gathered to confirm or refute the hypotheses (Barrows and Feltovich, 1987). Likewise, in the formulation of treatment plans, experts rely on past experience to determine what treatment approaches to use. This is in contrast to the novice clinician who has little prior experience on which to base hypotheses or select treatments. For the novice, each new patient is seen as a completely new "problem" that must be investigated.

20. Expert clinicians can be seen as using something other than a traditional problem solving process (Norman, 1988) because each new patient can be seen as similar to some prior patients. In the diagnosis and treatment process each patient is not, in Resnick and Glaser's description of a problem, "a task not previously encountered" (1976, p. 209). In contrast, novices do evaluate and treat patients ac-

cording to a problem solving method, since each patient is seen as a new "task." This problem solving process requires that information regarding the patient be gathered and integrated to formulate a diagnosis, or a list of symptoms that can be treated. Then the clinician must recall the various types of treatments that are available for treating the patient's problem, and integrate the information regarding each treatment's effectiveness with information from the patient evaluation to select an appropriate treatment regime.

Methods of Promoting Clinical Problem Solving

21. If the purpose of professional education is to train individuals to be problem solvers in their respective fields (Cyert, 1980), the educational preparation of health professionals must address this skill. Attempts to improve health professional students' clinical problem solving ability have taken several forms.

Note that in paragraph 21, Kathy goes on to another topic without tying the relevance of the expert-novice contrast discussed in paragraphs 19 and 20 to her study. Apparently, experts and novices use different paths to problem solving since the latter doesn't yet have categories for diagnosis. So what? Does that invalidate the use of her students? What are we to conclude?

The point of the literature review is not to cover everything that was said on the topic but to demonstrate how well you have chosen references that have some bearing on your study. It should display your competence in mastering this subject matter and original thinking in revealing that relevance. Until they are related to the study, paragraphs 20 and 21 don't do this.

22. [The next eighteen pages of literature review up to its summary, paragraph 23, were omitted.]

Summary

23. In summary, three distinct arguments can be made for using spatial learning strategies to promote problem solving ability. The first is made on the basis of the transfer-appropriate processing hypothesis (Bransford, Franks, Morris and Stein, 1979; Morris et al, 1977). According to this hypothesis, efficient studying requires that the initial processing of material be compatible with the ultimate testing conditions. Construction of spatial representations requires selection of important material; in problem solving one must be able to attend to relevant cues, disregarding extraneous content. Clinical problem solving requires that relationships between problems and symptoms be identified, similar to the building of internal connections and labeling of relationships used in spatial strategies. When relationships between concepts are not explicitly stated within the text of the material to be learned the studier must infer the nature of the relationship. Inference is essential in problem solving, as one must determine the cause of the patient's symptoms. It is

argued here that the cognitive strategies required for construction of a spatial representation of text material are consistent with the cognitive processes required by problem solving, indicating that these strategies are appropriate study tools for improving problem solving ability.

24. Second, according to Mayer's "qualitative" view of learning, inference is enhanced by study strategies which require building internal connections between concepts in the to be learned material. As noted above, when working with ill-structured problems such as those encountered in the health professions, inference is an essential element of the problem solving process. Likewise, building external connections between the to be learned material and prior knowledge enhances learning transfer, resulting in improved ability to solve novel problems (Mayer, 1984, 1988). Transfer of learning to new situations is an essential element of problem solving. Strategies that require generation of both internal and external connections have been shown to assist in problem solving (Bromage and Mayer, 1981; Mayer and Cook, 1984). Both internal and external connections are depicted on concept maps.

25. A final argument for the use of spatial learning strategies in general, and concept mapping specifically, for the improvement of problem solving skills, is that such strategies assist in representing the structure of the subject area. Knowledge of content structure is speculated to assist in transfer of learning and problem solving ability (Bruner, 1960). Mental models (Mayer, Dyck and Cook, 1984), the mental representations of relationships between elements in a content area, provide the background structure on which inferences can be drawn and problems can be "run" (de Kleer and Brown, 1983). Wittrock (1988) contends that the purpose of the mind is to create mental representations or models of the world, and the mental representations or models are used to solve problems. Spatial learning strategies, then, are seen as ways to acquire knowledge and build these representations.

Paragraphs 23–25. Ah, here we are told the relevance to her study of the topics in the literature review. She very nicely justifies her treatment for improving clinical problem solving! But connections of previous research to her study should be made throughout the review. Summaries should summarize—briefly restate and organize previous arguments, not surprise us with new material.

Methods

The methods section, paragraphs 26–49, is the heart of the proposal; what has gone before is further operationalized. It should cover the six facets of experimental design: participants, situation (participants and situation, as they often are, are linked in this instance), focus of action (treatment and independent and dependent variables), records (observations and measures), comparison and contrast (basis of sensing attributes and changes), and procedure. The proposal structure roughly follows the ordering of these facets.

Note that while "subjects" was appropriate in the day when this proposal was completed, today her advisors would suggest that she use words like participants *or* informants *to indicate a more equal status with the investigator and, in the latter case, their importance in providing the grist for the mill.*

Subjects

26. The study population consists of first and second year college students intending to major in a health profession. Sixty volunteers from the freshman physical therapy class at Ithaca College will serve as the study sample. If insufficient numbers of freshman students volunteer to participate in the study, students from the sophomore physical therapy class will be recruited for the study. Subjects will be told that participation in the study is strictly voluntary. They will be told that by participating in this study they will learn a study technique that may assist them in preparing for their physical therapy courses. Subjects will be randomly assigned to treatment groups using a table of random numbers.

Paragraph 26. Good! Using volunteers for the control as well as the experimental group and random assignment of individuals to groups control for a lot of potentially contaminating variables. Usually, one would also expect to see that the treatment will be randomly assigned to one of the groups, perhaps by flip of a coin. That ensures the researcher won't assign the treatment to the better group to give them a head start (but see footnote in next paragraph). As you will see in paragraph 40, however, she is going to test for factual knowledge of the material on physical therapy treatment that her students are to master as well as their critical-thinking ability. What if, by chance, the experimental group masters the subject matter considerably better than the control group? Or already are better critical thinkers? She would have great difficulty showing her experimental treatment worked.

On average, random assignment will make the groups equivalent. But to avoid the rare case where it fails to do so, she should have sorted the total group into three or four subgroups on the basis of their scores on factual knowledge of the experimental material. Then she should have sorted each of those subgroups on the basis of their critical-thinking scores. With three subgroups on each test, this would yield nine blocks of students. She would then randomly assign students within each block to experimental and control groups. That would have eliminated differential mastery of the reading material as well as differences in initial problem-solving ability as alternative explanations of apparent treatment effectiveness.[1]

1. As the dissertation data turned out, random assignment did sufficiently control for these variables—indeed, more often than not it does. But should the experimental group have started out markedly superior, we do not have satisfactory means for correcting for this head start. Rather than assignment of treatment to groups by a coin flip, a conservative approach assigns it to the lower scoring one. The treatment effect is assumed strong enough to overcome the handicap. At best, this yields a conservative measure of treatment effect, however, and it may not be possible where, as here, one is controlling for more than one variable (for more, see Cook and Campbell, 1979, pp. 103 ff.).

Materials

27. The content used as the basis for testing will be an approximately 2000 word passage on the physiological effects of thermal agents (heating and cooling treatment techniques), and a description of the different forms of thermal agents. The text passage is written in a style consistent with that used in physical therapy textbooks, with the citations of supportive research studies deleted, and language modified to accommodate subjects' limited experience with medical terminology (see Appendix A).

Paragraph 27. Great, she has it all ready to go and shows it to us in the appendix!

Instruments

Dependent Variable

Problem Solving. 28. A number of methods of assessing health professional students' abilities in problem solving have been developed. The Patient Management Problem (PMP) is a written test used to determine the method the test taker would use to assess and plan treatments using branched simulations. The simulations begin with a brief description of a patient, followed by questions regarding the type of information needed to diagnose the patient. The test takers' goal is to select appropriate test information to diagnose and plan an effective treatment. The information selected during the PMP is provided to the test taker, who then makes judgments regarding additional data required, the patient's diagnosis and/or appropriate treatment procedures. Information not requested is not provided to the test taker, thus simulating actual data collection procedures.

29. Goran, Williamson and Gonnella (1973) examined the relationship between performance on PMPs and actual clinical performance of physicians as documented in medical records. They found that significantly more tests were ordered on the PMP than were actually ordered in the same physicians' clinical practice, thus reflecting questionable validity of the PMP. Construct validity was established by Sedlacek and Nattress (1972) by having expert judges rate a series of decisions in a PMP in terms of their appropriateness. The inter-rater reliabilities ranged from .71 to .85.

30. Newble, Hoare and Baxter (1982) investigated the differences between orally presented PMPs and written PMPs on the premise that written PMPs provided increased cueing to test takers. They found that medical students and physicians with different levels of experience all requested more information when the PMP was presented in the written format vs. the oral (uncued) format. Further reported findings indicated that it appeared that medical students outperformed the more experienced physicians on the PMPs. Since one would predict that the physicians with the most experience should have the highest scores on the PMP, the authors questioned the validity of the PMP. However, the results on differences

between groups of physicians were not statistically analyzed. Wolf (1984) reana-lyzed data gathered by Newble, Hoare and Baxter (1982) to find that the PMPs did not discriminate between the various levels of physicians and students. Thus, while the findings did not support the contention that more experienced physicians should outperform less experienced students, the results did not indicate otherwise for this one PMP. A greater number of PMPs tested on a larger study sample may provide a better measure of the construct validity of the PMP (Wolf, 1984).

31. This type of study was conducted by Farrand, Holzemer and Schleuter-mann (1982), who examined the validity of PMPs by comparing the performance of certified nurse practitioners to nurses with basic registered nurse (RN) training. Their findings supported the hypothesis that the nurse practitioners' diagnostic per-formance should be superior to the less highly trained RNs.

32. While PMPs provide one method of assessing problem solving, the tech-nique has been criticized because it is unstandardized, and therefore difficult to construct and use. Each test taker receives different information and in a different sequence, according to the information requested. Another technique used to as-sess problem solving ability which is more standardized is the modified essay ques-tion (MEQ).

Paragraphs 28 through 31 set us up to accept the PMP as a dependent variable measure with a nice discussion that includes paragraph 31 indicating that for nurses, a group for whom the data are more relevant to physical therapists than the data for doctors, there is ev-idence attesting to its validity. But paragraph 32 veers into a series of problems with the PMP and raises the MEQ as an alternative. This leaves the reader wondering, "Why"?

In fairness to Kathy, we do find some of that information at the end of paragraph 33. There, having described the MEQ sufficiently so the reader will have some understanding of her choice, the PMP and MEQ are contrasted. In part, therefore, this is a matter of style. We very strongly advocate answering any question in the reader's mind raised—if possible, even before. Then their reading of the proposal continues with a positive attitude toward the project instead of it being continually tinged with questions.

But in terms of content as well as style, there is still reason for concern. It is not clear how the fact that all students get the same information is critical, especially since "seeking and choosing" information is part of the problem-solving process in the real world. Perhaps it is that "seeking and choosing" is more closely connected to diagnosis (which Kathy has excluded from her study) than to choice of treatment (her focus). If so, the MEQ may be more desirable. But whatever the reason, she should have explained it to her audience.

33. The MEQ has been used to assess medical (Knox, 1989; Irwin and Bamber, 1982) and physical therapy (Stratford and Pierce-Fenn, 1985) students' problem solving ability. Each MEQ consists of a brief written introduction of a patient case history followed by a number of questions based upon the presented information. The questions asked may test factual knowledge, or may test higher levels of cog-nitive objectives. Following the completion of the presented questions test takers

are presented with additional data regarding the patient, as well as additional questions to which they must respond. This process of data presentation followed by questioning is continued until all desired questions have been responded to. MEQs are typically presented in booklet format as written tests. Test takers are not allowed to read ahead in the test booklet, nor may they return to previously answered questions to make corrections or changes in their responses. MEQs differ from patient management problems (PMP) in that all test takers are provided with the same information regardless of their responses. In the PMP test-takers receive only the information requested. Therefore, with PMPs the test itself is individualized, while the MEQ is more standardized.

Paragraph 33. As readers, we'd like to know what Knox (1989), Irwin and Bamber (1982), and Stratford and Pierce-Fenn (1985) learned from their use of the MEQ, since they aren't cited again. Add a note like, ". . . gave no analysis of usage" to allay that question and keep us from wondering if the author had simply ignored their findings.

34. MEQs have been used as a major part of the assessment of students in the Newcastle Medical School in Australia (Feletti and Smith, 1986). In this application the MEQ was intended to be focused on problem solving ability, and the application of knowledge rather than a test of recall of prerequisite knowledge per se. Analysis of the actual MEQs given over a three year period, however, indicate that the percentage of items testing problem solving ability declined, with an increase in the percentage of items testing factual recall and data interpretation (Wolf, 1986). Irwin and Bamber (1982) likewise analyzed the content of MEQ examinations given at Queen's University in Belfast. As in the Newcastle study, the number of items testing higher levels of cognitive objectives (analysis, synthesis and evaluation) declined over a two year period, with a concomitant increase in the number of items testing recall and comprehension. Apparently, when MEQs are given over a period of years there is a tendency to increase the emphasis on factual knowledge, and decrease testing of higher level cognitive skills.

Paragraph 34. Once again nice information, but of what relevance to the project? This isn't a study that would extend over time.

35. The reliability of MEQs has varied according to the content area tests. Internal consistencies of MEQs used with physical therapy students ranged from .75 to .92 when adjusted to a 60-item questionnaire.

36. Disadvantages of the MEQ include the effort required to create an acceptable test (Knox, 1989). A difficulty appears when test takers use different approaches to the clinical problem presented than the test constructor, thus finding themselves out of sequence with the information presentation in the MEQ test booklet. Student feedback regarding the MEQs at Newcastle medical school indi-

BEISSNER

cate that the questions are sometimes perceived as ambiguous. Students also claimed that they felt a great deal of time pressure, and were uncertain of the degree of detail required to complete each item (Feletti and Smith, 1986). While acknowledging the difficulties with MEQs, Feletti contends that the test is a valuable standardized problem solving assessment tool, if other instruments are used to assess knowledge and data interpretation (Feletti and Smith, 1986).

We're glad her paragraph 36 alerts her audience to problems with the MEQ. But once again, she needs to relate the material to her study. How will these problems be solved? Will she structure the test so students don't get out of sequence? Or doesn't sequence make any difference in this study? How will she ensure that questions are not ambiguous? Will she pretest to set time limits generously?[2] Will examples indicate the level of detail wanted? It is getting to be an old refrain, but when questions are raised in the reader's mind, answer them or indicate why you can't.

37. In this study, a modified version of the MEQ will be used to assess subjects' ability to select appropriate treatment techniques. The standard MEQ presents test takers with a brief description of a patient, and, following a series of questions, additional information on the same patient is provided. This provides an intense examination of the ability to problem solve on a single patient.

Paragraph 37. When terms like modified version *are used, as in paragraph 37, one needs to clearly indicate the nature of the modification. We infer that her modification of the MEQ is that it will test only the treatment aspect of problem solving, but that needs to be made explicit.*

38. As noted previously this study will examine only the treatment planning aspect of problem solving. The subjects for this study do not have the background required to make decisions about simulated patients' diagnoses. The items on the investigator-developed instrument will consist of brief patient descriptions, referred to as case studies, similar to the type used for MEQ. The cases used in the study will be realistic examples of patients with musculoskeletal problems. For each case, an appropriate form of treatment will be one of the treatments covered in the text to be used in this study. Each case will be followed by two questions, asking the subject to a) identify one thermal agent treatment that is most appropriate for this patient, and to b) explain why that particular thermal agent is most appropriate for the patient. Sample patient descriptions of the type to be used in this study are provided in Appendix B.

2. She didn't pretest! In the discussion section of her dissertation, where she is explaining why the map scores did not relate to the dependent variable, she noted insufficient time as a possible reason. Pretesting pays!

Paragraph 38. Good use of the appendix again! But it would be even better if she included at least sample questions. Examples not only indicate careful prior thought but also give the dissertation committee a chance to apply their expertise through making concrete suggestions. After all, specialized know-how is one of the criteria for selecting members of a dissertation committee.

39. Validation of this testing instrument will be made with the use of three experts in the area of thermal agents. These experts will review the cases generated and respond to each item. The responses will be compared with those of the test maker for consistency in treatment selection. The experts' responses to the items will be used as the scoring key for the test. In addition the content experts will be asked to determine whether each item on the problem solving test requires the cognitive processes identified as important to problem solving. They will be provided with a brief description of the cognitive processes required in problem solving. For each item on the problem solving test experts will be asked to indicate whether each of the cognitive processes are required to correctly respond to the item. Those items that do not require the cognitive processes identified as essential to problem solving will be modified so as to include these processes.

Paragraph 39. Another instance—anticipate readers' questions and answer immediately! Here one wonders what happens when the "experts" disagree either with one another or with the test maker. If the readers didn't think of that question in this paragraph, it will be raised in their minds by the last sentence of the next.

Independent Variables

Factual Knowledge. 40. Factual knowledge on the reading will be assessed with an investigator-generated 20 item multiple choice test covering the content of the text. Items on this test will require strictly recall of content, with no inference. Validation of this test will again utilize the content experts, who will individually take the test. Items on which the content experts do not agree will not be used in the study.

Paragraph 40. Multiple choice-test construction is not always as easy as it looks. Pretesting of instruments (surveys, tests, observation forms) is essential to knowing whether they work as intended. In this instance, having experts take the test may have validated the correct responses and their relevance to the reading passage, but it did not serve as a pretest with subjects like those she would be using. The test constructed for the dissertation proved too easy; the mean score on the 17 item test was nearly 16 (no explanation was given for the drop from the proposal's 20 to 17 items). Therefore, the test did not discriminate well enough among the students for there to be a valid measure of factual knowledge. Pretesting, of course, would have discovered this problem before the final data were gathered.

Critical Thinking Ability. 41. Students' innate ability to reason critically may affect their performance on problem solving tests. Therefore, critical thinking ability will be measured with the Watson-Glaser Critical Thinking Appraisal (CTA) Form A (1980). This test is comprised of 80 objectively scored items. Five subscales of the appraisal assess inference, recognition of assumptions, deduction, interpretation, and evaluation of arguments, five elements of critical thinking. The test-retest reliability of the CTA is .73, while split-half reliabilities range from .69 to .85 for the five subscales. Construct validity of the CTA has been established by studies which tested traits presumed to be related to critical thinking ability.

42. This instrument has been used in previous studies of critical thinking in nurses (Matthews and Gaul, 1979; Pardue, 1987; Tiessen, 1987) and physical therapists (Slaughter, Brown, Gardner and Perritt, 1989).

Inventory of Learning Processes. 43. The chief hypothesis of this research is that use of study strategies which include building internal connections between concepts within text and relating content to prior knowledge will improve ability to problem solve. Since some subjects may already use study strategies that include building internal and external connections, the Inventory of Learning Processes (Schmeck, 1983) will be used to identify usual study methods. The Inventory of Learning Processes (ILP) is a self-report inventory which consists of 62 true/false items regarding students' study habits. Four subscales are included in the inventory. "Deep processing" consists of 18 items which assess the extent to which students evaluate, compare and contrast, and organize information as they study. "Elaborative Processing" is a 14 item subscale designed to determine the extent to which students relate new material to prior knowledge. The 23 items on the "Methodological Study" scale assess how much students report that they conform to practices recommended in "how to study" manuals. The final scale, "Fact Retention" in composed of 7 items. This scale assesses students' tendency to adopt study habits that encourage rote memorization.

44. The test-retest reliability of the ILP subscales, when tested over a two-week period range from .79 to .88. Internal consistencies range from .58 for the seven item "Fact Retention" scale, to .82 for "Deep Processing."

45. Test construct validity has been established through tests measuring traits expected to correlate with specific learning process subscales. For example, Schmeck and Ribich (1978) found a significant relationship between the Deep Processing scale of the ILP and total score on the Watson-Glaser Critical Thinking Appraisal. Since deep processing involves careful evaluation of data, and comparisons and contrasts between concepts, this relationship was predicted. Other predicted relationships between the ILP and other standardized assessment instruments include a positive relationship between reports of mental imaging and the Elaborative Processing scale, positive relationships between a measure of academic curiosity and the Deep Processing, Elaborative Processing and Study Methods subscales, and a negative relationship between the Deep Processing scale and anxiety measures (Schmeck and Ribich, 1978). The latter finding is con-

sistent with the Schwartz (1975) study which indicated that highly aroused (anxious) subjects tend to organize memory around superficial aspects of words, such as rhymes, while low arousal subjects organize memory more semantically.

Paragraph 45. The fact that the ILP deep-processing scale and the Watson-Glaser have a "significant relationship" is a positive factor for the validity of the ILP. But it raises the question of what new information the ILP is giving. A careful reader can hardly miss raising this question. It should have been addressed, if nothing else, by indicating the size of the correlation and the reliability of each test. Ideally, also include the proportion of reliable variance on the ILP deep-processing scale that is independent of the Watson-Glaser. (Help from a statistician might have been worth seeking here. Assistance of this and many other kinds is freely available for doctoral students at most universities; make use of them.)

Concept Map Scores. 46. Concept maps generated by the experimental group will be scored according to the standard procedure outlined by Novak and Gowin (1984). This procedure awards points for 1) the number of levels included in the concept map hierarchy, 2) the number of appropriate links identified on the map, and 3) the number of interrelationships identified. The latter measure of interrelationships can be taken as a measure of the degree to which the map maker developed internal connections while studying the material. Since the building of external questions is predicted to have an influence on problem solving ability, an additional measure for assessing the degree to which subjects relate the new material to prior knowledge will be added for this study.

Paragraph 46. How will that score be constructed, and what kind of reliability will it have? Note the number of things yet to be worked through in this proposal—the subject matter test, the MEQs with all their problems, and now this. It isn't overwhelming, but it is enough to raise warning flags for the readers. You want to keep the limit of to-be-worked-through items as low as possible, consistent with the kind of study you are doing. An exploratory study or a qualitative one, typically by its nature, has many. An experimental study, such as this one, typically would be expected to have few.

47. Concept maps will be scored by the researcher and a trained assistant. Interrater reliabilities for concept map scores will be determined using Pearson Product Moment correlations.

Paragraph 47. An intraclass correlation or Cohen's Kappa are the usual statistics for checking interrater agreement. (As noted above, if you aren't comfortable with statistics, have the proposal checked by someone who is; they would catch something like this.) The use of the Pearson product moment correlation to determine interrater reliability will show similarity of ranking of individuals, but will not catch the fact that one is an "easier" grader than the other. Because the intraclass does, it is usually preferred. When using other than the preferred method of analysis, always allay questions by telling why.

In this instance, Kathy is interested only in the relation of map scores to the MEQ. The fact that one rater grades higher than the other makes no difference so long as they agree on the rankings—they did, the correlation given in the dissertation was 0.96. Readers preferring to see an intraclass correlation or Kappa might consider this a flaw unless the proposal includes an explanation.

Procedure

48. Sixty freshman and sophomore physical therapy major volunteers will be solicited via a recruitment letter, and then randomly assigned to either the control or experimental group. Each group will then be divided into two subgroups according to subject availability for meetings. All subjects will participate in 3 sessions. In the first session subjects will be oriented to the study in general terms, and provided with an informed consent form. During this session all subjects will complete the Watson-Glaser Critical Thinking Appraisal, and the Inventory of Learning Processes. During the second session the experimental groups will receive training in the concept mapping technique. The training will follow the suggested outline provided by Novak and Gowin (1984) for training college students, with slight modification. The modification will be to include instructions to relate the text material being mapped to prior knowledge, and to reflect these connections on the concept map. The third session for the experimental group will be the study and testing session, in which subjects will be provided with a text passage on some aspect of physical therapy. Subjects will be instructed to study the passage, and to construct a concept map of the content. Subjects will be allowed one hour to study the material. Then, following a brief break all subjects will be asked to complete the post-test.

Paragraph 48. Don't leave material dangling! She'll divide experimental and control groups into subgroups "according to subject availability for meetings"? What happens then? She uses only those available for all three? Or is this to allow her to adjust session scheduling so subjects can attend them all? Probably the latter, but it isn't clear.

One gets so familiar with the material, particularly toward the end of proposal development, that it is easy to forget how ignorant the reader is. This happens also in the last sentence's reference to a posttest—a posttest of what? One can determine it is the subject matter test, but it should be explicit. Have the proposal read by an "ignorant" reader to catch these.

49. The first session for control subjects will involve completion of the same tests as for the experimental subjects. In the control's second session subjects will receive the text passage, and be instructed to study the material in their usual manner. On completion of the session all notes made during the study session will be collected. Following a brief break, control subjects will take the post-test measure. The third session will consist of training in the concept mapping technique as described above. During each session for both the control and experimental groups

the subjects will be advised not to discuss the content of their sessions with other study participants.

Data Analysis

50. Multiple regression analyses using the method of least squares will be the data analysis procedure. The dependent variable, score on the problem solving post-test, will be regressed against the following independent variables: Group Assignment, Factual Knowledge Score, Critical Thinking Appraisal score (CTA), Inventory of Learning Processes sub scores, and Concept Map Scores.

Independent Variables

Group Assignment(Gr)
Factual Knowledge(FK)
Critical Thinking Appraisal(CTA)
Inventory of Learning Processes Scores
    Deep Processing(DP)
    Elaborative Processing(EP)
    Concept Map Scores(CMS)
The resultant regression equation is:
$y1=b_o+b_1Gr+b^2FK+b_3CTA+b_4DP+b_5EP+b_6CMS$
where y1 = score on problem solving test.

Paragraph 50. Kathy's use of multiple regression analysis in place of the usual analysis of variance is excellent. Not only will it give her information as to which variables are statistically significant, but it will also indicate how much new variance is predicted by each variable. As previously, some discussion of the contrast with the typically expected analysis of variance method with the advantages of this one would be in order. So also would more information about how this will be applied.

Such details indicate one's capability in the area of analysis. A brief treatment, as here, makes the reader wonder whether the analysis is going to be a problem for this student. Allay such questions if you can, either by getting statistical help at the proposal level or by learning enough yourself to handle the problem competently.

Statisticians always prefer to be consulted BEFORE the data are gathered. That way they can avoid many problems that are just not solvable with available methods after the data are already in hand.

Appendixes omitted.

Recall that at the outset we raised questions about Kathy tackling a difficult problem, changing long-standing problem-solving patterns using concept mapping. Curious about the outcome? As it turned out, the experimental group did exceed the control by a statistically significant amount.

But the regression equation explained only 8 percent of the variance, so the effect was

BEISSNER

not very strong. Further, none of the other hypotheses were supported, including the fact that scores of the maps did not correlate with the score on the MEQ (her hypothesis 6). Thus, she was left in the anomalous position of having a positive result not supported by other explanatory variables. She offered a number of explanations, many relating to a lack of validity for the measures. Alternatively, her finding may have been a chance result (type 1 error). As Kathy lays out very nicely at the end of her dissertation, a number of additional studies (which she carefully describes) are needed.

So, our initial concern about being able to design a sensitive enough study to show a statistically significant main effect proved unfounded. While the study has other problems, that is the way research is; even experts, using their best wisdom and experience as a base, can't always predict how it is going to turn out—and thank goodness! Granted, their record at prediction may be considerably better than chance, but still researchers must decide for themselves, occasionally disregarding expert opinion to make important new discoveries. We need risk takers, and we want to encourage those of you who are such. But we also want to warn the bulk of you that one can lose a great deal of time, effort, and resources going down this path as well. Think carefully when warned about your choice of problem.

BEISSNER

A Quantitative Dissertation Proposal with Student Annotations

This dissertation's annotations are selections (sometimes edited for clarity) from those made by some of our students who used draft versions of this book. If these students can pick up these aspects in Dr. Phelan's proposal after reading this book, you can too. Comments are identified with the student's initials. To theirs, we have added our own comments, attributed to "Auth."

SELF-DIRECTED LEARNING'S IMPACT ON MBA STUDENTS AND THEIR ATTITUDES TOWARD PERSONAL DEVELOPMENT

by Thomas D. Phelan

Abstract

1. A current trend in corporate employee development is to maintain one's employability through the acquisition of knowledge transferable to various functions in the work place. Many corporations are encouraging employees to seek development opportunities on their own time, rather than on company time. Motivation to develop on one's own time may be related to the extent to which an adult learner is self-directed and to the extent to which educational providers address self-directedness in the design of courses. This study will examine the impact of self-directed learning on employees' behaviors which indicate a willingness to develop on their own time. A quasi-experimental design involving corporate employees enrolled in a site-based, evening MBA program will pretest and posttest their self-directed readiness while providing, as a treatment, training on self-directed learning techniques. Training on self-directed learning techniques will also be offered to the instructors in the program to establish congruence between what is presented to the learners and what is known by the instructors about the topic.

(DE) The first sentence is too general and does not relate to the dissertation topic or research question. The acquisition of knowledge transfer may be a part of the findings, but it is not appropriate as a lead-off statement.

(RAY) [I]f these employees are already in a development program are they the right ones to test? What about those employees contemplating beginning or who are putting off further development?

(Auth) We'd start the paragraph with the second sentence and clarify the study's goal by adding "of training" to the sentence beginning "This study will examine . . ." so it notes that it is "the impact of training in self-directed learning" that is being studied.

Significance of the Problem

2. A trend in corporations is to reduce hindrances to productivity by asking employees to develop on their own time rather than to disrupt production schedules by employees attending training on company time. Institutions of higher learning are contracting with corporations to provide undergraduate and graduate degree classes in the evening at locations on or near places of employment. When viewed as a cultural change in corporations, an important question is how do corporations motivate employees to develop on their own time. One popular incentive is for corporations to pay the tuition for such courses. Another possible motivator is to design the instruction so that adult learners have more control over the learning system, making attendance more attractive because the individual needs of the learners are addressed with learner input.

3. In essence, the principles and methods of self-directed learning, if understood and applied effectively, offer adult learners greater control over the instructional system. If corporate learners utilize self-directed learning methodologies, employees should be more motivated to attend and to develop on their own time. The result could be increased cost-effectiveness in training the work force, greater employee satisfaction while acquiring job-specific knowledge and transferable educational credentials, and increased productivity for the entire enterprise.

(SW) I found the first sentence of paragraph 2 to be very confusing. Is "reducing hindrances to productivity" (double negative) the same thing as "increasing productivity"? It's . . . hard to indicate the significance of a problem without defining the problem first— maybe the first two sections could be reversed, and redundant definitions of the problem eliminated.

(RAY) The statement "how do corporations motivate employees to develop on their own time" helps put the problem in perspective.

(Auth) Note the hypothesis buried in the middle of paragraph 3. It is nicely put in "if-then" format: "If corporate learners utilize self-directed learning methodologies, employees should be more motivated to attend and to develop on their own time." (Be on the lookout for "if-thens"; they are either hypotheses or statements of relationships. Either way, they usually play a significant role in the study.) Here is the underlying relationship to be tested in the study. (It might be clearer if it used "employees" both places instead of "corporate learn-

PHELAN

ers.") SJ noted: "I agree this might be [a] 'hypothesis' but then he didn't see its significance." This is a comment more on the organization than on the ideas. Readers aren't ready for the hypothesis in the section on problem significance. As SH put it, "Good summary paragraph, but he's making the assumption that using self-directed learning methodologies would increase motivation to develop. Might want to save this for . . . the Research Question section. . ." True.

When the hypothesis is stated, give it prominence. Italicize, underline, or label it; Phelan used underlining to emphasize points elsewhere.

Statement of the Problem

4. This research study is aimed at determining if knowledge acquired about self-directed learning techniques will favorably impact employee attitudes resulting in an increase in their motivation to develop on their own time. The problem in introducing self-directed study on an employee's own time to corporate employees is first, overcoming the strong tradition of other-directed learning employees gained in elementary, secondary and post-secondary schools, and secondly, dispelling the myth that corporate classroom training, on company time, is the corporate way for employees to learn. In addition to dealing with these two problems, there is the added problem of resistance to self-directed learning from corporate trainers who feel their jobs will be in jeopardy, and overcoming the barrier of corporate tuition assistance policies that reimburse only for traditional, highly organized credit earned through attendance at classroom-centered courses.

(Auth) Paragraph 4 could benefit from separation into two; a statement of the problem and then statements of difficulties to overcome. The first paragraph could state the problem as hypotheses to be tested (labeling them as hypotheses for emphasis), bringing down the hypothesis from paragraph 3 like this:

This study tests two hypotheses:

1. Training in self-directed learning methodologies can be done successfully.

2. If employees learn to utilize self-directed learning methodologies, they should be more motivated to attend training on their own time.

5. Furthermore, the problem exists as to whether or not an instructional intervention aimed at teaching employees about self-directed learning techniques will or will not have a positive effect on their attitudes toward development activities on their own time.

(MH) "Self directed learning" as defined by who? What is this exactly? If this is going to be the focus of the entire study then it needs to be defined up front. Good rationale for the argument and importance of the study. References would help strengthen the argument.

6. Recent writings reporting investigations in corporate culture change (Senge, 1990; Noer, 1993; Deal & Bolman, 1991) have indicated that corporate downsizing

has led to increased spans of control for corporate managers, leaving less time for on-the-job training, and less time for employees in leaner organizations to devote company time to training and development. To make matters worse, many of the corporate managers are recent appointees, having filled positions vacated by more senior managers who left due to early retirement incentives, downsized by attrition, creating a new demand for learning, particularly in the area of management skills. This dilemma has found the newest corporate leaders in great need of learning to acquire management skills, and very little company time to do so. It is a natural context for the application of self-directed learning concepts.

(SH) Paragraph 4–6. These three paragraphs are a nice example of beginning with the narrow scope of the study and moving out toward the problem at large. Gets the reader interested quickly, then elaborates on the problem. He also focuses on those who have some kind of stake in the problem (the learners themselves), corporate managers, and corporate trainers.

(Auth) That is one way to look at it. Another is that the beginning of the first paragraph deals with the definition of the problem and could be expanded. Then, in a new paragraph, the rest of paragraph 4 and paragraph 5 (the difficulties of the study's having an impact even if the ideas proved out), together with paragraph 6, could be built upon to further develop the significance of the study.

Literature Review Plan

7. Among the literature to be reviewed are the writings of Allen Tough, Malcolm Knowles and Roger Hiemstra, all researchers in adult learning, and the writings of Ken Blanchard, Steven Covey, Otto Kroeger and Peter Senge from the fields of human resource and organizational development. . . .

8. The original texts of Houle (1961), Knowles (1975), Tough (1979), Guglielmino (1977), Rogers (1983) and others who have contributed to the early thinking in self-directed learning have provided the foundation for the literature review. Later works by Piskurich (1993), Brockett and Hiemstra (1991), Knowles (1984), Brookfield (1984), Candy (1991) and Long et al (1995) will provide insight into determining current thinking. Recent dissertations in the field will also be examined through a compilation and review of selected dissertations by Huey Long and Terrence Redding at the University of Oklahoma. . . .

[The plan of the literature review extended six more paragraphs and was followed by the actual literature review of eighteen more paragraphs. The latter included a time line indicating the appearance of significant works in the self-directed learning literature. These have been omitted to save space.]

(SJ) I cannot find what is Tom's definition of self-directed learning.

(MH) I still think there needs to be a defining of self-directed [learning] terms (pick one of the authors' definitions and then use them as the lead into this section).

PHELAN

(SW) Is a literature review plan required. . . ?

(DE) The literature review plan is an interesting touch which I have never seen . . . before.

(SH) This is a good idea. . . . However, he could have probably done this in a couple of paragraphs.

(Auth) A plan is not required, but it always helps to provide the reader with a conceptual map of what comes next.

The Research Question

9. The question is whether providing a workshop on self-directed learning to adult learners in a corporate, site-based, evening division MBA program will impact the learners' attitudes toward attending development activities on their own time. The plan is to measure the self-directed learning readiness and motivation of employee's enrolled in the MBA classes taught by Jesuit Catholic University professors at Central City Power Corporation; provide a workshop on self-directed learning to learners; and measure self-directed learning readiness again, after information on self-directed learning techniques has been presented. Though the researcher's hypothesis is that exposure to self-directed learning techniques in a workshop will positively affect employee motivation to attend development programs beyond the hours of the normal work day, the null hypothesis, correctly stated will be, "Ho = Attitudes will remain the same after knowledge of self-directed learning techniques is acquired by corporate employees enrolled in the Jesuit Catholic University MBA program at Central City Corporation." The study will be quantitative using surveys, readiness instruments and follow-up interviews.

(JM) The question here suggests that the . . . workshop on self-directed learning . . . alone will change their attitudes? What if lecturers use self-directed learning techniques in their courses? How will this be measured? Will this also affect the learners' attitudes and behaviors?

(DE) More explanation of the design would help eliminate confusion on the part of the reader who may not be as sophisticated or current in his or her design knowledge (Auth. Maybe, but it is a little early to get into design details. The presence of the null hypothesis seems to suggest the design ought to be discussed—another reason to omit it here, see comment below.)

(SH) The research questions should be very specific in nature in order to guide the data collection and analysis. [For example:] "Do learners' attitudes toward attending development activities on their own time change after attending a workshop on self-directed learning?"

(MH) Is it necessary to state the Null hypothesis here? This does not seem to help clarify or strengthen the research question. "The study will be quantitative using surveys. . ." This seemingly could be expanded on. . . .

(Auth) The null hypothesis is neither a necessary (except as your advisor requires it for pedagogical reasons to ensure you understand the logic) nor a desirable part of the proposal.

It tells you nothing and is simply part of the statistical logic. In addition, this paragraph has a number of complex and lengthy sentences; avoid these where possible. Use word processing software and the grammar checker will highlight them for you; heed it.

Research Methods

10. Subjects for this study will be selected from approximately 130 corporate employees who have enrolled in an evening division MBA program sponsored by their corporation. All MBA classes are offered at the corporate training center through a contractual arrangement with the graduate school of a local college. Participants in the program elected to pursue the MBA with full knowledge that classes would be conducted outside of, and in addition to, regular working hours. The program offers employees a choice of five or six courses each semester. By special arrangement, the corporation's tuition assistance program will pay each employee's tuition for courses successfully completed.

(CC) I don't think the group you have targeted is the problem corporate America is interested in solving. They are already enrolled in a credit bearing, after hours, educational program. . . . How about allowing the company to designate a set of employees as those needing training that are not yet involved. Pretest them, offer [self-directed-learning] training, posttest, then tabulate the number of those employees that actually seek additional education in the year following your training.

(Auth) Great idea if he can afford to tack another year onto the data-gathering process. Except as the dissertation is part of a long-term effort, longitudinal studies are usually too time consuming and costly for dissertations.

11. Participants are permitted to enroll in the program upon application approval, and course selection is by recommendation of the college's department chair. Though participants may enter the program without submitting a GMAT score, they must take the exam before completing twelve hours of study.

(JM) Interesting background information on the MBA program without relating its significance to the research methods.

(Auth) Do these entrance requirements make it more likely that it is the self-developers who will apply to the program? Should this question of possible bias have been addressed?

12. Five sample groups (N=71) will be formed. Random assignment will be used to form the two treatment groups. Three of the sample groups will be from employees currently enrolled in the site-based MBA program in which all classes are held in the evening on the employees' own time. The fourth group, a control group, will be selected employees from the corporate information technology group who are not enrolled in the MBA program. A modified Solomon Four-Group design (Huck, et al., 1974) will be used in the quasi-experimental design. Such a design provides for the use of a Pretest, Treatment, and Posttest with precautions taken to

PHELAN

reduce the threat to validity should the Pretest influence the treatment and Posttest. The design is illustrated below:

Group 1 (n=14)	O_1	X	O_2
Group 2 (n=11)		X	O_3
Group 3 (n=11)			O_4
Group 4 (n=12)	O_5		
Group 5 (n=22)	O_6		O_7
Pilot 6 (n=9)		X	O_8
Pilot 7 (n=5)		X	O_9
Pilot 8 (n=14)	O_{10}	X	O_{11}
Total (n=98)			

(SJ) What about putting paragraph 14, a . . . definition of the Solomon four group design, before paragraph 12?

(JM) This section would be more complete if it had provided more details on what the pretest, posttest and treatment would entail. Even though mention is [later] made of these. . . ,the information is still inadequate.

(SH) While it is nice to see how he will analyze the data, no variables have been defined and no measurement instruments have been introduced. Maybe this whole section (paragraphs 10–18) could be organized a little better with section headings like Variables, Subjects, Instruments, Pilot Study, etc.

(MH) I am not sure of what the Pilot 6–8 are doing in the design.

(Auth) The paragraph below comments on Groups 1–5 but never mentions the Pilot, nor what is derived from these data.

All these student comments reflect a need for better organization and more explanation. Putting material in charts and tables isn't enough; it must be explained. The next paragraph makes a beginning.

13. Group 1 undergoes Random assignment (R), Pretest (O_1), Treatment (X) and Posttest (O_2). Group 2 receives no Pretest, but does receive treatment and Posttest (O_3). Groups 3 and 4 are similar in makeup, but group 3 subjects were randomly assigned to receive a Pretest measurement, whereas Group 4 was given the same measurement at a date after the treatment was administered to Groups 1 and 2. This was done to see if anything had affected a non-treatment group over the time period between Pre-test and Post-test. It is possible, at a later time, to present the treatment workshop to these two groups, plus the Posttest, should additional information be required from a Pretest, treatment, Posttest study group. Group 5 is the control group, receiving both Pretest and the Posttest, but having no enrollees in the MBA program. They are similar in their job function to the Information Technology group studied by Durr at Motorola. (Durr, 1994.)

(unknown) Why are the pretest scores not going to be used in the analysis? (Auth. Actually, they are; see paragraph 17 below. No doubt this referred to certain pretest measures, but this isn't made clear. And if no attention is to be paid to the pretests, why give them? Clearly, they are intended to serve some purpose. There is a lot to clear up here.)

(Auth) With the exception of the second sentence of paragraph 13, the functions of the various groups and what they protect against are not explained. Neither is the function of the pretest indicated. Will pretests be used to derive gain scores, or are only the posttest scores going to be analyzed?

(MH) Why are the controls selected from a different group?

(Auth) The explanation of the function of the control group is inadequate; there is no reason to assume readers are familiar with Durr (1994).

14. "The Solomon four-group design is a combination of the pretest-posttest and posttest-only control group design. The first two groups . . . represent the pretest-posttest control group design and the last two groups represent the posttest-only control group design." (Huck. 1974. pp. 254–255.) It was used as a model for the design of this study.

15. "A two-way analysis of variance . . . should be used to compare the four groups of posttest scores. Pretest scores will not be part of the statistical analysis" (Huck. 1974. p. 255), The design is shown in Table 13.1.

(MH) By just quoting Huck, it makes it seem as though you don't understand the analysis process. If this isn't the case, you should expand on the desired results from your multiple ANOVAs.

(Auth) The earlier comment about moving up paragraph 14 makes sense as you read it here. Further, paragraph 14 does not tell you how the Solomon is modified nor why. More organizational problems—paragraph 15 intrudes in the design discussion, coming as it does before the table summary of the design. That table summary would have been a perfect basis for discussing how the Solomon was modified and why the changes were made.

(MH) What is the meaning of the treatment, pretest, posttest yes and no thing? Is this to show where the ANOVA is going to be applied? If so this needs fuller description.

TABLE 13.1

The Solomon Four-Group Design as Adapted for This Study

		Treatment Yes	No
Pretest	Yes	Grp 1	Grp 3
	No	Grp 2	Grp 4 & 5
Posttest	Yes	Grp 1 & 2	Grp 4
	No		Grp 3 & 5

PHELAN

16. "A significant F for the interaction source of variation indicates that the effectiveness of the treatment varies according to whether or not the subjects have been pretested." (Huck, 1974. p.255.)

(Auth) Again, quotations from the expert need to be related to this particular study.

17. A paired t-test statistical treatment and analysis of results will be used to interpret differences between pretest scores and posttest scores on the Learning Preference Test (Guglielmino, 1991) given to the same subjects before and after treatment. A statistical significance at the $p<.05$ level will be sought to reject the Ho that there is no difference in the attitudes of corporate employees toward developing on their own time after employees enrolled in an MBA program attend a workshop on self-directed learning and professors teaching in that program attend a training session on how to incorporate self-directed learning activities into their courses.

18. The proposed Pretest and Posttest is the "Self-Directed Learning Readiness Scale (SDLRS)" (Guglielmino, 1977). (copy in appendix)

(JM) What does the Learning Preference Test measure, and is it used differently from the SDLRS?

(SH) A one-sentence paragraph is not enough to inform us of the SDLRS instrument.

(MH) There needs to be more said about this measure. Is it widely used? Is it valid? Is it reliable with the group you are working with?

(Auth) Including a copy in the appendix is a good idea.

19. As a follow-up to the quantitative pre-tests and post-tests and the treatment workshop, focus group interviews were conducted with two of the pilot groups and volunteers from the MBA students. To establish appropriate questions, thirty-two professionals from adult education, corporate training, adult learning and training research, corporate executive leadership, career development and authors in related fields were asked to list three observable behaviors they felt indicated an employee was motivated to development on that employee's own time. . . . Specifically, the following question was asked of thirty-two (32) professionals in the fields of corporate management, corporate training, career development and adult education, "Would you help by listing three behaviors, which, if observed, would indicate to you that a corporate employee appeared motivated to develop, learn, or study on that employee's own time?" Fifteen (15) responded with the following answers:

Enthusiam, openness, inquiry or questioning; (Krain)

One who takes the initiative to seek out learning opportunities . . . (Syntell

Asking for advice about continuing education opportunities at nearby community colleges or universities (Calibrese)

[Several pages of quotations from responses appeared here.]

(JM) Asking the experts was a good idea. . . .

(TA) I would recommend that the extensive list of specific comments received from content experts . . . be placed in the appendix. . . . I did, however, like how these items were grouped to create patterns for participant focus group discussions. This was a creative way to develop a new instrument.

(Auth) Note the break in the presentation from design into the description of questions for further data collection without, unfortunately, any titling or sectioning to warn the reader. Signposts are important in helping readers understand where to place material in the overall picture.

Nowhere earlier were we told to expect data from focus groups nor what their purpose would be. Undoubtedly, these data are to serve a purpose; a proposal that is a chain of reasoning should mention the focus groups and their purpose early in the basic plan so that this section and the following detail contribute to the central purposes of the study. As it stands, one has to infer the use of these data. In paragraph 22 we find that they are congruent with Hoyle's previous findings and the attempt to relate them to Hoyle's types of learners. Presumably, then he will use these data to guide questions to ask learners in the follow-up interviews with students and faculty and perhaps use the learner types to categorize them. But this is never stated, so we must infer this. It would have made a nice package and tied in this whole section. Here it is ancillary and takes up an inordinate amount of space in the proposal in contrast to the main thrust of the study.

Although the student comments are somewhat critical of this part of the proposal, the students apparently didn't feel sufficiently confident to trounce it as thoroughly as it deserved. That comes with practice.

20. This input was studied for categorical similarities, and six categories were identified which had four or more listings. They are:

1. Attends training, development or seminars (9 responses)
2. Talks about, questions, discusses or asks about learning opportunities (9)
3. Exhibits self-directedness in learning or other areas (9)
4. Explores job enrichment opportunities (8)
5. Reading or subscribing to relevant literature (7)
6. Attitude reflects interest in learning (4).

(MH) Who else looked at the data? Was it just you?

21. With these descriptor categories as guides, focus group interview questions were prepared to be asked at focus group meetings with employees who par-

PHELAN

ticipated in either treatment, test or control groups. The question pool consisted of the following questions:

1. What factors encourage you to study on your own time?
2. What barriers are there to studying on your own time?

[33 additional questions were listed here]

(MH) There is no mention of the IRB in this study. Isn't it necessary to contact them when you are using human subjects?

(Auth) Yes, it is okay to indicate IRB clearance is to come, but it is even better to already have their approval.

22. Upon examination of the comments six groups of behaviors were formed, which then were matched to Houle's classifications of learners who were Goal Oriented, Activity Oriented and Learning Oriented (Houle, 1961). It became evident during discussions held in the pilot groups that Houle's descriptions and reports of concerns facing adult learners were as relevant [now] as they were in 1960. Pilot group participants related especially to Houle's findings about peer and family rejection of continuing education as a credit to those involved. In fact, the 1995 adult learners expressed every bit as much criticism of their continuing education efforts as were expressed by Houle's subjects prior to his 1961 publishing of The Inquiring Mind.

(JM) I do not understand the significance of the information presented in paragraph 22.

23. Focus group interviews were tape recorded on five different occasions and transcribed for detailed review.

(MH) Why did you pick the five different occasions that you recorded? Was the selection random? Were there specific topics being covered at those sessions? What is a detailed review and who performed it?

(Auth) In addition, this paragraph should come before the previous one.

Once again, note the lack of organization and headings. Why isn't paragraph 24 with 26 under the "Treatment Workshop" heading? Inserting headings not only helps the reader, but had the writer tried to insert headings, he would have noticed the misplacement of material and, likely, better organized it. Another reason to use them.

24. The proposed treatment is a workshop on self-directed learning methodology to be offered to the MBA professional instructional staff and a self-directed learning readiness workshop to be offered to Group 1 and Group 3 of the subjects in the MBA program. The design and development of the workshop materials will be completed and piloted by the dissertation author in the spring of 1995. An out-

line for such a workshop has been suggested by Knowles (1975), Tough (1979) and Guglielmino et al. (1991a). The SDL training will occur in May of 1995 for the MBA professors and in September 1995 for the MBA students.

25. A quantitative statistical analysis of results will include a two-way factorial ANOVA, a summary of means and standard deviations of posttest scores.

(JM) This . . . should have been mentioned earlier. (Auth. See paragraphs 14–17; how about in there somewhere?)

(MH) What results from where? You did not talk about any kind of instrument that was developed for the treatment workshop. Is there going to be a special instrument developed for this purpose? Or are you still talking about the SDLRS?

The Treatment Workshop

26. *[The treatment workshop was described in more detail in an appendix.]*

Management Plan

27. The management plan and time schedule follows:

January 1995	Dissertation committee formed;
February 1995	Experimental Design completed;
March 1995	All necessary approvals for access obtained from Syracuse University, Niagara Mohawk and Le Moyne College; Begin writing the following: 1. What the study is about. 2. What the problem is and its significance. 3. Where the study fits into the body of previous work and how it will contribute to it.
October 1995	First measurement of learner attitudes and self-directed learning readiness (Pre-test);
October 1995	Workshop on Self-directed learning (Learner Treatment)
October 1995	Second measurement of learner attitudes and self-directed learning readiness. (Post-test);
November 1995	Write section on the following: 4. What did I do?
December 1995	Follow-up interviews with professors and students; Write the sections on: 5. What did I find? Initial analysis of data: 6. How do the findings relate to what I expected? To previous work?
January 1996	Analysis of data;
January-March 1996	Write section on: 7. How to put it all together?
April 1996	Preparation of defense and defense of dissertation.

PHELAN

(SH) The management plan is a good idea. However, only 1 month is allowed for data analysis, and only 4 months are allowed for writing about the findings and preparing for dissertation defense. These two time frames should be increased.

(MH) This seems like a general outline that could use greater detail. The more you think through the details before the study the less apt you are to run into problems during the study.

(Auth) Overall, a proposal should develop as a chain of reasoning. This one doesn't. One doesn't get a sense of one section building on another. Not only are segments not inter-related, but also they aren't always in a logical order. There is little foreshadowing—"Oh, yes, I was expecting this, now let's see how you've developed it"; the reader has only a general idea of where the study is going.

Students were asked for paragraph by paragraph comments. You'll probably agree with us that they did a really good job of spotting most of the problems in the proposal. Had an overall statement about it been requested, they would probably have come up with something like the above.

PART SIX

Funded Proposals

Some seek funding to support their dissertation research as a matter of necessity in order to be able to complete their degree. In most instances, the easiest sources of support to tap are those within your own institution—assistantships and fellowships, and sometimes there are special funds for this purpose.

Those of you who plan on seeking positions in higher education should especially seek such support whether your financial needs impel you to do so or not. Seek assistantships for the opportunity to work closely with faculty members either on their research or your own. You'll benefit from the apprenticeship; they'll get to know you better, which is valuable when you need their help in finding a position. Seek funding outside your institution for the experience of preparing such proposals (including making a budget and work plan if you didn't do so for your committee) and of going through the competitive process. Invaluable knowledge and seasoning is gained in interacting with funding personnel, trying to understand their demands, getting feedback on your proposal, and, if you are successful, negotiating the grant or contract with them. Seek funding to have the experience of handling a research budget and, perhaps, in order to do a better study than you would be able to otherwise do.

Seeking funding for faculty research is of tremendous importance in most large universities; it is a skill that can be developed. Your chair and committee will be especially pleased to see you seeking this experience at this early stage. And whether or not you succeed, though it is a special plus if you do, the experience will mark your résumé for special attention in later job competition.

Specially designated funding for doctoral students and less experienced applicants is available in many governmental programs. Look for those in your research area. Nearly all programs will allow you to enter their regular competitions as well. Though your rivals may be more experienced, a good idea well presented (as suggested in this book) can carry the day.

You may find it helpful to enter the competition jointly with a faculty member, especially one who has already received funding. In most competitions you'll need a faculty sponsor in any event. Most committee chairpersons will be delighted to serve as sponsor.

The chapter in this section is devoted to suggesting ways you can seek funding. Nearly all major institutions have offices intended to assist faculty in this task, and generally they will also gladly assist graduate students. We hope that you find this advice helpful and wish you every success.

CHAPTER 14

Finding Funding

CHAPTER CONTENTS

Are you considering submitting your first proposal for funding? If you have followed the advice of the previous chapters, you are in a good position to do so. You have all the parts needed to submit to most agencies, except perhaps for a budget and possibly a work plan! You need only arrange it in their outline or fill in their form if they have one. What advice can we give you? First, the proposal is used as a basis for judging the kind of work that you will do, so careful preparation of the proposal is clearly one message. Second, there are several places in the proposal where you have a special opportunity to show your skills:

- The conceptualization of your problem is the first of these. Your ability to conceptualize your problem in a framework that places it in a position of importance in its field is the first sign that you have a good understanding of your field and what you intend to do in it.
- Your handling of the review of the literature is the second place where you can demonstrate your command of your field. When you present your project in appropriate perspective in relation to the other relevant work, your ability shows. So does your ability to select only the appropriate literature and weave it into the fabric of your proposal.
- Similarly, when you present a study design and procedure that, in studies where it is appropriate, eliminate alternative explanations of a relationship you wish to demonstrate, explicitly recognize those explanations that were not eliminated and tell why a compromise was made and the basis for it.

Handling well those aspects of the proposal will carry you a long way. But what else can you do? The biggest hurdle to funding is finding someone with an interest in what you want to do and with resources available within your time frame of study. That is the first task and is key to success.

SEARCH CURRENT GRANTS

Search for funders that are already supporting work in your area. This calls for a listing of grants. There are at least two at the present time that include both government and private grantors. One, which appears to be only in print at the present time, is the *Annual Register of Grant Support.* The other, available online, is *Dialog@Site*'s database of grants. These may be available through your institution's library or its office of grant support (see below). The former is issued annually; the latter is available by subscription. The latter, being online, is the easier and faster to screen.

Federal

If these are not available, or with the results of what you found, search for federal programs, the largest funding source. Find those with missions that include your interest. Before actually applying, find out all you can so you can make sure your project is appropriate, or can be made so. Fit is critical; units have no authority to fund projects beyond their mission statements. Mission statements are available at their Web sites, or you can look them up in the *Catalog of Federal Domestic Assistance* (online at http://cfda.gov [accessed October 1, 2004]). For more targeted searching, try these: the Department of Education (http://www.ed.gov/rschstat/landing.jhtml?src=el [accessed October 1, 2004]), the Department of Health and Human Services (http://www.hhs.gov/grants/#grant [accessed October 1, 2004]), and the National Science Foundation (http://www.nsf.gov/home/menus/funding.htm [accessed October 1, 2004]; see especially the site for graduate students and postdocs: http://www.nsf.gov/home/menus/grads.htm [accessed October 1, 2004]).

Look for research funding announcements; these will typically have the name, phone, and e-mail address of the contact person. Get in touch with persons in your research area about programs that do not appear to be broad enough to include your interest and ask where you might find funding for your interests. They may recommend other programs or have suggestions as to how you might reconfigure your ideas to fit existing programs.

Foundations

Some researchers prefer to seek foundation funding even though government funding might be available. There is much less bureaucratic "red tape," there is less reporting, and the proposal is usually simpler. The Foundation Center is the place to start (see http://fdncenter.org [accessed October 1, 2004]). The center's *Foundation Directory* requires a fee or subscription for access, but the "SearchZone" (click on it) is free. The center's publications and instructional materials are very useful, so browse them. Once you have identified possibly relevant foundations, screen them further by seeing what kind of grants they have been giving by checking their Web sites (use a search engine to find the URL). Another source you can gain access to for a fee is to the *Chronicle of Philanthropy*'s "Guide to Grants" at http://philanthropy.com/grants (accessed October 1, 2004) where they list foundation grants for the previous three years. Again, your library or office of grant support (see below) may provide access for both of the above.

USE PROFESSIONAL ASSOCIATIONS

Some professional associations have aids to finding funding for their members. For example, the American Psychological Association (APA) has such an aid (http://www.apa.org/science/researchfunding.html [accessed October 1, 2004]). While visiting the APA site (http://www.apa.org [accessed October 1, 2004]), click on "students" and browse the useful materials provided. Among these is *GradPSYCH* magazine, which may have articles of interest. Using a federal grant, APA has also developed *A Search Tool for Research Funding in the Behavioral and Social Sciences*, which is available from the above APA science site and at http://www.decadeofbehavior.org/fundsource/ (accessed October 1, 2004). Ask faculty about other professional associations.

Some associations have a grants or governmental affairs person whose main responsibility is lobbying. They have learned the bureaucracy and know the nature of programs as well as the personnel. These individuals are targeted to your own and closely related fields; they nearly always personally know the people you want to contact. Their information and advice can be invaluable, but remember, they can't favor you over persons from other institutions. Some professional organizations have grant-writing workshops. These can be helpful not only in giving advice, but also in getting you started writing.

EXAMINE SUCCESSFUL PROPOSALS

Look at some successful proposals. For example, browse the abstracts of the Grantsmanship Center's collections on CD-ROMs at http://www.tgcigrantproposals.com (accessed October 1, 2004). A CD-ROM can be ordered for a small fee. Try your department head; ask for some at your institution's grants support office (see below). Some federal agencies will release copies of successful proposals. Ask about this possibility by phone or e-mail. Use the sites listed above to find contact persons, or, if unsuccessful, try using http://firstgov.gov (accessed October 1, 2004) as the portal to find relevant personnel and programs.

USE YOUR INSTITUTION'S GRANTS SUPPORT OFFICE

The most important suggestion in this list is that nearly all doctoral granting institutions have a grants support office; ask for its help. They go by various names, grants administration, sponsored program office, etc.; at state universities, they are often foundations or separate corporations. Ask faculty or department chairs to find yours. Personnel in these offices may be able to provide a number of things:

1. *A person who is familiar with the nature of proposals in your field, either on their staff or, more likely, in your institution.* If the latter, they will probably be willing to help you to contact that person.

2. *A file of previously successful proposals* from your institution that you can examine for ideas.

3. *A library of other helpful materials* on writing proposals and getting funding for them. They are likely to have some of the compilations of successful proposals that are available. Some institutions also have internal publications that describe the procedures to follow to make grant submission and administration go smoothly in their bureaucracy.

4. *Information on where to find funding,* both governmental and foundation. Most of these offices have access to information services that require fees and/or subscriptions. For example, they may have copies of *The Annual Register of Grant Support* or a subscription to the Foundation Center so you can access their files for relevant foundations, and also to the Chronicle of Philanthropy so you can search its "Guide to Grants."

5. *Funds to visit appropriate agencies or a foundation* to try out your ideas in person. Knowing that departmental budgets rarely have extra money for travel, some institutions have an incentive fund to help individuals get started. Nothing is so reinforcing as finding a sponsor interested in one's ideas, and that comes from making personal contacts.

6. *Contacts with persons in agencies and foundations,* either from their own personal knowledge or from knowledge of who has such contacts in the institution, so you don't go in "cold."

7. *Help with the budget.* What is brand-new to you is the daily responsibility of these offices. This is the one area where you should be able to count with certainty on their help; it is in their interest to get you funded adequately.

8. *Set-up grants from your institution to get your research started.* Often such grants are just for equipment, but sometimes they can be used for personnel and supplies as well. Such a grant can get your research under way so you have something to show an agency. These investments show an institutional commitment to your work and indicate the institution's confidence in you—a display not lost on potential sponsors. And sometimes, by funding a significant portion of your project, an institution can make it feasible for the sponsor to pick up the remaining expenses.

You need never be ashamed of a proposal that you worked through carefully and prepared as well as you could and then had turned down. Even when we do our best, some of us fail. But even that has its positive aspects: One is that we learn from our failures. A second is that it shows we weren't afraid to try. People respect that; they know that those who don't try, don't learn. Everyone respects a best effort. A best effort is apparent, and agency and foundation staff will typically be most helpful to you. Your having made that kind of effort contributes to the reputation you are building with that agency; they know you will try again, and they want you to succeed. Find the reasons for the rejection and resubmit. But here's hoping that you succeed the first time!

Additional Readings

References

Index

Additional Readings

The materials listed below augment what has been presented in the preceding chapters in various ways. They are arranged alphabetically, but if arranged in priority, the Dead Thesis Society's Web site would top the list.

Becker, H. S. (1998). *Tricks of the trade: How to think about your research while you're doing it.* Chicago: University of Chicago Press.

A thoughtful book modeling how the author, an experienced, careful researcher, asks questions. Its chapters on imagery, sampling, concepts, and logic trace the research process with wise advice and examples. Very helpful read for all researchers.

Bolker, J. (1998). *Writing your dissertation in fifteen minutes a day: A guide to starting, revising, and finishing your doctoral thesis.* New York: Holt.

A book on how to handle yourself to get the writing done. Good advice like setting attainable goals, providing motivation, writing to think, parking on the downhill side. Common sense, yes, but it usefully reinforces much of what one knows.

Cone, J. D., and Foster, S. L. (1993). *Dissertations and theses from start to finish: Psychology and related fields.* Washington, DC: American Psychological Association.

Except for the methods section, which is oriented toward quantitative methods, it provides generally applicable advice from problem finding to publishing the dissertation. Ably combines advice at the conceptual level so you know what the target is, with brief examples at the detail level to show you how to do it. The proposal as such receives less attention than books devoted to it and references need updating, but among books covering the process as a whole, this is one of the best.

Dead Thesis Society (n.d.). An online resource at: http://freewebhosting.hostdepartment. com/d/deadthesissociety/ (accessed October 1, 2004).

This is probably *the most important resource in this section.* Click on the tabs at the right of the home page to see its offerings. The tab "Resources" has links to other support groups and advice on thesis writing (and ads for services), thesis defense, time management, supervision, and general survival (including comic relief). The "Research" tab links to research reports on the general topic. The "Discussion" tab provides a sign-in to join the discussion groups for advice and support. *Don't wait until in trouble to become familiar with this site; consulting it for material relevant to whatever your dissertation stage can be very helpful.*

Fitzpatrick, J., Secrist, J., and Wright, D. J. (1998). *Secrets for a successful dissertation.* Thousand Oaks, CA: Sage.

>Having completed their doctorates, these three women share what they wish they'd known. Quite frank about the perils of faculty politics and other problems, they concentrate more on what one needs to do to get through than academics.

Foundation Center (n.d.). *Short online course in proposal writing.*
http://fdncenter.org/learn/shortcourse/prop1.html (accessed October 1, 2004).

>The Foundation Center has prepared this short course primarily for nonprofit programs seeking funds. But the essentials would apply as well to a research proposal.

Glatthorn, A. A. (1998). *Writing the winning dissertation: A step-by-step guide.* Thousand Oaks, CA: Sage.

>Written by an experienced advisor and intended for teachers and administrators who have not previously done research, it is indeed a step-by-step guide, down to spelling out what paragraphs should appear in each section and in what sequence. Easy to dismiss by those with experience, it will be just the hand-holding that is needed for some just starting out.

Hawley, P. (1993). *Being bright is not enough: The unwritten rules of doctoral study.* Springfield, IL: Charles C. Thomas.

>Intentionally written from the student point of view by a former faculty member, its intent is to reduce ABDs by giving insights to faculty viewpoints, illuminate unvoiced institutional expectations, and give practical advice regarding problem handling. Each step is examined from both personal and academic sides. Her personal experiences were broadened by interviews with students and faculty.

Heath, A. W. (1997, March). The proposal in qualitative research [41 paragraphs]. *Qualitative Report (online serial), 3(1).* http://www.nova.edu/shss (accessed October 1, 2004). Click on "SHSS Scholarly Journals," choose "The Qualitative Report," and click on the article index; Heath is the first article in volume 3, number 1.

>A generic outline for a four-section proposal: Introduction, Research Paradigm, Research Method, and Preliminary Biases, Suppositions, and Hypotheses. Subheadings are proposed for each section.

Kerlins, B. (n.d.). *Research proposals.* http://kerlins.net/bobbi/research/qualresearch/proposals.html (accessed October 12, 2004).

>A useful collection of materials by Bobbi Kerlins. Hold your cursor on "Research" in the panel at the left of the screen for links. Among these, select "Qualitative Research"; further choices will appear. The above URL has taken you to the Proposal's one. Links to other helpful sites are at the end of Proposals' text. Explore other links in the "Research" and "Qualitative Research" panels. The "Quant Corner" links to quantitative research resources; "Discussion Groups" to qualitative research discussion groups to which you can subscribe.

Levine, S. J. (2003). *Writing and presenting your thesis or dissertation.*
http://www.learnerassociates.net (accessed October 12, 2004).

>S. Joseph Levine's site (Michigan State University), among other documents, contains two of interest: "Writing and Presenting Your Dissertation" and "Guide for Writing a Funding Proposal."

Locke, L. F., Spirduso, W. W., and Silverman, S. J. (2000). *A guide for planning dissertations and grant proposals* (4th ed.). Thousand Oaks, CA: Sage.

An excellent book that concentrates on the proposal. Includes chapters on funding and grant proposals. Four proposals are reproduced with extensive annotations: one experimental, one qualitative, one quasi-experimental, and one a request for funding.

Piantanida, M., and Garman, N. B. *The qualitative dissertation.* Thousand Oaks, CA: Corwin Press.

A thorough, very well-done discussion of the qualitative dissertation process from "Cycles of Deliberation" to "Life after Dissertation." Includes a number of helpful exemplars.

Proquest Digital Dissertations.

http://www.il.proquest.com/hp/Products/Dissertations.html

(accessed October 1, 2004).

Excellent place to get an idea of what dissertations in one's field look like. This site accesses dissertations from all universities that send them to UMI, probably most of North America's. Search the past two years without charge; the whole database is available to subscribing universities.

Pyrczak, F. (2000). *Completing your thesis or dissertation: Professors share their techniques and strategies.* Los Angeles: Pyrczak Publishing.

A compilation of tips from seventy-one professors; most reinforce good practice, many are mundane but useful as reminders, a few embarrassingly terrible.

Reis, J. B., and Leukefeld, C. G. (1998). *The research funding guidebook: Getting it, managing it and renewing it.* Thousand Oaks: Sage.

Uses the National Institutes of Health format as a basis for discussing how to apply for funds, but that format is similar to most government agencies. Helps one see the proposal from the funder's point of view.

Rudestam, E. R., and Newton, R. R. (2001). *Surviving your dissertation: A comprehensive guide to content and process* (2nd ed.). Newbury Park, CA: Sage.

An excellent discussion of the dissertation process with a good chapter on computer usage. More oriented to quantitative than qualitative work, but most topics apply to both.

Sternberg, D. (1981). *How to complete and survive a doctoral dissertation.* New York: St. Martin's Press.

Like Hawley above, this book concentrates on the problems of the dissertation process, especially how to manage oneself, with copious solution suggestions. More comprehensive than Hawley and very well written. References to such things as computer use are out of date, but the general advice is not.

Substance Abuse and Mental Health Services Administration (SAMHSA). *Developing Competitive SAMHSA Grant Applications.* http://www.samhsa.gov/grants/index.html (accessed October 1, 2004). Click on "Grants-Writing Training and Technical Assistance Workshops for Grassroots Faith and Community Based Groups."

An *extremely* detailed step-by-step how-to for the grant writer. Following all its minute parts may seem tedious, but it picks up aspects others don't. Intended for organizations and demonstration projects, adapt its sound advice to your project, and an idea with merit will shine! A hidden gem.

References

American Psychological Association (2001). *Publication manual of the American Psychological Association* (5th ed.). Washington, DC: Author.

Backer, T. (1977). *A directory of information on tests.* ERIC TM Report 62-1977. Princeton: ERIC Clearinghouse on Tests, Measurement and Evaluation, Educational Testing Service.

Balay, R. (Ed.) (1998). *Guide to reference books* (11th ed.). Chicago: American Library Assn.

Bangert-Drowns, R. L. (1986). Review of developments in meta-analytic method. *Psychological Bulletin, 99,* 388–399.

Bauer, D. G. (1984). *The "how to" grants manual.* New York: Macmillan.

Becker, B. J. (1994). Combining significance levels. In H. Cooper and L. V. Hedges (Eds.), *The handbook of research synthesis.* New York: Russell Sage Foundation.

Bogdan, R. (1971). *A forgotten organizational type.* Unpublished doctoral dissertation, Syracuse University.

Boruch, R. F., & Wothke, W. (Eds.) (1985). *Randomization and field experimentation* (New Directions for Program Evaluation, No. 28). San Francisco: Jossey-Bass.

Bushman, B. J. (1994). Vote-counting procedures in meta-analysis. In H. Cooper and L. V. Hedges (Eds.), *The handbook of research synthesis.* New York: Russell Sage Foundation.

Campbell, D. T., & Stanley, J. C. (1963). Experimental designs for research on teaching. In N. L. Gage (Ed.), *Handbook of research on teaching.* Chicago: Rand McNally. (Also available from the publisher as a monograph under the chapter title.)

Cantor, R. (1994). *The president of the United States as "public educator": A new historical perspective.* Unpublished dissertation proposal, School of Education, Syracuse University.

Carifio, J., & Baron, R. A. (1977). Soliciting sensitive data anonymously: The CDRGP technique. *Journal of Alcohol and Drug Education, 23* (2), 47–66.

Cohen, J. (1988). *Statistical power analysis for the behavioral sciences* (2nd ed.). New York: Academic Press.

Converse, J. M., & Presser, S. (1986). *Survey questions: Handcrafting the standardized questionnaire* (Quantitative Applications in the Social Sciences, No. 63). Beverly Hills: Sage Publications.

Cook, T., et al. (1992). *Meta-analysis for explanation: A casebook.* New York: Russell Sage Foundation.

Cook, T., & Campbell, D. T. (1979). *Quasi-experimentation.* Chicago: Rand McNally.

Cooper, H. M. (1985). Literature searching strategies of integrative research reviewers. *American Psychologist, 40,* 1267–1269.

Cooper, H. M. (1987). Literature searching strategies of integrative research reviewers: A first survey. *Knowledge, Creation, Diffusion, Utilization, 8,* 372–383.

Cooper, H. M. (1989). *Integrating research: A guide for literature reviews* (2nd ed.). Newbury Park, CA: Sage.

Cooper, H. M. (1998). *Synthesizing research: A guide for literature reviews* (3rd ed.) (Applied Social Research Methods Series, vol. 2). Thousand Oaks, CA: Sage.

Cooper, H., & Hedges, L. V. (Eds.) (1994). *The handbook of research synthesis.* New York: Russell Sage Foundation.

Duke, N. K., & Beck, S. W. (1999). Education should consider alternative formats for the dissertation. *Educational Researcher, 28* (4), 31–36.

Eisner, E. W. (1976). Educational connoisseurship and criticism: Their form and function in educational evaluation. *Journal of Aesthetic Education, 10* (3–4), 135–150.

Eisner, E. W. (1981). On the differences between scientific and artistic approaches to qualitative research. *Educational Researcher, 10* (April), 5–9.

Eisner, E. W. (1984). Can educational research inform educational practice? *Phi Delta Kappan, 15* (7), 447–452.

Fabiano, E., & O'Brien, N. (1987). *Testing information sources for educators* (TME Report 94). Princeton: ERIC Center on Tests and Measurements, Educational Testing Service.

Fetterman, D. M., Kaftarian, S. J., & Wandersman, A. (Eds.). (1996). *Empowerment evaluation: Knowledge and tools for self-assessment and accountability.* Thousand Oaks, CA: Sage.

Fleiss, J. L. (1994). Measures of effect size for categorical data. In H. Cooper and L. V. Hedges (Eds.), *The handbook of research synthesis.* New York: Russell Sage Foundation.

Fournier, D. M. (1993). Reasoning in evaluation: A distinction between general and working logic (Doctoral dissertation, Syracuse University, 1992). *Dissertation Abstracts International, 55/03A,* 0527.

Glass, G. V., McGaw, B., & Smith, M. L. (1981). *Meta-analysis in social research.* Beverly Hills: Sage Publications.

Glass, G. V., & Smith, M. L. (1979). Meta-analysis of research on class size and achievement. *Educational Evaluation and Policy Analysis, 1* (1), 2–16.

Goldman, B. A., & Mitchell, D. F. (1995–2003). *Directory of unpublished experimental measures* (Vols. 1–8). Washington, DC: American Psychological Association.

Gronlund, N. E. (2001). *Measuring student achievement* (7th ed.). Boston: Allyn & Bacon.

Guba, E. G., & Lincoln, Y. S. (1987). The countenances of fourth-generation evaluation: Description, judgment, and negotiation. In D. S. Cordray & M. W. Lipsey (Eds.), *Evaluation studies review annual* (Vol. 11). Newbury Park, CA: Sage.

Hastings, P. K., & Southwick, J. C. (Eds.) (1974). *Survey data for trend analysis: An index to repeated questions in U.S. national surveys held by the Roper Public Opinion Research Center.* Storrs, CT: Roper Public Opinion Research Center.

Hedges, L. V. (1982). Estimation of effect size from a series of independent experiments. *Psychological Bulletin, 92* (2), 155–162.

Hedges, L. V., & Olkin, I. (1985). *Statistical methods for meta-analysis.* Orlando: Academic Press.

Hopkins, K. D. (1998). *Educational and psychological measurement and evaluation* (8th ed.). Boston: Allyn & Bacon.

Hunter, J. E., & Schmidt, F. L. (1990). *Methods of meta-analysis: Correcting error and bias in research findings.* Newbury Park, CA: Sage.

Hunter, J. E., Schmidt, F. L., & Jackson, G. B. (1982). *Meta-analysis: Cumulating research findings across studies.* Beverly Hills: Sage Publications.

Joint Committee on Standards for Educational Evaluation (1994). *The program evaluation standards* (2nd ed.). Thousand Oaks, CA: Sage.

Kaufman, R. A. (1979). *Needs assessment: A concept and application.* Englewood Cliffs, NJ: Educational Technology Publications.

Kounin, J. S. (1970). *Discipline and group management in classrooms.* New York: Holt, Rinehart and Winston.

Krathwohl, D. R. (1988). *How to prepare a research proposal: Suggestions for funding and dissertations in the social and behavioral sciences* (3rd ed.). Syracuse: Syracuse University Press.

Krathwohl, D. R. (1994). A slice of advice. *Educational Researcher, 23* (1), 29–32, 42.

Krathwohl, D. R. (1998/2004). *Methods of educational and social science research: An integrated approach* (2nd). New York: Longman; reissued, Long Grove, IL: Waveland Press.

Lee, R. M. (2000). *Unobtrusive methods in social research.* Buckingham, U.K.: Open University Press.

Light, R. J. (1984). Six evaluation issues that synthesis can resolve better than single studies. In W. H. Yeaton & P. M. Wortman (Eds.), *Issues in data synthesis* (pp. 57–73) (New Directions for Program Evaluation, No. 24). San Francisco: Jossey-Bass.

Light, R. J., & Pillemer, D. (1984). *Summing up: The science of reviewing research.* Cambridge: Harvard University Press.

Lipsey, M. W. (1989). *Design sensitivity: Statistical power for experimental research.* Newbury Park, CA: Sage.

Lipsey, M. W., & Wilson, D. B. (2000). *Practical meta-analysis* (Applied Social Research Methods Series, vol. 49). Thousand Oaks: Sage Publications.

Mansfield, R. S., & Busse, T. V. (1977). Meta-analysis of research: A rejoinder to Glass. *Educational Researcher, 6,* 3.

Martin, E., McDuffee, D., & Presser, S. (1981). *Sourcebook of Harris national surveys: Repeated questions, 1963–1976.* Chapel Hill: University of North Carolina Press.

Mauhs-Pugh, T. J. (1992). *Rural school consolidation in New York State, 1914–1992: The rhetoric of quality.* Unpublished dissertation proposal, School of Education, Syracuse University.

Miles, M. B., & Huberman, A. M. (1994). *Qualitative data analysis: A sourcebook of new methods* (2nd ed.). Thousand Oaks, CA: Sage.

Novak, J. D., & Gowin, D. B. (1984). *Learning how to learn.* New York: Cambridge University Press.

Patton, M. Q. (1997). *Utilization-focused evaluation: The new century text* (3rd ed.). Thousand Oaks, CA: Sage.

Raudenbusch, S. W. (1984). Magnitude of teacher expectancy's effect on pupil IQ as a function of credibility of expectancy induction: A synthesis of findings from 18 experiments. *Journal of Educational Psychology 76* (1), 85–97.

Reed, J. G., & Baxter, P. M. (1994). Using reference databases. In H. Cooper and L. V. Hedges (Eds.). *The handbook of research synthesis* (pp. 57–70). New York: Russell Sage Foundation.

Reed, J. G., & Baxter, P. M. (2003). *Library use: A handbook for psychology* (3rd ed.). Washington, DC: American Psychological Association.

Reif-Lehrer, L. (1995). *Grant application writer's handbook.* Boston: Jones and Bartlett.

Romiszowski, A. J. (1981). *Designing instructional systems.* London: Kogan Page; New York: Nicholas Publishing.

Rosenthal, M. L. (1994). The fugitive literature. In H. Cooper and L. V. Hedges (Eds.). *The handbook of research synthesis* (pp. 85–94). New York: Russell Sage Foundation.

Rosenthal, R. (1991). *Meta-analytic procedures for social research* (rev. ed.). Beverly Hills: Sage Publications.

Rosenthal, R. (1994). Parametric measures of effect size. In H. Cooper and L. V. Hedges (Eds.), *The handbook of research synthesis.* New York: Russell Sage Foundation.

Rosenthal, R., & Rosnow R. L. (1975). *The volunteer subject.* New York: John Wiley.

Rosenthal, R., & Rubin, D. (1982). Comparing effect sizes of independent studies. *Psychological Bulletin, 92* (2), 500–504.

Rossi, P. H., & Lyall, K. C. (1976). *Reforming public welfare: A critique of the negative income tax experiment.* New York: Russell Sage Foundation.

Rowe, M. B. (1974). Relation of wait-time and rewards to the development of language, logic and fate control. Part I: Wait-time. *Journal of Research in Science Teaching, 11,* 81–94.

Scriven, M. (1972). Pros and cons about goal-free evaluation. *Evaluation Comment, 3,* 1–4. Reprinted in *Evaluation Practice, 12,* 55–62.

Shadish, W. R., & Haddock, C. K. (1994). Combining estimates of effect size. In H. Cooper and L. V. Hedges (Eds.), *The handbook of research synthesis.* New York: Russell Sage Foundation.

Shadish, W. R., Cook, T. D., & Campbell, D. T. (2002). *Experimental and quasi-experimental designs for generalized causal inference.* New York: Houghton-Mifflin.

Shadish, W. R., Cook, T. D., & Leviton, L. C. (1991). *Foundations of program evaluation: Theories of practice.* Newbury Park, CA: Sage.

Shannon, D. M., Johnson, T. E., Searcy, S., & Lott, A. (2002). Using electronic surveys: Advice from survey professionals. *Practical Assessment, Research & Evaluation, 8* (1). Retrieved October 1, 2004, from http://edresearch.org/scripts/seget2.asp?want=http://edresearch.org/ericdc/ED470202.htm.

Stufflebeam, D. L., & Shinkfield, A. J. (1985). *Systematic evaluation: A self-instructional guide to theory and practice.* Boston: Kluwer Nijhoff.

Toulmin, S. E. (1958). *The uses of argument.* New York: Cambridge University Press.

Turner, C. F., & Krauss, E. (1978). Fallible indicators of the subjective state of the nation. *American Psychologist, 33,* 456–470.

Wachter, K. W., & Straf, M. L. (Eds.) (1990). *The future of meta-analysis.* New York: Russell Sage Foundation.

Wax, M. L., & Wax, R. H. (1979). *Fieldwork: Some didactic remarks for educational researchers.* St. Louis: Washington University.

Webb, E. J., Campbell, D. T., Schwartz, R. D., & Sechrest, L. (1981). *Nonreactive measures in the social sciences* (2nd ed.). Boston: Houghton-Mifflin.

White, H. D. (1994). Scientific communication and literature retrieval. In H. Cooper and L. V. Hedges (Eds.). *The handbook of research synthesis* (pp. 41–56). New York: Russell Sage Foundation.

Whyte, W. F. (1993). *Street corner society: The social structure of an Italian slum* (2nd ed.). Chicago: University of Chicago Press.

Wilson, P. (1992). Searching: Strategies and evaluation. In H. D. White, M. J. Bates, and P. Wilson (Eds.), *For information specialists: Interpretations of reference and bibliographic work* (pp. 153–181). Norwood, NJ: Ablex.

Witkin, B. R. (1994). Needs assessment since 1981: The state of the practice. *Evaluation Practice, 15*, 17–27.

Wortman, P. M. (1994). Judging research quality. In H. Cooper and L. V. Hedges (Eds.), *The handbook of research synthesis* (pp. 97–109). New York: Russell Sage Foundation.

Yin, Robert K. (1984). *Case study research: Design and methods* (Applied Social Research Methods Series, vol. 5). Beverly Hills: Sage.

Index

Dr. David R. Krathwohl is Hannah Hammond Professor of Education Emeritus, School of Education, Syracuse University. A former dean of the school, he has also served at the University of Illinois–Urbana/Champaign and Michigan State University. He is a former president of the American Educational Research Association and of the Educational Psychology Division of the American Psychological Association. He was a fellow at the Center for Advanced Study in the Behavioral Sciences. He is the author of *Methods of Educational and Social Science Research: An Integrated Approach* (2nd ed.) and *How to Prepare a Research Proposal* (3rd ed.). He is also an author of Bloom's *Taxonomy of Educational Objectives: Cognitive Domain,* senior author of *Affective Domain,* and coeditor with Lorin Anderson of *A Taxonomy for Learning, Teaching, and Assessing: A Revision of Bloom's "Taxonomy of Educational Objectives."*

Dr. Nick L. Smith is currently Professor of Education, School of Education, Syracuse University, and previously held positions at the University of Nebraska Medical Center and the Northwest Regional Educational Laboratory. In addition to having received distinguished research or service awards from the Association of Teacher Educators, the American Psychological Association, and the American Evaluation Association, he is also a former president of the Evaluation Network and 2004 president of the American Evaluation Association. He is author or coauthor of more than fifty refereed articles and editor or coeditor of eight volumes, including *Varieties of Investigative Evaluation.*